Henry Jackson Van Dyke

The Church, Her Ministry and Sacraments

Lectures Delivered on the L. P. Stone Foundation at Princeton Theological Seminary

in 1890

Henry Jackson Van Dyke

The Church, Her Ministry and Sacraments

Lectures Delivered on the L. P. Stone Foundation at Princeton Theological Seminary in 1890

ISBN/EAN: 9783337169657

Printed in Europe, USA, Canada, Australia, Japan

Cover: Foto ©Lupo / pixelio.de

More available books at **www.hansebooks.com**

THE CHURCH:

HER MINISTRY AND SACRAMENTS.

LECTURES

DELIVERED ON THE L. P. STONE FOUNDATION AT PRINCETON
THEOLOGICAL SEMINARY IN 1890.

BY

HENRY J. VAN DYKE, D.D.

PASTOR OF THE SECOND PRESBYTERIAN CHURCH OF BROOKLYN.

NEW YORK:
ANSON D. F. RANDOLPH AND COMPANY,
38 WEST TWENTY-THIRD STREET.

TO

MY TWO SONS,

WHO WERE THE HOPE OF MY EARLY MANHOOD,
AND ARE THE JOY AND CROWN OF MY LATER YEARS,

This Book

IS AFFECTIONATELY DEDICATED.

PREFACE.

THE absorbing duties of the pastoral office in a great city may be regarded as both a hindrance and a help to the discussion of the subjects involved in these Lectures. They are a hindrance because they leave so little time and strength for patient and thorough investigation beyond the limits of ordinary preaching; and yet they are a help, because they constantly present in a concrete and practical form the questions which go to the roots of all theories and controversies concerning the Church, the Ministry, and the Sacraments. Every man who claims to be a minister of Christ and a steward of the mysteries of God must often ask himself whether his claim is well founded, and for his own peace of mind must find some solution of the problems which this question involves. And so also in the administration of the sacraments, he must often ask and answer the inquiry what these holy ordinances mean, and to whom they are to be dispensed. If these Lectures show that their Author has not been exempt from the hindrances referred to, he trusts that their defects, of which he is painfully conscious, will find some compensation in the help which comes from the practical experience of a long pastoral life, and from the earnest desire to settle the questions which underlie such a life-work according to the Word of God.

The Author is well aware that the views here expressed differ in some respects from the prevailing practice and opinions in the Presbyterian Church. They are likely to provoke criticism in two directions. His views of the Divine origin and authority of the visible Church and its ministry, and of the obligation and efficacy of the sacraments, will be regarded by many as *High-church*. The name is of little importance. The Author believes that these views are scriptural; and he feels sure that they are in full accord with the teaching of the Westminster Confession of Faith.

On the other hand, the breadth and comprehensiveness of his views as to the constitution of the visible Church, and his readiness to subordinate differences in doctrine, church government, and forms of worship to the desire for greater unity among Christians, will be criticised and rejected as *Broad-churchism* by those who hold to what is called *jure divino* Presbyterianism. Here again the name is of little importance. The Author has long felt that the present attitude of Christian denominations is unscriptural, and hurtful to the cause of Christ, and especially that the relations of the Episcopal and Presbyterian churches are too much controlled on both sides by misunderstandings, unreasonable prejudices, and the bitter memories of past controversies which ought to be forgiven and forgotten. A careful study of the creeds of Christendom, and especially a comparison of the standards of the Presbyterian and Episcopal churches, brings the full conviction that the agreements are unspeakably greater than the differences, and that it is the high duty of every one who is loyal to Christ to magnify the one and minimise the other. I claim to be a minister, not only of the Presbyterian Church, but of the one visible Church of Christ; and the larger relation dominates and moulds my thoughts and desires. I long for the time when all the ministers and churches of Christ shall cease their rivalries and their witness-bearing against each other and unite in the larger and more important work of testifying the grace of God in all the world to every creature, and in co-operation for the triumphant establishment of Christ's kingdom in all the earth.

How this consummation is to be reached, I do not undertake to dictate or to prophesy; but sure I am that the wish, if it shall attain to the height and depth and breadth which the Scriptures warrant and enjoin, will be father not only to the thought, but also to the deed. The obstacles in the way are but wood, hay, and stubble, when compared with the one Foundation on which we all build, and in whose praise our hearts and tongues unite. If in the more controversial parts of these Lectures anything shall be found inconsistent in fact or in spirit with these views, it will be a cause of sincere regret.

It may be proper, though hardly necessary, to add, that while these Lectures were delivered in the Theological Seminary at Princeton, N. J., by invitation of its Faculty, no one but their Author is in any way responsible for them.

HENRY J. VAN DYKE.

BROOKLYN,
May 27, 1890.

CONTENTS.

LECTURE	PAGE
I. THE HOLY CATHOLIC CHURCH	1
II. THE KINGDOM OF CHRIST	24
III. THE UNITY OF THE VISIBLE CHURCH	48
IV. THE CHURCH MEMBERSHIP OF INFANTS	74
V. ORDINATION TO THE MINISTRY	115
VI. THE LORD'S SUPPER	162
VII. THE ADMINISTRATION OF THE SACRAMENTS	192
APPENDIX	223
INDEX	250

THE MINISTRY

AND

SACRAMENTS OF THE CHURCH.

LECTURE I.

THE HOLY CATHOLIC CHURCH.

GOD'S thoughts are so far above our thoughts that they cannot be at once and completely expressed in man's words. The diffuseness and variety of the Scriptures, and the progressive development of its doctrines, are necessary conditions of a verbal revelation. Divine inspiration redeems human words from their common use, breathes into them a new life, and sanctifies them to higher ends, from which we may not drag them down by insisting upon their radical as their true meaning. The English word "church" may be derived from Κυρίου οἶκος; but it does not follow that what we understand by the "House of God" comprehends all the Divine idea of the Church.

Nor do we get much light from the etymology of the words in the original Scriptures translated "church" in our English version. The *kahal* of the Old Testament and the *ecclesia* of the New literally signify an "assembly." Hence there are some who insist that we ought to disabuse our minds of all later accretions to their meaning, and regard the Church simply as an assembly of Christians. But why should this dismantling process stop at a *Christian* assembly? Why not strip the words bare to their original meaning? The *kahal* of the Old Testament is applied to the army of Pharaoh and to the company of Korah,[1] as well as to the congregation of Israel. And so also in the New Testament the Greek word *ecclesia* is applied to a meeting of citizens called by civil authority, and even to a mob like that which was gathered in the theatre at Ephesus.[2] The logical conclusion of the etymological argument is that any and every assembly of people is a church.

Neither is the Divine idea of the Church completely defined when you add to a Christian assembly the element of a Divine call. It is true that the etymology of *ecclesia*, and of its Hebrew equivalent, suggests, and the connection in which they are used generally conveys, the notion of an assembly constituted by authority and selection. It is also true that the κλητοί, those who are effectually called of God, will be the sole constituents of the Church in its ultimate glory, and that God knows infallibly who they will be.

But it does not follow from this that the Church consists only of those who love God and are the called according to His purpose. It is frequently spoken of in Scripture as a mixed assembly, including not only real, but also nominal, Christians. And this mixed society is the true Church; because its existence is a reality, its organization is a fact, its duty and destiny are the fulfilment of a Divine purpose.[3]

[1] Numbers xvi. 16; Ezek. xvii. 17.
[2] The assembly (ἡ ἐκκλησία) was confused. — *Acts* xix. 32.
[3] God hath ever had and ever shall have some church visible upon earth; not only because He had thousands which never bowed

The Church is never spoken of in Scripture as an ideal thing. It is always a concrete reality,—a living organism. It is composed of individuals; but their composition into the Church limits their individuality and knits them together in one body.[1]

The truth is, that no one definition ever has been or ever can be constructed to cover all the facts and revelations recorded in Scripture concerning the Church. The best analysis of the complex idea that ever has been made is presented in the twenty-fifth chapter of the Westminster Confession. *First*, the Church consists of all those who have been or ever will be saved through Christ, out of whom there is no salvation. All these are knit together in God's apprehension, by the purpose of His grace in regard to them, by their personal relationship to Christ, and by their common destiny. This is the Holy Catholic Church invisible.

Secondly, the Church consists of all those throughout the world who at any particular period profess the true religion, together with their children. This is the visible Church, which is also Catholic under the Gospel, not

---

the knee to Baal, but even they whose knees were bowed to Baal were also of the visible church of God. — HOOKER: *Ecc. Pol.*, book iii. chap. i. 8.

[1] There are precepts in the New Testament addressed, not to believers separately, but to believers associated and joined together in a corporate capacity. There are duties enjoined upon the whole society, and not upon the separate members composing it. There are powers bestowed upon the community which cannot be exercised by its separate members, and promises which cannot be fulfilled in their individual experience. There is a system of offices and ordinances described in Scripture as belonging to the Church, which can be appropriated only by a body whose many members are subordinated and compacted together in a living organism. — BANNERMAN: *Church of Christ*, i. 2.

being confined to one nation, as it was before under the law.

Thirdly, the Church consists of "particular churches;" that is to say, of local communities of Christians associated and organized for worship, instruction, and holy living. That such local associations are recognized in Scripture as "churches," is too obvious to require proof; and we expect to make it equally plain that the recognition of these "particular churches" is entirely consistent with the doctrine that there is only one Church. This threefold division may easily be reduced to two, because all local or particular churches are only parts of the one Catholic *visible* Church, and, so far as their members are true Christians, parts also of the one Catholic Church *invisible*. This idea is often expressed by calling them "branches" of the Church,—a mode of speech which has been sarcastically termed "the *vegetable* theory." But the sarcasm is more witty than wise; for Christ Himself likened the kingdom of heaven, which is His Church, to a small seed growing into a great tree, in whose *branches* the birds of the air lodge. The comparison of the Church to a tree is, of course, figurative; but how profound and true to fact is the figure! It expresses not only the idea that the visible Church is a living organism, growing upon a common root, sustained and expanded by common influences, but that every part of it is a representative and miniature of the whole. The branch is not only connected with the tree, but is a small tree in itself, for the typical form of the tree is traceable in every limb and in every leaf; so that this "vegetable theory" is not only conformable to Scripture, but exquisitely beautiful in its conformity to nature. This point will come up again for consideration. It is referred to now only to show that the recognition of local and particular associations of Christians as true churches does not contradict the doctrine of the one Holy Catholic Church.[1]

It should be further observed that the distinction between the visible and the invisible Church is formal rather than real.[2] They are not two separate churches, but one church under two distinct characters; the invisible Church being spiritually united to Christ, the visible being externally united to Him for the sake of the other.[3]

I. The Catholic, or Universal, Church, which is invisible, consists of the whole number of the elect that have been, are, or shall be gathered into one under Christ, the Head thereof. It is the comprehensive title

[1] The Congregational, or Independent, theory denies the existence of the visible Church regarded as one body. We find this theory where we would least expect it, — in Episcopal writers. Shrinking back from the extreme that there is no invisible Church, they go to the opposite extreme, — "dum vitia vitant, in contraria currunt." Thus Dr. Litton says: "There are only two really distinct senses which the word [church] bears in Scripture, according as it is used to signify either one or more Christian societies, or the Church which is described as the Body or the Bride of Christ. . . . Between a local church or a collection of such churches there is no vital organic connection, such as exists between the members of the human body and the head, or between the branches of the tree and the tree itself." (Church of Christ, pp. 218, 223.) This is altogether too *Low Church* for us. Some Presbyterians may adopt it, but it is not the doctrine of our standards nor of the Reformers. The Body and Bride of Christ is both an invisible and a visible organization.

[2] Christ hath not two churches, one visible and the other invisible, but one Church, which in one aspect is visible, and in another aspect invisible. — WALKER: *Scottish Theology and Theologians*, p. 123.

[3] Bannerman, Church of Christ, i. 9. See also Macpherson, On Confession of Faith, p. 143; and Calvin on Holy Catholic Church, Institutes, book iv. chap. i. 7.

of all those whom the Father has given to the Son (John xvii. 2); of all those who shall ever believe on Him (John xvii. 20); of all the sheep who will ever hear His voice and follow Him; to whom He will give eternal life, and whom He will bring from many folds into one flock under one Shepherd (John x. 16–28). In other words, the Church under this aspect includes *the whole results of the work of redemption.* No one can deny that this body of the redeemed is in fact invisible to us, and that it will continue to be so until Christ comes again, "to be glorified in His saints and to be admired in all them that believe" (2 Thess. i. 10). Nor can any one who believes in "the determinate counsel and foreknowledge of God" deny that the whole number of the redeemed is and always has been distinctly present to the Eye that sees all things at one view. Neither again can it be denied that this body of the redeemed is repeatedly designated in the Scripture as the Church. Many passages cited in support of this position are disputed, and we are free to confess that Protestant zeal has pushed its quotations on this point too far; but there are other passages which admit of no dispute. Where has there ever been, and how can there possibly be, on earth a visible company of believers commensurate with the Church which is Christ's Body, "the fulness of Him that filleth all in all"? (Eph. i. 23.) The Body of Christ is, indeed, frequently used as a descriptive title of the visible Church, including both real and nominal professors of His name (Eph. iv. 4–12; 1 Cor. xii. 12–25). But in such passages as the one just quoted, where the Body of Christ is said to be "the fulness of Him that filleth all in all," —and this is further explained by the prediction of that "peace through the blood of His cross" in which

He will "reconcile all things unto Himself, whether they be things in earth or things in heaven" (Col. i. 20), — the reference manifestly is to the comprehensive and everlasting results of redemption.

Where now, but in God's all-seeing vision, is "the general assembly and church of the first-born which are written in heaven" (Heb. xii. 23)? To these dim eyes, which see only through a glass darkly, it is invisible; and never can we behold it until we come to the city of the living God, the heavenly Jerusalem, — and not then, in its completeness, until all those that "are written in heaven" are gathered in from every nation and kindred and tongue. The denial that the Church, in the Scripture use of the name, reaches far beyond any earthly and visible organization, compels those who make it to contradict themselves, and leads to unwarranted limitations of the grace of God. Dr. Goulburn, one of the ablest and most candid writers on that side of the question, may be taken as a representative of all. He says, "The 'invisible Church' is erroneous and unscriptural phraseology. The Church of Holy Scripture, whether under the old or new dispensation, is *always a visible body, which may be known and seen,* established in the earth to bear testimony to God's truth, and intrusted with the administration of His word and ordinances."[1]

What we object to in this statement is not its recognition of the Church as a Divine institution in the world, nor its description of the ends which that Divine institution is designed and fitted to secure. We hold as strenuously as any Roman Catholic or Anglican Churchman that "our Lord Jesus Christ came not simply to teach certain religious doctrines, but to found a

[1] Goulburn's Holy Catholic Church, p. 2.

society, and that He did what He came to do."[1] We also believe that "a church is not an aggregation of believers, but a body or society of believers;" and that "a body is not a heap of members, but a system of members knit together into one organization, and pervaded by one life."[2] And we believe further that this Divine institution under the New Testament is the enlarged continuance of "the church in the wilderness" (Acts vii. 38), the one superseding the other as the full-blown day swallows up and abolishes the morning twilight. But we object to the assertion that the Church of God is *always* and *only* a visible society, as contrary alike to Scripture and to facts which all Christians admit. Dr. Goulburn himself is compelled to modify, and virtually to take back, this assertion, when he says that "the Church, as a visible body called out of the world, *must not be confounded with the smaller invisible body contained within it of the elect people of God.*"[3]

Here then is the admission that the elect people of God are a body, "not a heap of members, but a system knit together into one organization, and pervaded by one life." It is this body which we call the Invisible Church. It is not merely the name for which we contend, important as that is to the consistent interpretation of Scripture, but we protest against the theory which limits the facts represented by that name, makes the body of God's elect smaller than the body of the visible Church, and the number of those who are "written in heaven" less than the names upon the Church rolls on earth. The opposite of this is true. The number of those who will be saved is unspeakably greater than the number of those who profess to be Christians. And

---

[1] Goulburn's Holy Catholic Church, p. 7.
[2] Ibid., p. 9.   [3] Ibid., p. 27.

this is perfectly consistent with the teaching of our Confession, that "out of the visible Church there is no ordinary possibility of salvation."[1] No *ordinary* possibility. We are to work out our own salvation, and to labor for the salvation of others in the use of Divinely appointed means, and in connection with Divinely established institutions. For "to the Catholic visible Church Christ has given the ministry, oracles, and ordinances of God, for the gathering and perfecting of the saints in this life to the end of the world, and doth by His own presence and spirit according to His promise make them effectual thereto."[2] But the visible Church and its Divine ordinances are not their own end, they are only means to a higher end. They are means which *we* are bound to use, and by which our agency is limited. But God is not bound or limited by them. "He worketh when and where and how He pleaseth."[3] What the *extraordinary* possibilities of salvation are, and what will be their precise results, it is not for us to determine. We can only express the conviction that no human soul will be lost whom it is possible for God to save, consistently with His own attributes, with the freedom of the human will, and with the best interests of the intelligent universe. "No man is lost for the want of an atonement, or because there is any other barrier in the way of his salvation than his own most free and wicked will."[4] The Holy Catholic Church invisible was in the beginning, is now, and ever shall be greater than any visible society on earth. We cannot agree with Edwards that "they who are visibly or seemingly of the one only Church of Christ are many more than they who are really of His

[1] Westminster Confession, ch. xxv. 2.
[2] Ibid., 3. [3] Ibid., ch. x. 3.
[4] A. A. Hodge's Outlines of Theology, p. 420.

Church, and so the visible or seeming church is of larger extent than the real."[1] There are not few that be saved. Only the mind of a Pharisee could ask the question or give it an affirmative answer.

The assembly of the redeemed, as seen by John in the Apocalypse, is "a great multitude, which no man could number, of all nations, and kindreds, and peoples, and tongues" (Rev. vii. 9). It is no new discovery of modern thought, but the legitimate outgrowth of the theology of the Reformation, as opposed to the narrow dogmatism of the Church of Rome, that the great majority of the human race will be saved through Christ. It was no advocate of a new theology, but Dr. Charles Hodge, who said: "We know from the Bible itself that God is no respecter of persons, but in every nation he that feareth God is accepted of Him. No one doubts that it is in the power of God to call whom He pleases from among the heathen, and to reveal to them enough truth to secure their salvation."[2] It is in the works of the same eminent expounder of the Reformed theology that we find the clearest and most Scriptural defence of the doctrine that all who die in infancy, baptized or un-baptized, are redeemed and saved through Christ.[3] This doctrine is intimately connected with our subject; for if all who die in infancy are saved, they belong to the body of God's elect and to the Church of the First-born, which are written in heaven. "I tell you," says Dr. Alexander Hodge, "that the infinite majority of the Spiritual Church of Jesus Christ came into existence outside of all organization. [He means, of course, all visible and earthly organization.] Through

[1] Qualifications for Full Communion Work, i. 96.
[2] Theology, iii. 476.
[3] Hodge's Theology, i. 27.

all the ages, — from Japan, from China, from India, from Africa, from the isles of the sea, — multitudes, flocking like birds, have gone to heaven of this great company of redeemed infants of the Church of God."[1]

The doctrine of the salvation of all dying infants is not a mere abstract theory, invading the secret things which belong to God. It is necessary to the consistent interpretation of Scripture and to the vindication of God's character as a righteous Judge and a loving Father. While it comes home to our dearest affections and hopes, and touches our tenderest sorrows with the finger of Christ, it magnifies the grace of God and sets the high mystery of Divine fore-ordination in its true light as a help and not a hindrance to the salvation of men. It throws a gleam of hope over all our efforts to extend the triumphs of the visible Church on earth. The visible is pervaded and enveloped by the invisible. Around and above the valley of conflict and the sacramental host, the mountains are full of horsemen and chariots of fire. The fruit of the travail of Christ's soul satisfies His infinite love.

It is not our business either to define or to depend upon the extraordinary possibilities of salvation. Our business is to preach the Gospel to every creature. We may not hold out any hope which that Gospel does not clearly set before us. But at the same time it is not our prerogative, and it does not belong to the commission of the visible Church, to shut the gates of mercy on mankind by excluding any from salvation which the Gospel does not expressly exclude. Christ has cosmic relations which, because they do not come within the

[1] A. A. Hodge's Popular Lectures.
For a fuller discussion of the salvation of infants, see Appendix, Lect. I. (A).

sphere of our agency and responsibility, are but occasionally hinted at in Scripture. But these hints are very precious. They are gleams of light from a glory that is now inaccessible and beyond our comprehension, but which we shall one day behold and inherit. Such passages as the following are rainbows on all the dark clouds of the future: "And I, if I be lifted up, will draw all men unto Me" (John xii. 32); "God is the Saviour of all men, specially of those that believe" (1 Tim. iv. 10); He "is not willing that any should perish, but that all should come to repentance" (2 Pet. iii. 9); "All things were created by Jesus Christ, in heaven and on earth, visible and invisible; all things were created by Him and *for* Him, and He is before all things, and by Him all things consist; and He is the head of the body, the Church; for it pleased the Father that in Him should all fulness dwell; and having made peace through the blood of the cross, by Him to reconcile all things to Himself" (Col. i. 16–20); "That in the dispensation of the fulness of times He might gather together in one all things in Christ, both which are in heaven and which are on earth, even in Him" (Eph. i. 10). Such passages are not to be flung aside as though they had no meaning; and while their dim transparency is not to be so interpreted as to contradict plainer declarations of Scripture, nor to include any whom the Gospel excludes from its benefits, nor to deny the definite purpose of God in regard to those whom He has chosen in Christ before the foundation of the world (Eph. i. 4), they may and ought to be used to enlarge our conception of the Divine purpose of redemption and of the Church, which is "the fulness of Him that filleth all in all."

II. One extreme begets another. On both sides of

every controversy men are apt to lean backwards. To the assertion that the Church spoken of in the Old and New Testament is "always a visible society," the extreme controversial response is that the Church, *as such*, is not a visible society at all. The argument by which this extreme position is defended may be summed up in the following propositions: (1) None but those who truly repent and believe are ever denominated κλητοί (the called); and as the ἐκκλησία consists of the κλητοί, the Church must consist of true believers. (2) No external visible society, as such, is holy; and therefore the Church of which the Scriptures speak is not a visible society, but the communion of saints. (3) The Church as the communion of saints *is one;* as an external society it is not one; therefore the Church is a company of believers, and not an external society. (4) Unity of faith is one of the attributes of the true Church, which cannot be predicated of any external society calling itself the Church of God.

To the first of these propositions, — that "the Church must consist of true believers," — it will be sufficient to answer that it begs the question under discussion, and contradicts a multitude of Scriptures, in which the Church is described as including both true and nominal believers.

The assumption which underlies all the other statements is, that the attributes given in Scripture to the Church, regarded as the whole body of true believers, do not apply *in any sense* to the whole body of *professed* believers. This assumption is contrary to the received maxim, that a mixed body may be designated by the attributes of one of its elements; as in the case of the human and Divine person of Christ, and the person of man, consisting of both soul and body.

Holiness is an attribute of all true believers; but every believer is also a sinner,—no believer on earth is perfectly holy. Does it follow, therefore, that there are no true believers in the world? The same logic which proves that the Church, as such, is not a visible society, because the Church is holy, whereas no visible society is *perfectly* holy, is of equal force to prove that the Church is not "the communion of saints," because no saint on earth is perfectly holy. If the continuance of sin in believers individually, and consequently in the whole body of believers, does not preclude that body from being called "the holy Catholic Church," neither does the continuance of sinners among professed believers preclude the whole body of professed believers from being called the holy Catholic Church, nor from inheriting the promise of final and complete sanctification.

When Paul wrote his epistles "to the church of God which is at Corinth, to them that are sanctified in Christ Jesus, called to be saints, with all that in every place call upon the name of Jesus Christ our Lord, both theirs and ours" (1 Cor. i. 2), he certainly addressed a visible society, to whom his letters could be read, and he certainly did not intend to preclude from his appellation of the whole body the sinners whose unholiness he rebuked, and whom he hoped to reclaim from their backsliding. The whole nominally Christian communion is addressed as "*the church of God* which is at Corinth," and this is broadened in its application so as to include professing Christians, in all ages and lands, by the comprehensive clause, "with all that in every place call upon the name of Jesus Christ our Lord, both theirs and ours." If Paul had meant to discriminate, in the use of the word "church," between true and nominal believers, it would have been easy for him to do so. His comprehensive words do not need to be guarded by any limitations we can impose upon them.

Following his example, we are permitted and bound to call the whole body of professed believers on earth "the Holy Catholic Church," because in the judgment of charity the great mass of those who call upon the name of our Lord Jesus Christ are accepted of him, and because, whatever may be the destiny of particular individuals in its membership, its destiny as a body is to be finally washed, sanctified, and glorified. Its holiness is not yet complete. Nevertheless, the process of its sanctification makes continual progress. As Calvin beautifully says, "the Lord is daily smoothing its wrinkles and wiping away its spots."[1]

The same reasoning applies equally to the *unity of faith* which is another attribute of the true Church. There is just as much division and diversity of doctrinal opinion among true believers as there is among nominal Christians. Peter and Paul certainly belonged to the communion of saints; yet how they differed and disputed with each other! If unity of faith is a mark of the true Church, and if that unity is destroyed by existing doctrinal differences, then there is no such thing as the Church of God, visible or invisible, outside of heaven. The truth is, unity of faith does not depend upon exact agreement in doctrine, nor is it destroyed by the conflict of creeds. "The profession of the true religion" is at once the distinctive note and the bond of the visible Church. In the mind of God and in the experience of believers there must be, though we are not able sharply to define it, an essen-

[1] Institutes, book iv. chap. i.17.

tial *minimum* of truth, sufficient for salvation, and therefore sufficient for the unity of the Church. It is remarkable that Calvin, in attempting to define this essential truth, says nothing about what is peculiar to Calvinism.

"For all the heads of true doctrine are not in the same position. Some are so necessary to be known that all must hold them to be fixed and undoubted as the proper essentials of religion, — for instance, that God is one; that Christ is God, and the Son of God; and that our salvation depends on the mercy of God; *and the like.* Others, again, which are the subjects of controversy among the churches, do not destroy the unity of the faith."[1]

We have an admirable and universally accepted summary of essential truth in the Apostles' Creed, which was adopted — or rather retained — by all the Reformers. Calvin made it the basis of his Institutes. This creed of creeds, as we understand it, recognizes the Holy Catholic Church as a visible body. "The communion of saints" is not merely explanatory of "the Holy Catholic Church," still less is it a tautology, expressing the same idea in another form. The first statement describes the Church as visible, and the second as invisible. To identify the two is to mar the simplicity and

---

[1] Calvin's Institutes, book iv. chap. i. 12.

The unity of the visible Body and Church of Christ consisteth in that uniformity which all persons belonging thereunto have, by reason of that *one Lord* whose servants they all profess themselves, by reason of that *one faith* which they all acknowledge, and by reason of that *one baptism* wherewith they are all initiated. The visible Church is therefore one in outward profession of those things which supernaturally pertain to the very essence of Christianity, and are necessarily required in every particular Christian man. — HOOKER: *Ecc. Polity*, book iii. chap. i. 3, 4.

beauty of the creed, and to obliterate what is essential to its completeness as a symbol of the Catholic faith.[1] But whether this is true of the Apostles' Creed or not, it is certainly true of the Scriptures. They recognize the Church as both invisible and visible. And in both aspects it is a living organism, whose head is Christ, and whose members are His Body. As the soul without the body could not accomplish its life-work on earth, nor inherit its full redemption in heaven (see Rom. viii. 23), so the Church of the living God, regarded simply as an invisible communion of saints, or as a manifestation of faith in the lives of individuals, could not be "the pillar and ground of the truth" (1 Tim. iii. 19) on earth, neither could it "make known to the principalities and powers in heavenly places the manifold wisdom of God" (Eph. iii. 10). We contend, therefore, that the visible Church is just as much a *true* church as the invisible. It is "not a mere abstract idea, a convenient expression for the number of all those who visibly profess the faith of Christ throughout the world. It is made up of all those who, visibly professing the faith of Christ, *are constituted by that profession into one corporate body*, and stand in one outward covenant relationship to Christ. This, so far as regards the visible Church, is the primary and usual application of the term in Scripture. The application of it to local churches or separate congregations is only a subordinate and secondary meaning."[2]

The first announcement that the visible Church, under its New Testament form, was about to be established, was made by John the Baptist when he preached in the wilderness of Judæa, saying, "Repent ye, for the

[1] Appendix to Lecture I. (B).
[2] Bannerman, Church of Christ, i. 44.

kingdom of heaven is at hand" (Matt. iii. 2). The same announcement was repeated by Christ at the beginning of His public ministry (Matt. iii. 17). The *kingdom* of God, of Christ, and of Heaven, as we shall undertake to show in a future lecture, are synonymous, and interchangeable with the *Church* of God and of Christ.

The first reference in the New Testament to the Church under the name of the *ecclesia* is found in the promise of Christ to Peter, "On this rock I will build My Church" (Matt. xvi. 18), or, as it might be more accurately rendered, "I will build the Church for Myself." This gives the true emphasis to the promise; for at the time it was uttered, Jesus and His disciples had been excommunicated from the existing Church, and He was on his way to be crucified. He did not during His life set up a visible society apart from the Jewish church of the time, but He made preparations for doing so after His death. And now, with the shadows of death and apparent failure thickening about Him, He says to Peter, as the spokesman and representative of the chosen twelve, "I will build the Church *for Myself,* and I will build it *on thee.*" Our first glimpse of the actual fulfilment of this promise is in the record of the day of Pentecost: "Then they that gladly received his word," the word preached by Peter, " were *baptized:* and the same day there were *added* [to Peter and the rest of the Apostles] about three thousand souls. And they continued steadfastly in the Apostles' *doctrine and fellowship,* and in *breaking of bread,* and in *prayers.* And the Lord added to the *Church* daily such as were being saved" (Acts ii. 41, 42, 47).

Here, then, we have the Church of Christ fully organized and equipped, with its living ministry, its assemblies for worship, its administration of baptism and the Lord's Supper, — still abiding indeed under the shadow of the Old Testament Church, and recruiting from it, but having a separate organic life of its own; and to this visible Church God adds those who were being saved, as the Divinely appointed means of saving them. From this time on to the end of the inspired history the Church is a body conspicuously visible, both as a society for the propagation of the Gospel and as an object of persecution. Saul "made havoc of the Church" (Acts viii. 3). "Herod stretched forth his hand to vex certain of the Church" (Acts xii. 1). "Prayer was made without ceasing of the Church unto God for Peter" (Acts xii. 5). Paul exhorts the elders of Ephesus "to feed the Church of God, which He hath purchased with His own blood" (Acts xx. 28). What candid reader can fail to see in this record of trial and of triumph, and in the conspicuous ministry of the Apostle by whom this visible society was first gathered and organized, the exact fulfilment of the Saviour's promise, "Thou art Peter, and on this rock I will build My Church, and the gates of hell shall not prevail against it"?[1]

Taken in their obvious and natural sense, how easy Christ's words are to be understood; and so far as they apply especially to Peter, how fully are they justified by the facts recorded in the Acts of the Apostles! He was not separated from the others, neither was he exalted above them as an infallible primate. Paul

---

[1] This interpretation plainly doth agree with the matter of fact and of history, which is the best interpreter of right and privilege in such cases; for we may reasonably understand our Saviour to have promised that which in effect we see performed. — ISAAC BARROW: *Works*, iii. 104.

certainly did not recognize any such primacy when he "withstood Peter to the face because he was to be blamed" (Gal. ii. 11). But he was distinguished as the first and most successful in setting up the New Testament Church among both Jews and Gentiles, as is clearly shown in the account of the day of Pentecost, and in opening the door of the Church to the Gentiles in the case of Cornelius (Acts x.).[1] If this interpretation seems to belittle while it preserves the integrity of a saying which has filled the world with the noise and smoke of controversy, it is only because this controversy has distorted and exaggerated the saying to proportions that were not dreamed of for five centuries after the Saviour's death. We have dwelt on this passage, not for Peter's sake, but for the sake of the Church. It is the most emphatic and conspicuous of those Scriptures which show that Christ came not merely to preach a doctrine and to establish forces by which the world is to be regenerated, but to

---

[1] The position taken by Peter fully justifies this highly figurative language of the Master. During all His public ministry Peter stood by His side. He was with Him on the Mount of Transfiguration, and in the Garden of Gethsemane at the moment of His arrest. He stood on Mount Olivet on the day He was taken up. When the Holy Spirit fell on the disciples, he was there to tell sinners of the Crucified whom God had made both Lord and Christ, and to invite them to come to Him by faith and repentance. In those glorious days when the Church was increased by daily additions of such as were being saved, Peter occupied the most conspicuous place. To join the Church was for a man to unite himself to Peter and to the Apostles who were about him. They were foundation-stones as well as he, for the Church is built upon the Apostles; but he is a rock as compared with them, — that is, he is distinguished among them for talents, labors, and success. — DR. THOMAS WITHEROW: *Form of the Christian Temple*, p. 440.

embody the truth and conserve these forces in a visible society, — even a Church against which the gates of hell shall not prevail.[1]

Nor is this the only passage whose testimony in favor of the visible Catholic Church has been spiritualized away. Take, for example, the words of Paul in Gal. iv. 26: "Jerusalem which now is, is in bondage with her children; but Jerusalem which is above is free, which is the mother of us all." By the Jerusalem which is above and free, the Apostle does not mean heaven, or the final state of the blessed, about which we sing so sweetly, "O mother, dear Jerusalem;" neither did he mean the invisible "Church of the first-born, which are written in heaven." He meant the visible Church under the New Testament dispensation, which is free from the yoke of bondage to the ceremonies of the Levitical law; and this Church he calls by the endearing name of "mother." Seventeen centuries ago, Cyprian said, " He cannot have God for his father who has not the Church for his mother." Do we think this an exaggerated statement, suited only to those whom we call *High Churchmen* by way of reproach? Then Calvin was a High Churchman, for he appropriates Cyprian's words without any qualification. "To those to whom God is a father, the Church must also be a mother. This was true not merely under the law, but even after the advent of Christ, since Paul declares that we are the children of the new, even a heavenly Jerusalem, in Gal. iv. 26."[2] Again, he says still more explicitly: "As it is now our purpose to discourse of the *visible Church*, let us learn, from her single title of *mother*, how useful, nay, how necessary, the knowledge

---

[1] See Appendix to Lecture I. (C).
[2] Institutes, book iv. chap. i. 1.

of her is, since there is no other means of entering into life, unless she conceives us in the womb and gives us birth, unless she nourishes us at her breasts, and, in short, keeps us under her charge and government until, divested of mortal flesh, we become like the angels."[1] We do not accept the inferences of Cyprian and of Calvin in regard to the absolute necessity of having the visible Church as our mother, but we cannot deny the correctness of their interpretation of Paul's words. It is evident from the whole context that by "the Jerusalem which is above and is the mother of us all," the Apostle means the visible Church under its New Testament form. The freedom which he claims for her is deliverance from the yoke of the Levitical law, which no one ever imagined to be imposed upon the Church invisible. If by the "mother of us all" the Apostle meant the elect people of God in all ages, then his plea for freedom would apply to the Old Testament saints as well as to Christians; and the inevitable conclusion would be that he condemned circumcision and the observance of the Levitical law under the Old Testament dispensation,— which is absurd. But that he refers to the visible Church under the New Testament, and pleads for the freedom of its members, is evident from what follows: "Stand fast therefore in the liberty wherewith Christ hath made us free, and be not entangled again with the yoke of bondage. Behold, I Paul say unto you, that if ye be circumcised, Christ shall profit you nothing" (Gal. v. 1, 2).

Thus Paul believed in the Holy Catholic Church, and dignified her position and magnified her offices by calling her "the mother of us all." When we come to discuss the unity of the visible Church, we shall show that he calls her also "the Body of Christ" (in 1 Corinthians

[1] Institutes, book iv. chap. i. 4.

xii. and Ephesians iv.). Meantime, if it offends either our theology or our taste to confer such high titles upon a society which contains false as well as true professors of religion, let us remember that Christ Himself taught the same thing when He said, "I am the true vine;" and proceeds to show that in this vine there are unfruitful branches, whose end is to be burned.

LECTURE II.

THE KINGDOM OF CHRIST.

"THE visible Church — which is also catholic, or universal, under the Gospel, not confined to one nation, as before under the law — consists of all those throughout the world that profess the true religion, together with their children, *and is the kingdom of our Lord Jesus Christ*, the house and family of God."

This statement of the Westminster Confession is exceeding broad. There is nothing secular nor sectarian in it. It admits no limitations of time or place. Rising above all distinctions based upon forms of Church government, modes of worship, and formularies of doctrine, it is as wide and as elastic in its embrace as the ever-extending bounds of Christendom. (1) It recognizes all who profess Christianity as members of the visible Church of Christ. It leaves open the questions: What is essential to Christianity? and What constitutes a profession of the true religion? But we think no candid answer to these questions can exclude from the Holy Catholic Church the members of the Church of Rome, of the Eastern Church, or of any of the Christian denominations which have grown out of the Protestant Reformation.[1] (2) Our

---

[1] Calvin recognizes the Roman Catholic Church, aside from the papacy, as part of the visible Church of Christ. "But as in pulling down buildings the foundations and ruins are permitted to remain, so God did not suffer Antichrist either to subvert His Church from

THE KINGDOM OF CHRIST. 25

definition recognizes the children of all who profess the true religion as members of the Church of Christ. They are not brought into it by conversion, nor do they join it by their own voluntary professions, but they are born into it, and their baptism is the recognition of their Christian birthright. This vital principle will be demonstrated and emphasized in a future lecture. (3) Our definition separates the visible Church from all forms of human government and from the origin and destiny of all earthly empires. It is not confined to any nation, nor identified with any national policy. It is not the Republic of God in America, and the king-

its foundations or to level it with the ground, but was pleased that amid the devastation the edifice should remain, though half in ruin. While therefore we are unwilling to concede the name of church to the Papists, we do not deny that there are churches among them" (Institutes, book iv., chap. ii. 11, 12).

In accordance with these views, Calvin and all the Reformers refused to be re-baptized.

The Westminster Confession does not call the Roman Catholic Church, but only the Pope, "that Antichrist, that man of sin and son of perdition that exalteth himself in the Church against Christ and all that is called God." Both Calvin and Luther adopt the same questionable exegesis of 2 Thess. ii. 4; but they turn it into an argument to prove that the Church of Rome is still *the temple of God*, otherwise how could the Pope exalt himself in that temple?

" The claims of the Roman Church rest upon a broader and more solid base than the papacy, which is only the form of her government. The papal hierarchy was often corrupt, as the Jewish hierarchy, and some Popes were as corrupt as Caiaphas; but this fact cannot destroy the claims nor invalidate the ordinances of the Roman Church, which from the days of the Apostles to the Reformation has been identified with the fortunes of Western Christendom, and which remains to this day the largest visible Church in the world. To deny her church character is to stultify history and nullify the promises of Christ" (Schaff, History of the Christian Church, vi. 533.)

dom of God in Great Britain. It is everywhere the *kingdom* of our Lord Jesus Christ, governed by its own laws, and subject to its one Divine Head. The attempt to defend any form of Church government by its real or supposed resemblance to the civil institutions of any country (as, for example, when the polity of the Presbyterian Church is commended upon the ground that it resembles the Constitution of the United States of America) can be justified only upon the admitted principle that "there are some circumstances concerning the worship of God and the government of the Church common to human actions and societies, which are to be ordered by the light of Nature and Christian prudence, according to the general rules of the word, which are always to be observed."[1]

The candid application of this principle sweeps away from all existing denominations of Christians the exclusive claim to a *jure divino* Church government, but it leaves untouched the fact that Christ, as King and Head of His Church, hath appointed therein a government in the hands of church officers, distinct from the civil magistrate.[2] As the religion of Christ is designed for and suited to all mankind, the Church of Christ has the world for its empire, and all nations and kindreds for its subjects. (4) And this brings us to the crowning point in our definition: The visible *Church* of Christ is the *kingdom* of Christ. To demonstrate this doctrine and apply some of its inferences is the design of the present lecture.

I. That the Church of Christ is the kingdom of Christ is evident from the fact that He uses the two words as synonymous and interchangeable. When He

[1] Westminster Confession, chap. i. 6.
[2] Ibid., xxx. 1.

said, "Thou art Peter, and on this rock I will build My *Church*," He immediately adds, "and I will give to thee the *keys of the kingdom of heaven.*" Can any unbiassed reader deny that the kingdom whose keys were given to Peter is one and the same thing with the Church which was to be built on him? The keys of death and hell are in Christ's own girdle (Rev. i. 18); the key of heaven, — the right to admit or exclude from the final abode of the saints, is in His own hands. There He shuts, and no man opens; He opens, and no man shuts. And so also the entrance into the invisible Church is absolutely with Christ. He is Himself the door (John x. 7). But the *keys* — that is, the *doctrine* and *discipline* — of the kingdom of heaven on earth are committed to Peter and the rest of the Apostles and to all whom they represent; and the kingdom in which they exercise their office of binding and loosing — that is, of *forbidding* and *allowing* — can be none other than the visible Church of Christ.

The same truth is evident from the claim of Jesus of Nazareth to be the Messiah. He made these claims with a full knowledge of the character and work attributed to Him in the Messianic prophecies. He was to come indeed meek and lowly; but nevertheless He was to come as a king; and to those who beheld the glory of the only begotten Son, full of grace and truth, His essential royalty and the glorious majesty of His kingdom were the more resplendent by contrast with the meanness of His outward condition. They who received Him fell down and worshipped, saying, "Rabbi, Thou art the Son of God, Thou art the King of Israel;" and He accepted their homage.

Moreover, in His teaching He constantly declares that His messiahship involves the actual setting up of that kingdom which shall never be destroyed (Dan. ii. 44).

How explicit are these words: " Verily I say unto you, there be some standing here which shall not taste of death *till they see the Son of Man coming in His kingdom*" (Matt. xvi. 28).[1] This prediction stands in immediate connection with the saying to Peter, " On this rock I will build My Church, and I will give unto thee the keys of the kingdom of heaven." It evidently refers to the same thing. No ingenuity of interpretation can make " the Son of Man coming in His kingdom " mean the second coming of the Son of Man " in the glory of His Father with the holy angels, to reward every man according to his works " (Matt. xvi. 27); because the point and emphasis of the prediction is that its fulfilment should occur during the *lifetime* of some who were *standing there*. Neither, again, can it be made to refer to the coming of God's kingdom and the reign of Divine grace through Christ in the souls of individual men. What Christ predicted was a new and visible thing. It was not merely an experience, but a phenomenon. They were to *see* the kingdom coming with power. To quote Christ's words, " the kingdom of heaven cometh not with observation, but is within you," or the words of Paul, that " the kingdom of God is not meat nor drink, but righteousness and peace and joy in the Holy Ghost," as a proof that the Church, or kingdom, is not a visible organization, is about as candid and conclusive as it would be to cite the saying of Napoleon III., " The Empire is peace," to prove that the Second Empire of France was only a private experience in the hearts of Frenchmen.[2]

---

[1] Mark has it, "Till they have seen the kingdom of God come with power " (Mark ix. 1). In Luke it is more briefly expressed, "Till they see the kingdom of God " (Luke ix. 27).

[2] Nor are these predictions concerning the coming of the Son of

The visible Church must in fact be the kingdom of Christ, because He is its Sovereign Head. When the Father "bringeth His first-begotten into the world, He saith, Thy throne, O God, is for ever and ever." And when the Son of God had by Himself purged our sins, He sat down on the right hand of the Majesty on high, "being made so much better than the angels, as He hath by inheritance obtained a more excellent name than they" (Heb. i. 8, 4). In the religious teaching of our day this inherited kingship and royal authority of the Son of God is too much ignored. What sometimes claims to be pre-eminently the preaching of Christ and Him crucified, is but half the Gospel. His priestly functions in sacrifice and intercession are too exclusively insisted upon. Christ is greater than His cross. His sacrifice, while it is the centre, is not the circumference of Christianity. He is a teacher sent from God. The rest He gives to the soul is not obtained simply by coming to Him, but by taking His yoke upon us and learning of Him. The Sermon on the Mount is addressed to His disciples; its beatitudes delineate their character; its exposition of the moral law lays down the rule of their life; and the morality it enforces is an essential part both of the result and the process of salvation. Christ's kingship underlies both His pro-

Man in His kingdom, in the near future, inconsistent with the fact on which Christ constantly insisted, — that His kingdom had already come. "The law and the prophets were until John: since that time the kingdom of God is preached, and every man presseth into it" (Luke xvi. 16). "The kingdom of God is *within* you," or, as it is more correctly rendered in the Revised Version, "*among* you" (Luke xvii. 21). It was in its germ a present reality. Its future coming was but the development of what already existed. The Church which was visibly inaugurated at the day of Pentecost had been previously constituted and organized in the family of Christ.

phetic and His priestly office, and imparts an infinite value and efficacy to both. He is a royal priest after an order more ancient than Aaron's, a royal prophet after the type of David. While grace is poured into His lips, He girds His sword upon His thigh and rides forth in His glory and majesty. He is exalted a Prince and a Saviour. He is able to save to the uttermost, because all power is His. And this exaltation is not the conference of a new dignity, but simply a return, as the Head of a redeemed people, to the glory He had with the Father before the foundation of the world. His humiliation on earth did not annul His authority, but only obscured its outward manifestation for a time. When He lay as a swaddled infant in the manger, "the government was on His shoulder," and both angels and wise men recognized Him as the Prince of Peace. When He stood in the dignity and glory of His humiliation before Pilate, with a crown of thorns more resplendent than gold, inlaid with drops of blood more precious than all royal gems, He witnessed a good confession. "Thou sayest it,—*I am a king*. To this end was I born, and for this cause came I into the world, that I should bear witness unto the truth" (John xviii. 37). This claim was the ground on which He was condemned and crucified. And this is still the point at which He is accepted or rejected. No one can take Christ for a Saviour without confessing Him to be the Son of God and the king of Israel.

Now, if Christ is a King in His glory before the world was,—in His humiliation, in His exaltation,—where and what is His kingdom? It is not the universal sovereignty of God, whose throne is established in the heavens, and whose dominion ruleth over all,—for that kingdom neither comes nor goes,—it is not set up, nor increased, but is from everlasting to everlasting. Neither, on the other hand, is it, as Dr. Bruce and others maintain, merely "the reign of Divine love exercised by His grace over human hearts believing in His love, and constrained thereby to yield Him grateful affection and devoted service."[1] For the reign of Divine love was not first set up or proclaimed in the ministry of Christ, nor were believers under the new dispensation the first to respond to the love of God. This Divine and gracious dominion over the human heart began at the closed gate of Paradise, and runs through all dispensations. What Christ established and proclaimed was a new embodiment and a more visible incorporation of the same reign of Divine love, according to the promises which God "spake by the mouth of His holy prophets, which have been since the world began" (Luke ii. 70).

The kingdom which Daniel prophesied should be set up in the days of the Son of Man,[2] whose approach was announced by John the Baptist,[3] which Christ Himself declared to be near at hand,[4] and which He commanded His disciples to go forth and proclaim;[5] the kingdom which He promised that the men of that generation should see before they tasted death,[6] and which they did see in its power on the day of Pentecost; the kingdom of God which Paul preached by the space of three years in the church at Ephesus;[7] the kingdom whose keys were given to Peter and the other Apostles as the representatives of all church officers, and for whose increase all Christians are to pray and to labor, — can be none other than the visible Church of Christ.

[1] Bruce on the Kingdom of God, p. 46.
[2] Dan. ii. 44. [3] Matt. iii. 2. [4] Matt. iv. 17.
[5] Matt. x. 7. [6] Matt. xvi. 28. [7] Acts xx. 25, 31.

Our Lord's parables outline the history of His kingdom from the days of His own ministry to the day of judgment. In the *Sower* we are taught that "the word of the kingdom," which is the same thing with the Gospel, will be diversely received, according to the moral condition of the hearers; in the *Tares* and the *Drag-net*, that good and evil are to co-exist in the kingdom until the final judgment at the end of the world; in the *Mustard-seed* and the *Leaven*, that the kingdom of God is destined to grow both inwardly and outwardly, invisibly and visibly; in the *Seed* springing up into the blade, the ear and the full corn in the ear, that the progress and triumph of the kingdom is not by the sudden annihilation of evil, but by the slow and steady unfolding of good. Where is there, or where can there ever be, a fulfilment of these prophetic descriptions, if it is not recorded in the history of the visible Church?

And yet the visible Church is not the kingdom of Christ in any *exclusive* sense. The kingdom is synonymous with the Church in both its aspects, visible and invisible. Christ reigns in the souls of all true believers as well as in the organized body of professed believers. The grace which is bestowed on men, above and aside from all human agency, "through the Spirit which worketh when and where and how He pleaseth," [1] is the exercise of His kingly power. And so also the indirect influences which the Gospel and the institutions of Christianity exert upon and through the literature, the civil institutions, and the commerce of the world, — all belong to the kingdom of Christ. Christ Himself speaks both of the Church and of the kingdom as invisible to men when He compares it to leaven hid in three measures of meal, and to the seed that grows

[1] Confession, chap. x. sect. 3.

in secret. But to infer from such passages that the kingdom of God and of heaven is always, or even pre-eminently, invisible, is to narrow the meaning of Scripture and miss the main point of its parables. The kingdom of heaven is like a grain of mustard-seed which grows into a great tree, so that the birds lodge in its branches. Is not such a tree a visible object? It is like a field in which an enemy sows tares among the wheat. Is not such a field a visible reality? It is like a net cast into the sea and gathering fishes of every kind. Is such a net only an ideal and invisible thing?

We have said that the Church and the kingdom are synonymous and interchangeable terms. By this it is not meant that there is no difference at all between them. Synonyms are not an arbitrary and wanton multiplication of words, with no variableness in their meaning. The Scriptures do not give different names to the same conceptions, but they do give different names to different aspects of the same things. Just as the infinite fulness of Christ is indicated and measurably expressed by the great variety of His titles, so in the Church, which is His Body, as there are diversities of gifts and operations, there is also a diversity of names.

II. What, then, is the precise ground of the distinction between the Church and the kingdom of Christ? What ideas does this title add to our conceptions of the Church, and by what facts is that idea illustrated? This is a far-reaching question, and the answers are various. They are not always distinctly given; they overlap and shade into each other. But they may be summarized with sufficient clearness in the following propositions: (1) The term "kingdom" indicates the relation which the visible Church should sustain to the

State; (2) The kingdom represents the moral and spiritual forces of Christianity, aside altogether from its positive institutions; (3) The Church is called the kingdom by way of anticipation, the one being only preparatory to the other; (4) The Church and the kingdom are identical; the kingdom expressing the Divine authority by which the Church exists and acts, and the Divine power by which she will ultimately triumph. This we hold to be the true theory.

1. The most prevalent theory, and that which has exerted the mightiest influence upon the whole course of history during the Christian era, is that the term "kingdom" as applied to the Church indicates the *relation which the Church should sustain to the State.* Assuming that the State is Divine in the same sense and to the same extent that the Church is Divine, and that their ultimate design is the same; assuming also that the kingdoms of this world are to become the kingdoms of our Lord and of His Christ, not to be dashed in pieces as a potter's vessel, but to be preserved and perpetuated as kingdoms, — Christians have prayed, and intrigued, and fought, and deluged the earth with Christian blood, and illuminated it with the fires of persecution, in order to realize the idea of a Christian State. The practical results of these attempts are the inevitable fruit of the doctrine. For if the State is Divine, and its ultimate design is the same with that of the Church, then the civil magistrate, whose symbol is the sword, is as much the ambassador of Christ as the minister of God's Word; and he must not bear the sword in vain as the appointed means of propagating the Church. Once admit the principle that the civil magistrate, whether he be king or constable, has any official relation to the Church and any official duty *in* the Church, and the conclusion is irresistible that all

dissent from the religion of the State is an offence to be punished by civil pains and penalties, the toleration of such dissent is a sin against God, and religious persecution becomes the highest duty. Persecution does not belong to any one form of Church government or doctrine. Persecutors have not been blind and unreasoning lovers of human blood. They have reasoned correctly, and had the courage of their convictions. But their premises were unscriptural and wrong, in the assumption that the State is Divine, and co-ordinate in its ends with the Church. The attempt to realize the idea of a Christian State has been made in each of the three possible directions, — (1) by subjecting the Church to the State; (2) by subjecting the State to the Church; and (3) by a confederation or covenant between them. The first of these experiments was made under the most favorable circumstances in the days of Constantine; and twelve centuries after it had failed, in the very convulsions which were the evidence and the result of the failure, the Reformers made the same experiment again in Germany and in Great Britain. The civil magistrate, whether elector, king, or emperor, by virtue of his office as a ruler in this world, and without regard to his personal character or qualifications, was declared to be the head of the Church; and the holy sacraments of the Church were made the qualifications for civil office and the tests of political loyalty.

The second attempt to realize the kingdom of God, — namely, by subjecting the State to the Church, — was made on a grand scale by the Church of Rome; and its success seemed to be complete when the Pope dissolved royal marriages, released subjects from allegiance to their sovereigns, took away and bestowed crowns at his will, and received tribute for kingdoms as feudal dependencies. Then, in the eyes of devout Churchmen, the kingdoms of this world seemed to have become the kingdoms of our Lord and of His Christ. We all know that the triumph was the signal for revolution and defeat; that aside from its corruptions in doctrine and morals, this magnificent structure of the Church as a world empire was built on the sand, and destined to decay. And yet, strange to say, in the Reformation, which was the most violent symptom of that decay, Calvin repeated in Geneva, on a smaller scale, essentially the same experiment to realize the kingdom of God, by identifying the State with, and at the same time subjecting it to, the Church. With what success this attempt was made, the condition of that city where his grave is searched out and honored chiefly by strangers, sufficiently declares.[1]

The most illustrious example of the third form of the experiment, by a union and co-ordination of Church and State under a solemn league and covenant, belongs to the history of the Westminster Assembly. We may not say, perhaps, that this assembly wrought better than they knew; but certain it is,— for the event has proved it,— that they wrought differently and better than was intended by the statesmen and politicians at whose bidding they assembled. Their theological work, of which the Long Parliament was so impatient, is not perfect;

---

[1] The principles which underlay Calvin's theological and ecclesiastical system have been a powerful factor in the growth of civil liberty. Nevertheless, in the constitution which he created at Geneva, the jurisdiction of the Church was extended over the details of conduct to such a degree as to abridge unduly the liberty of the individual. The power of coercion which was given to the civil authority subverted freedom in religious opinion and worship.— FISHER: *History of the Christian Church*, p. 329.

how could it be under their circumstances? But it is the most permanent, because the best, part of their performance. The political and ecclesiastical peace which they made between the churches of England and Scotland as established by law, and which in the intention of the Parliament was the chief object of the Assembly, lasted just twelve years, and the Presbyterians of Scotland were the most efficient agents in its abolition; though doubtless in this they were deceived and betrayed by putting confidence in princes. The Confession which was imposed upon England by Act of Parliament, and enforced by civil pains and penalties, was never cordially accepted by the great mass of the people, who repudiated it at the first opportunity.[1] And in Scotland the blue banner of the Covenant has waved ever since over a divided Church, whose divisions have grown chiefly out of its connection with the State. The Solemn League and Covenant, so far as it was a pledge to God for holy living, is alive to-day, and will live forever; but in so far as it was an attempt to co-ordinate Church and State in a national covenant which would realize the kingdom of God, it is as dead in the hearts of the great mass of

[1] The Westminster Confession was framed on the basis of a close alliance of Church and State. The assembly was itself the creature of the Long Parliament, appointed and paid by it, and amenable to its authority. The Confession, which was sent to the Parliament under the title of "the Humble Advice," assigns to the civil government the right and duty of calling synods, protecting orthodoxy, and punishing heresy. It thus sanctions the principle of religious persecution; and the Long Parliament acted on this principle by the expulsion of about two thousand clergymen from their livings for nonconformity to Puritanism. The Church of England after the Restoration fully repaid the act of intolerance, with interest, by expelling and starving the Puritan ministers, such as Baxter and Bunyan, for nonconformity to Episcopacy. — SCHAFF: *Essay on Creed Revision*, p. 7.

the people as the Decrees of Constantine. The Presbyterian Church in this country never could have been organized under the Westminster Confession without a radical revision of its doctrine as to Church and State, the repudiation of the essential principle of the Solemn League and Covenant, and the substitution of the sublime truth that "the Lord Jesus Christ, as king and head of the Church, hath therein appointed a government in the hands of Church officers *distinct from the civil magistrate*," and that to these officers, and to them alone, "the keys of the kingdom of heaven are committed." [1]

These attempts to unify the Church and the State in order to realize the kingdom of Christ have all been miserable failures, because they embody an unscriptural and impracticable principle. Even under the Mosaic economy, the theocracy was a failure; it did not establish the kingdom of God from the river to the ends of the earth. But the failure was not on God's side, for He never intended that economy for more than a temporary repository of the truth, until Shiloh should come. And Shiloh could not come, according to His promise and purpose, until the lawgiver had departed from the feet of Judah. The very condition for the setting-up of His world-wide kingdom was the abolition of the Jewish theocracy, the scattering of that covenanted nation, and the casting down of its temple till not one stone is left upon another. The throne of David, on which Peter declares that Christ was seated on the day of Pentecost, is not in Jerusalem, but in heaven.

The noblest of all these attempts to realize the kingdom of Christ, and that which has the best support of Scripture and of reason, is the experiment to subject

[1] Confession, chap. xxx. 1, 2.

the State to the Church, whether it be tried on a large scale in Rome, or on a small scale in Geneva. By all means, if the Church must have a head on earth in order to show her unity and royalty as the kingdom of Christ, let it be a pope, and not a kaiser, — Innocent III. rather than Henry VIII.; John Calvin rather than John the Elector of Saxony.[1] But, thank God, we are not shut up to this hard alternative. "There is no other head of the Church but the Lord Jesus Christ." Whatever may be our views as to the *Anti*christ, let us cling with a positive and loyal adherence to Christ as the only king in Zion.

Is there then no such thing as a Christian nation? And in order to its final triumph, must not the Church of Christ exert her benign and transforming influence upon all human institutions and relations, whether political, commercial, or social? Yes, certainly; this is the very end for which she is endowed and set up in in the world. But she is not authorized nor fitted to do this by direct control, — by "intermeddling with civil affairs which concern the commonwealth," by dictating the laws of trade, or even by regulating the personal and domestic life of men, except as they are regulated in the Word of God, which she is to declare and enforce upon those who voluntarily submit to her government and instruction. Her authority is purely ministerial and declarative. But how mighty is it on that account! The Gospel is the power of God; the sacraments are effectual means of grace and salvation through the presence and blessing of Christ; and these are her Divinely given instruments. The Church can

[1] In principle, a magistratical headship is still more indefensible than a pontifical headship. — WALKER: *Scottish Theology and Theologians*, p. 135.

influence the State only by influencing the several individuals of which the State is composed; and the State can aid the Church only by protecting the several individuals of which the Church is composed, as citizens in the exercise of their freedom to worship God and propagate the truth. When the Gospel is preached to every creature, and just so far as every creature is brought under its dominion, the State not only, but every Divine and human institution and relation and pursuit of human life, will be pervaded and controlled by Christian influences. This is God's plan for the regeneration of human society and of the world, and it is not only sealed with His authority, but backed by His power. "All power," says Christ, "is given unto Me." What will He do with it? Will He dethrone Cæsar? Will He revenge Himself upon Pilate? Will He regulate the civil, commercial, and social affairs of nations? No. He simply says: "Go ye therefore into all the earth, and preach the Gospel to every creature, baptizing them, and teaching them to observe whatsoever I have commanded you." His all-power works through His Gospel and His sacraments.

2. At the opposite extreme from the theory that the Church of Christ is called His kingdom,—to indicate its relation to the kingdoms of this world,—is the notion that the kingdom represents the moral and spiritual forces which constitute the life of the Church, aside altogether from the forms, whether of government, worship, or Church activity, through which they operate. According to this theory, the kingdom of Christ represents the influence which the Church exerts upon the hearts of men and upon human society, as *distinct from the relation she sustains to God, and the piety she cultivates towards Him.*

Thus Dr. Candlish says: —

"Both the Church and the kingdom of God are represented in the New Testament as having a twofold aspect, — external and internal, visible and invisible. The distinction is not that the Church is external, and the kingdom of God spiritual, — for each has both characters, — but that the Church describes the disciples of Christ in their character as a *religious* society, the kingdom of God as a *moral* society. The special functions of the Church are the exercises of worship, and have to do with the relations of men to God; those of the kingdom are the fulfilment of the law of love, the doing of the will of God in all departments and relations of life."[1]

In accordance with these views, he afterwards defines the kingdom of Christ "as a cosmopolitan society of brotherly love."[2] In order to justify this distinction between the Church as religious and the kingdom as moral, and to defend his definition from the charge of narrowing the function of the Church, Dr. Candlish insists that "Christian worship, for which the Church is united, is not a mere performance of external rites and ceremonies," but includes "doing good and communicating, visiting the fatherless and the widows in their affliction, and keeping oneself unspotted from the world."[3] This is sound doctrine, but it obliterates the distinction it is adduced to defend. The Church even in her exercises of worship has to do with the law of love towards men, as well as with her relations to God. The first and great commandment of the law cannot be separated from the second, which is like unto it. The idea of a religious life as separate from the discharge of

[1] Candlish, Kingdom of God, p. 205.
[2] Ibid., p. 240.
[3] Ibid., p. 207.

daily duty in all human relations, has no sanction in the Word of God; and the specific function of the Church, for the performance of which her worship is at once the preparation and the pledge, is to preach the Gospel to every creature, and let her light shine into the darkened hearts and homes of men.

3. Intimately connected with the notion that the Church is religious while the kingdom is moral, is the theory that the Church is called the kingdom only by way of *anticipation*, — that the one is *preparatory* to the other, the Church visible being the *training-school* for the perfecting of moral character, and the Church invisible the *germ* that is to develop at last "into the full and perfect moral society which is the kingdom of God."[1] This distinction between the Church and the kingdom is imaginary; and the restriction of the latter title to a full and perfect moral society is altogether arbitrary. In the Divine conception and purpose, as revealed in Scripture, the Church is a no less perfect ideal than the kingdom. It is her destiny to be cleansed and made glorious, without spot or wrinkle; she is Christ's Body; and it is *in the Church* that "God is to receive glory by Jesus Christ throughout all ages, world without end."[2] It does not expound, but only confuses, the Scriptures to depart from their uniform use of names, and to set up distinctions which they do not recognize. Christ and the Apostles apply both names to the visible society of Christians in its present imperfect form. The influence which this society is designed and fitted to exert, covers all human relations, whether to men or to God. Morality, in the broadest sense of the word, is an essential part of religion. The Gospel is good-will towards

[1] Candlish, Kingdom of God, p. 203.
[2] Ephesians v. 27; i. 23; iii. 21.

men, as well as glory to God. The Church will not grow into the kingdom of God, nor the kingdom of God into the Church; but the Church, which *is* the kingdom of God, will grow out of its present imperfect state into its final completeness and glory. And this growth is not from the visible into the invisible, but in the opposite direction. The invisible and the spiritual is the vital force, the moulding power, the infallible security for the continuance and ultimate completeness of the visible, — just as the seed is the vitality of the tree, as the leaven works in and assimilates the meal with which it is incorporated, as the vine-stock sustains the vine from which the non-fruitful branches are expurged. In the Church, which is the body of Christ, there will be a perfect realization of the transforming power Milton attributes to saintly chastity, —

"Casting a beam on th' outward shape,
The unpolluted temple of the mind,
And turns it by degrees to the soul's essence,
Till all be made immortal."

The image of the earthly will be transfigured into the image of the heavenly, and become more manifestly real, more resplendently visible, by the change. The word "kingdom," as applied to the Church, expresses the Divine authority and power by which this transformation will be accomplished. That power is not the less real and mighty through God because its weapons are not carnal, but spiritual. The name and the essential idea of a kingdom belongs to the Church in both its aspects, but is more insisted upon in its application to the *visible* Church, because it is through its agency so far as any *human* agency is employed, that God will accomplish His purposes in the regeneration of the world, and because its complete visibility is the main fact in the final and perfect triumph of the Church. The unsearchable riches of Christ are to be preached unto the Gentiles, to the intent that unto the principalities and powers in heavenly places might be *made known by the Church* the manifold wisdom of God, that all men and angels " may see what is the fellowship of the mystery which from the beginning of the world hath been hid in God." This is the consummation for which we pray when we say, " Thy kingdom come." [1] This is the doctrine of the Westminster Confession concerning the mission and destiny of the Church. " To this catholic visible Church Christ has given the ministry, oracles, and ordinances of God for the gathering and perfecting of the saints in this life to the end of the world, and doth by His own presence and Spirit, according to His promise, make them effectual thereunto." [2]

III. In open and square opposition to this doctrine we have the *Millenarian*, which is the revival and perpetuation of the ancient *Chiliastic* theory. According to this theory the visible Church and the kingdom of

[1] In one sense the kingdom is already come, — it is established in *spiritual* power, and all its forces are at work. But, as Saint Augustine has expressed it, " Non adhuc regnat hoc regnum ; " for it has yet to grow like the mustard-seed, to work its way like the leaven through all the institutions of the world; it has yet to bear its universal witness to all the nations: only so can the kingdom come in its glory. All this is expressed in the double use of all the characteristic Gospel terms, as of things already enjoyed, and yet of things still to be hoped for. We *are* sons, yet " we wait for the adoption ; " we *are* redeemed, yet we " wait for the redemption of our bodies ; " we *are* saved, yet our " salvation draweth nigh," and is " nearer than when we believed." But it is because the present Church is a simple anticipation of the Church as it is to be — the same society at an earlier stage — that even now it is called the kingdom of heaven. — GORE : *The Church and the Ministry*, p. 43.

[2] Westminster Confession, chap. xxv. sect. 3.

Christ have no vital connection; they are neither contemporaneous nor co-operative. The one is simply the antecedent, but not in any active or efficient sense the preparation, for the other. The kingdom of Christ is a *third* dispensation, distinct from the Church under both its Old and its New Testament economy. The coming of this third dispensation will not be a development, but a catastrophe. The kingdom came near and was offered to the Jews in Christ's day; but they rejected the offer, and crucified their King, and therefore the setting up of the kingdom was postponed to the second coming of Christ. Meantime the visible Church is established, and maintained as a temporary expedient. Her mission is to preach the Gospel to all nations for "a witness *against* them." Under this Gospel dispensation the world is not to grow better, but worse, until Christ returns again to destroy it by the brightness of His coming, and to set up His kingdom on its ruins. Under all the variety of form and coloring in which this theory has been held, its foundation-principle is the doctrine that the kingdom of God is not to be established, nor even inaugurated, upon earth by means of agencies and influences now at work, but is to come by "a sudden supernatural interposition, that will usher in a new dispensation and break all continuity between the present and the millennial age."[1] We cannot enter at length into the discussion of this theory, nor is it necessary to do so. Its sufficient refutation lies on the surface of the New Testament and in the most familiar words of Christ. He called His Church, which He promised to build, "the kingdom of heaven," and delivered the keys of its doctrine and discipline to His living Apostles. He used the phrase, "preaching the kingdom

[1] Candlish, Kingdom of God, p. 336.

of God," as synonymous and identical with the preaching of the Gospel. He constantly spoke of the kingdom as a present reality, "in the midst" of those who heard Him, and told His hearers what it was like, and how it would reach its final consummation at the day of judgment.

The New Testament knows of only one decisive break in the continuity of this dispensation of the Gospel and of the Spirit. The harvest is the end of the world. The day of judgment will wind up the affairs of this world, "gather out of His kingdom all things that offend, and them that do iniquity," banish the wicked into everlasting punishment, and welcome the righteous into life eternal. Moreover, — and this is our main objection to this millenarian theory, — the precepts of Christ in regard to the administration of His ordinances and the extension of His Church are all backed with the promise of success, not with the prophecy of failure. These are all optimistic, not pessimistic. The agencies He instituted in His Church are Divinely adapted and made efficient for their end, and that end is the triumph of His redeeming love. God in Christ *is* reconciling the world unto Himself, and has committed the word of reconciliation to His ministers as to the ambassadors of a king. The preaching of the Gospel to all nations is not merely for a witness *against* them, it is the instrument of their conversion. Its burden is not the cry of Jonah, "Yet forty days, and Nineveh shall be destroyed," but the yearning call of redeeming love, "Look unto Me, and be ye saved, all ye ends of the earth." It is to be preached, not in the spirit of a witness who testifies against those who are to be destroyed, but in the spirit of one who persuades men, and in the confidence of one who believes that the result of his persuasion will be their salvation. The ground of this confidence is the authority of Christ, and the Divine power by which that authority is enforced. And this authority and power, crowning Him as the Head of the visible Church, underlying and pervading all the oracles, ordinances, and sacraments which are committed to her, make the visible Church, in all the stages of her history, from her inauguration at the day of Pentecost to her coronation at the day of judgment, "the kingdom of our Lord Jesus Christ, the house and family of God."

LECTURE III.

THE UNITY OF THE VISIBLE CHURCH.

BECAUSE the Holy Catholic Church consists of all those throughout the world who profess the true religion, some have hastily inferred that the visibility of the Church is nothing more than the visibility of the individuals who belong to it, and that its unity is merely an ideal aggregation of its members. They might as well say that because a city or State consists of the whole number of its inhabitants, therefore it is nothing more than an imaginary collection of those who are born or adopted into it. The United States of America consists of sixty millions of people; therefore these people *are* the United States; and since their unity depends ultimately upon their opinions and sentiments, their unity is altogether inward and invisible. This reasoning, which is manifestly absurd when applied to a kingdom of this world, is no less so when applied to the kingdom of Christ. Citizenship necessarily implies an organized State. The professing Christian is "no longer a stranger and foreigner, but a fellow-citizen with the saints, and of the household of God." A member of the Church, as the name implies, is a part of a body, which, though it has *many* members, is *one* body. This is Paul's reasoning. He says to the Church of God, which is at Corinth, including both worthy and unworthy members, "Now ye are the *body of Christ*, and members in particular" (1 Cor. xii.

27). It is in this same body that God has set apostles, prophets, and teachers. To make it mean the invisible Church of the elect, leads to endless contradiction and absurdity. "For upon that supposition no minister could ever exercise his office towards any non-elected man, the pastoral relation could never be fixed without knowing beforehand who are the elect of God; or else no person, however blasphemous and abominable, could be kept out of a church, because such a blasphemer and injurious may possibly be a chosen vessel."[1] The same remarks apply to the interpretation of the fourth chapter of Ephesians, where the Apostle tells us "there is one body, and one Spirit" (verse 4). The body is not the Spirit, but that in which the Spirit dwells, through whose members He works and manifests His presence. It is to this same body that Christ, in His ascension, gave gifts; namely, "apostles, prophets, evangelists, pastors, and teachers, for the perfecting of the saints, for the work of the ministry, for the edifying of the body of Christ" (Eph. iv. 11, 12). These ascension gifts were not bestowed upon the "Church of the first-born, which are written in heaven," neither is the work of the ministry confined to those who are members of the mystical body of Christ, and known only to God; nor are these gifts and this work of the ministry peculiar to any congregation of professed believers, nor to any combination of such particular churches. The one body can be nothing less than the visible Catholic Church. The truth of this position is further demonstrated by the scope and design of the Apostle's argument in both of the passages to which we have referred. That design is, positively, to "keep the unity of the Spirit in the bonds of peace" (Eph. iv. 3), and negatively, that there "be no schism in

[1] Dr. John M. Mason, Works, ii. 287.

the body" (1 Cor. xii. 25.) The unity of the Spirit is not a mere spiritual unity, which has no outward embodiment and expression. It is the same unity for which Christ prayed, "that they all may be one; that *the world may believe that Thou hast sent Me*" (John xvii. 21). How can the world be convinced by a unity which they cannot see? The antithesis of unity is *schism*, or division, which is an outward and visible thing. There never has been, nor *can* be, any division in the ideal body of the elect, which is known only to God. "A schism which cannot be perceived is no schism; and the moment you render it perceptible, you are in a visible church."[1] The visible Church, therefore, is the one body of Christ, in which Christ prays and Paul exhorts that there may be no divisions.

What constitutes this visible Church one body? The question is twofold. It may refer to the life, or to the organization in which that life is incorporated. A clay model, or even a marble statue, however express and admirable, is not a human body. Man formed of the dust of the earth did not become a living being till God breathed into his nostrils the breath of life. A corpse is not a human body, in the full sense of the word. No sooner does the life leave the earthly house of this tabernacle than it begins to dissolve. The analogy between the human body and the Church, the body of Christ, is complete. The Holy Spirit, given to the visible Church at her inauguration on the day of Pentecost as a permanent endowment, is admitted on all sides to be her life and the vital bond of her unity. By this gift God does not limit Himself to her agency, but He guarantees her continued life as a Divine institution in the world, and her ultimate

[1] Mason, Works, ii. 287.

attainment of the ends for which she was established. What then is the organization, or, if we may so speak, the *anatomy* of the body in which the Holy Spirit dwells? This is a question of great importance, and we desire to answer it explicitly. Our inquiry is not concerning the outward garments in which men have arrayed her, some of which are "beautiful" (Isaiah lii. 1), and others more fit for a harlot than for the Bride of Christ. But stripped of all human additions, whether lawful or unlawful, what is the Divine constitution of the visible Church?

We say, *first* of all, that the adoption of a formulated creed or confession is no part of that constitution. This, of course, is not intended to deny the lawfulness, nor even the necessity, of creeds under existing circumstances. We only say that creeds or confessions, in the technical sense of the words, are no part of the Divine constitution of the visible Church, and therefore not essential to her unity. The conclusive proof of this position is the fact that for more than three hundred years after her establishment the Christian Church had no creed beside the simple and ever-varying confession of Christ connected with the sacrament of baptism. The Church under the Old Testament never had any creed aside from the Word of God, nor is any express warrant for creeds found in the New Testament Scriptures. To make "the form of sound words" or "the faith once delivered to the saints" synonymous with any denominational confession, is a monstrous usurpation.

We say, *secondly*, that no particular form of church government is essential to the existence and unity of the visible Church. The proof of this position is that, aside from certain great principles, *no definite form of church government is laid down in the Word of God.*

On this point we agree most heartily with Dr. Charles Hodge : —

"The Church is to be governed by principles laid down in the Word of God, which determine within certain limits her officers and mode of organization; but beyond these prescribed principles, and in fidelity to them, the Church has a wide discretion in the choice of methods, organs, and agencies. . . . Christ in His infinite wisdom has left His Church free to modify her government, in accordance with these general principles, as may best suit her circumstances in different ages and nations."[1]

As there is no definite form of church government prescribed in the precepts of Christ, neither is there any enacted in the example of the Apostles. The plain fact is, that the Apostles did not follow the same plan at all times. They varied the organization of churches to suit different places and occasions. No man can deduce any of the existing forms of church government in their detailed arrangements, or even in their distinctive features, from the facts recorded in the Acts of the Apostles, nor from the precepts given in the Epistles; and the wisest expositors have given up the hopeless attempt. There is nothing in the New Testament to prove the primacy of Peter, whom Paul withstood to the face. Even if we recognize in James the diocesan bishop of Jerusalem, there was certainly no such bishop in the church at Ephesus when Paul told the elders of that church that the Holy Ghost had made *them* the *episcopoi* (which the Revised Version properly renders the bishops) of that flock. Moreover, it is not possible to show that among these presbyter bishops at Ephesus, or among "the prophets and teachers" at Antioch (Acts xiii. 1), or among the "bishops and deacons" at Philippi

[1] Hodge's Polity, p. 277.

(Phil. i. 1), there ever were what we call "ruling elders."[1]

We say, *thirdly*, that the organization and unity of the visible Church does not consist in nor depend upon any prescribed and uniform mode of worship. The elements of worship are prescribed, but not the form. The preaching of the Gospel, the reading of the Scriptures, prayer, the singing of Psalms and hymns and spiritual songs, the administration of the sacraments, and the offering of

[1] The claim which the Presbyterian standards make for the ruling eldership as an integral part of church government, is very moderate. The Form of Government (chap. iv.) says: "Ruling elders are *properly the representatives of the people*, chosen by them for the purpose of exercising government and discipline in conjunction with pastors or ministers. This office has been understood by a great part of the Protestant Reformed churches to be designated, in the Holy Scriptures, by the title of governments and of those who rule well but do not labor in word and doctrine." The Puritan doctrine as laid down by Thomas Cartwright (in his "Ecclesiastical Discipline"), "that nothing ought to be established in the Church which is not *commanded* in the Word of God," has been practically abandoned by all denominations of Christians. The interpretation of 1 Tim. v. 17, which makes it prove "that there was in the Apostles' days a formal distinction among those who bore the common name of presbyter, — that some were set apart to the work of both teaching and ruling, and others to that simply of ruling, — is certainly not expressly said, and has often been disputed as well by Presbyterian and Independent writers as by Roman Catholics and Episcopalians" (Fairbairn's Pastoral Epistles, p. 213). Ruling elders "are *properly* representatives of the people." This is their peculiar function. And the authority for their appointment is the divine right of the people, as distinguished from the ministry, to participate in the government of the Church, and their discretionary power to choose their own representatives. (See Hodge's Polity, p. 262.) The recognition of this right is no longer, if it ever was, a *distinctive* feature of Presbyterianism. Congregationalists and Baptists always acknowledged it practically, and Methodists and Episcopalians have incorporated lay-representation into their forms of government.

gifts, — these are all warranted and enjoined in Scripture. But the form under which these are to be observed or administered is left discretionary. The Puritan principle, that nothing is to be permitted in our worship which is not expressly commanded or sanctioned in Scripture, is itself contrary to both the examples and the precepts of Scripture; there is not a body of Christians on earth who have not violated it; and the attempt of the different denominations to justify their forms and ceremonies — or even their professed lack of forms, which often covers the most rigid formality — by an appeal to the Word of God, leads to a continual wresting of the Scriptures, which brings them into contempt.[1]

If the organization and unity of the visible Church does not consist in the adoption of creeds, nor in forms of government, nor in modes of worship, wherein does

---

[1] There has been a remarkable change during the past fifty years in all non-liturgical denominations in regard to forms of worship. This change is very marked among Presbyterians. The Directory for Worship is advisory rather than obligatory. Ministers and elders are not required to adopt nor to approve it. In its recommendations it concedes a large liberty as to the *forms* of worship, and in our day this liberty is being largely used. Fifty years ago the use of the Apostles' Creed and the responsive reading of the Psalms was unheard of, and would not have been tolerated in any of our churches; and even the occasional use of the Lord's Prayer and the Ten Commandments in our public assemblies was looked upon with disfavor. But a change has come noiselessly but manifestly, as the outbreak of the foliage in the spring. This change began in our Sunday-schools. We have trained a generation to the use of simple liturgical forms, and the logical result has followed. We must reform our Sunday-schools after the prevailing customs of fifty years ago, or we must disown our own children at the church door, and send them elsewhere for the gratification of tastes we have cultivated in them, or, as the only remaining alternative, we must continue in the course upon which we have entered, and give the people some audible share in our public worship.

it consist? What constitutes all those throughout the world who profess the true religion, the one Body of Christ? We answer that four things are essential to the organization and life of a *particular* church; and the same things are equally characteristic and efficient in the Holy *Catholic* Church, of which every particular church is the miniature and the type: (1) The Confession of Jesus Christ as the Son of God, the Saviour of men, and the Supreme Head of the Church.[1] (2) A living ministry, called of God's Spirit, and ordained to their work according to His appointment. (3) The faithful preaching of the Gospel. (4) The due administration of the sacraments.[2] This statement is but the

---

[1] Sufficient emphasis has not been laid upon the confession of Christ as a formative and unifying principle of the Church. Peter's confession, "Thou art the Christ, the Son of the living God," secured Christ's "Blessed art thou, Peter, and on this rock I will build my Church" (Matt. xvi. 18). Neither the benediction nor the promise is confined to Peter. "Whosoever shall confess me before men, him will I also confess before my Father in heaven" (Matt. x. 32). "If thou shalt confess with thy mouth the Lord Jesus, and believe in thy heart that God raised him from the dead, thou shalt be saved" (Rom. x. 9). "Whosoever shall confess that Jesus is the Son of God, God dwelleth in him, and he in God" (1 John iv. 15).

Such confession not only conditions the acceptance of the individual with God, but unites the confessors in a community before the world.

[2] There is no essential difference between the definitions of the visible Church given by Christians of all denominations, except that which relates to the supremacy of the Pope. Bellarmine, the great Roman Catholic authority, says, "The Church is the society of men united by the profession of the same faith, and the communion of the same sacraments, under the government of legitimate pastors, and especially of the only vicar of Christ on earth, the Roman Pontiff" (Bellarmine, On the Church, book iii. chap. 2).

Strike out the clause relating to the Pope, and what remains is

analysis and expression in another form of what Paul teaches in the fourth chapter of his Epistle to the Ephesians, "There is one body, and one Spirit." It is the indwelling and power of the Spirit that makes and keeps the body one; but that oneness is wrought out and made visible by the acknowledgment and possession of "one Lord, one faith, one baptism, and one Divinely given ministry."[1] If it be objected to this statement that it excludes from the visible Church some who, like the Quakers, profess Christianity, and yet reject the ministry and the sacraments, we answer, that their profession is incomplete. As interpreted by themselves, it denies not only the lawfulness of an ordained ministry

accepted by all Christians who believe in any Church. "The Church is the whole society of Christians throughout the world, including all those who profess their belief in Christ, and who are subject to lawful pastors " (Palmer, On the Church, i. 28).

To this corresponds the definition of the Thirty-nine Articles: " The visible Church of Christ is a congregation of faithful men, in which the pure Word of God is preached, and the sacraments be duly administered according to Christ's ordinance in all those things that of necessity are requisite to the same " (Art. 19).

The Westminster Confession teaches precisely the same thing when it says: " The Catholic visible Church consists of all those throughout the world who profess the true religion, together with their children " (chap. xxv. 21); for it teaches also that the profession of the true religion includes the observance of the sacraments and submission to lawful pastors. The question at issue between the Episcopalians and other denominations, as between them and the Roman Catholics, is, *Who are lawful pastors*, and what constitutes *the due administration of the sacraments?*

[1] The same elements appear in the analysis of the great commission (Matt. xxviii. 19). " All power is given unto Me in heaven and in earth. Go ye therefore, and teach [disciple] all nations, baptizing them in the name of the Father, of the Son, and of the Holy Ghost: teaching them to observe all things whatsoever I have commanded you: and, lo, I am with you alway, even unto the end of the

and of the administration of the sacraments, but the very existence of any such body as the visible Catholic Church. They do not claim to be members of it. Why should we force upon them names and privileges which they repudiate, especially when we freely admit that their exclusion from the visible Church does not shut them out from the Church of the first-born which are written in heaven?

We come now to the practical question, how far these views correspond with the existing state of things. Is the Church one in fact, as it is in our theory? And if not, which is wrong, the facts, or the theory? Whether what is commonly understood by "organic union" — *i. e.*, the consolidation of all Christian denominations in the world, or in any particular country, under one statement of doctrine and one administration of government — will ever be practicable, we are not competent to say. It is enough to observe that it is not practicable now. Such a consolidation has been the dream of the Church of Rome for fifteen centuries. The attempt to enforce her exclusive claims has produced little more than schism, strife, and bloodshed. She stands to-day stripped of her temporal power, simply as one of the denominations of Christendom. She is not in fact the

world." Here we have the sacraments, the preaching of the Gospel, the Divinely ordained ministry, and the confession of Christ's supremacy, necessarily involved in the acceptance of the ministry and sacraments. The same elements are apparent in the description of the infant Church in Acts ii. 41, 42. "Then they that gladly received the Word were baptized: and the same day there were added [to what? To *the Church*, v. 47] about three thousand souls. And they continued steadfastly in the Apostles' doctrine and fellowship, and in breaking of bread, and in prayers." The Greek has the article, and ought to be translated "*the* bread," and "*the* prayers," which plainly means the holy communion and public worship.

Catholic Church. "Catholic *Rome*," says Bishop Hall, "is an absurd Montanistic solecism, an attempt to find *orbem in urbe*." She is herself largely responsible for the existing divisions of Christendom, and for their bitter fruits. She made the schism of the Reformation (if it was a schism), not only by refusing to reform abuses which the best of her own adherents recognized, but by casting out and anathematizing those who would gladly have remained in her communion. Luther did not excommunicate the Pope till the Pope had excommunicated him. She cultivates and scatters broadcast the wrath and bitterness which are the worst fruits of schism, by her denunciation of all who do not acknowledge her authority as above the authority of God speaking in the Holy Scriptures. In her attitude towards Christians outside of her fold she covers herself with curses as with a garment. Jesus Christ came not to condemn the world, but that the world through Him might be saved. The Roman hierarchy, claiming to be His sole representative on earth, condemns to eternal death all who do not submit to its authority. In the decrees of the Council of Trent, *Anathema sit* (Let him be damned) is applied to the rejection of more than three hundred points of belief, most of which are utterly without warrant of Scripture. God has not committed such judgment to men. It is not the prerogative of any man or church to excommunicate any one from heaven, nor to pronounce upon any the awful sentence of damnation.

The Puritan dream of a visible church on earth composed only of the elect and the regenerated, begets a new Popery scarce less offensive than the old. In its attempts to gather up the tares it roots up the wheat also, and when it is in league with the secular power, leads inevitably to persecution.

The fires of Smithfield and the flames that burned Servetus were kindled by the same torch. The Act of Conformity, by which in 1662 thousands of Presbyterian and Congregational ministers were expelled from the English churches, was but a repetition of the same treatment Episcopalian ministers had received from the Presbyterian Parliament under "the humble advice" of the Westminster Assembly. The divines of the seventeenth century all believed in the enforcement of Church government and worship by the State. They all held that religious toleration was a damnable heresy; and the only question at issue between them at this point was who should get possession of the whip of small cords and drive all the others out. Let us thank God that we live in a more enlightened age, when "the right of private judgment in all matters that respect religion" is recognized by all Protestant Christians "as universal and unalienable."[1] And let us carry out the same principle in the doctrine and discipline of the Church itself. The function of the Church is purely ministerial and declarative. She has no right to make any new law to bind men's consciences; she has no right to make anything a term of communion which God has not declared in His Word to be a term of salvation; and in the application of these terms to individuals, she can only accept their credible professions, without pretending to judge their hearts. If the anathemas of the Council of Trent are revolting in their usurpation of Divine prerogatives and their lack of the loving spirit of Christ, no less revolting are the rash judgments of individuals or of ecclesiastical assemblies, making every difference of opinion a heresy, and every deviation from a humanly prescribed ritual a ground of

[1] Presbyterian Form of Government, chap. i. sect. 1.

exclusion from the Church. Dr. Alexander Hodge said in one of his last public utterances, "there is nothing more outrageously vulgar and profane than the coarse and careless shouting out of threats of damnation against heedless sinners by an orthodox ranter."[1]

There may be nothing more vulgar and profane, but there is something more presumptuous and inconsistent with the unity of Christ's Body, when a minister of Christ exalts his sect into *the* Church, sneers at all worship which is not offered under its forms, and denies the validity of all sacraments which are not administered according to its orders. How far this intolerant spirit is the legitimate fruit of the existing divisions of Christendom, and how far these divisions are the outgrowth of such a spirit, is a problem we are not competent to solve. But the question whether the organization of Christians under different and rival forms of government, confessions of faith, and modes of worship, can be justified by Scripture or by the practical workings of the system, presses for an answer upon every thoughtful Christian soul. It is *the* question of our time, rising above all past theological and ecclesiastical controversies. Does the Scripture recognition of Christian congregations in particular neighborhoods as *churches*, and the further recognition of the whole body of such churches in one city or country as *the Church* of that city or country, justify the organization of denominational churches on the principle of elective affinity? Are elective affinity and local convenience only different applications of the same principle? The best possible argument in the affirmative of this question is presented by Dr. Charles Hodge. Starting with the postulate that "there is nothing in

[1] Popular Lectures on Theological Themes, p. 416.

independent organization, in itself considered, inconsistent with unity, so long as common faith is professed and mutual recognition preserved," he proceeds to show that the Episcopal Church in England and in this country are one, and the Presbyterian Church of Scotland and in this country are one, notwithstanding their separate organizations; and all that is needed to make the Episcopal and Presbyterian churches in Great Britain and the United States one, is their mutual recognition." From these premises he proceeds to argue that if independent organization, on account of different *locality* or civil relations, is compatible with unity, so also is independent organization on account of diversity of language or diversity of opinion, provided such diversity does not violate unity of faith. "Diversity of opinion is indeed an evidence of imperfection, and therefore such separations are evil, so far as they are evidence of want of perfect unity in faith; but they are less evil than hypocrisy or contention, and therefore the diversity of sects is to be regarded as incident to imperfect knowledge and imperfect sanctification. *It is to be deplored;* yet the evil is not to be magnified above its just dimensions."[1] And this is all that can be said in defence of existing denominationalism. The proviso of "mutual recognition," which conditious the whole argument, is sadly wanting in practical fulfilment. Nor can it be denied that the unity of faith, though it be not destroyed, is greatly obscured by the magnifying of minor differences. The proposition that diversity of sects is "a less evil than hypocrisy and contention," is undeniable; but is not this choice between evils a sorry defence for the Christian Church? Would it not be better to choose neither? The conclusion is irresist-

[1] Hodge's Polity of the Church, p. 43.

ible that denominationalism is *an evil to be deplored*. But *do* we deplore it as we should? Do we not rather glory in it? A living Princeton divine said recently in private conversation, "Denominations are an advertisement of universal ignorance." The words were well chosen. It is not a *confession*, but an *advertisement* of ignorance; and the ignorance is not of that kind which humbles, and is sometimes supposed to be the mother of devotion. It is rather that half knowledge which perverts vision, puffs up and behaves itself unseemly. Every Christian, and especially every minister, ought to look the existing facts squarely in the face. To do this we must cease our self-eulogies, the undue magnifying of human systems, and the worship that is paid at sepulchres full of dead men's bones. We must assume a position above traditional prejudices, controversies, and resentments. We must imbue our minds with the essential facts and principles of the Gospel, with the perishing need of the world, with the great commission of the Church to go and preach the Gospel to every creature. We must put the name of Christ above every name.

Paul speaks to the whole Christian Church as he did to the saints at Corinth: "Now this I say, that every one of you saith, I am of Paul; and I of Apollos; and I of Cephas; and I of Christ. Is Christ divided? was Paul crucified for you? or were ye baptized in the name of Paul?" Which being interpreted, means, " Every one of you saith I am of John Calvin, I am of Martin Luther, I am of Arminius, I am of Cranmer, I am of Augustine, I am of Cyprian, I am of all the Fathers, I am of Peter, the first of the Popes. Were any of these crucified for you, or were ye baptized in their name?" Laying aside all theories, look at the concrete facts as they exist before our eyes. We cannot take in the world at one view;

let us look at a single locality as the type of the whole.
Here is a town, not a hundred miles away from any of
us. It has one thousand inhabitants, or about two hundred families, — just enough to make one self-supporting church, able to sustain its minister and contribute
to the sending of the Gospel to the unevangelized. But
instead of one such church, it has five sickly organizations, with as many half-starved and discontented ministers, sustained in whole or in part by aid from some
Missionary Board. One of these churches has a steeple
surmounted with the cross, — the common symbol of
Christianity. The others, if they have steeples at all,
have crowned them with a weather-cock. All these
churches claim to be Christian; but they all bear denominational names, and each is a rival of the others.
Now, the evil of this state of things does not consist
only nor chiefly in its waste of Christian resources, but
the chief evil is its demoralizing effect upon religious
experience and Christian character. It narrows men's
souls by concentrating on a sect the sympathies and
affections which ought to expand upon the whole body
of Christ; and this effect is the most shrivelling when
men succeed in deluding themselves into the belief that
their sect *is* the body of Christ. It creates false tests
and standards of personal piety. It mars the symmetrical growth of the soul in the knowledge of Christ, by
magnifying certain doctrines to the neglect or denial of
others. The notion that it is the mission of different
denominations to bear witness to *particular phases* of
Divine truth, might be well enough if the people to
whom this witness is borne were brought under the influence of all the witnesses. But to subject one Christian to the teaching of Divine Sovereignty, and another
to the insistence upon human freedom, cultivates two

different types of character, neither of which is according to the truth. The idea of a "witness-bearing church,"—that is, a body of Christians with a special Divine commission to bear testimony against *other bodies of Christians*, while it is pleaded in defence of denominationalism, is in fact one of the worst fruits of the system. The effect of the system upon the sacraments is no less to be deplored. It obscures the true meaning of these holy ordinances by contracting the table of the Lord to the close communion of a party in His Church, and by making baptism the badge of a sect; so that one says, "I was baptized an *Episcopalian*," and another, "I was baptized a *Presbyterian*," and another, "I was baptized a *Baptist*." The effect of denominationalism upon the ministry is no less deplorable. It too often degrades the servant and ambassador of Christ into the hired man of a voluntary association, and suspends his reputation and influence upon his success in making proselytes from other "societies." That minister must be a strong man who, in adjusting his work to such conditions, does not lose somewhat of the spirit of his high commission, and shrivel his own mind to the dimensions of a *Gossip*.[1]

These evils are greatly aggravated by their complication with social distinctions and family pride. Denominational lines, in such communities as we have described, are very apt to follow the lines of class distinctions and to deepen them with "the Gospel plough." Religious societies become social clubs, and get rid of the question about seating the poor man in vile raiment

---

[1] "Gossip" is an ecclesiastical term,—a corruption of "Godsib." It was first applied to sponsors in baptism; and its development into its present popular use is not without historic significance. See Brewer's "Dictionary of Phrase and Fable."

by making it practically certain that he will not come into the same assembly with the man in goodly apparel and a gold ring. "The Salvation Army," or any other outside effort, is good enough for him. And so we look with complacency upon the spasmodic movements of zeal without knowledge, and even patronize them from a distance, as a salvo to our conscience, not perceiving that the plea for their necessity, and indeed fact of their existence, is a standing reproach to the Church. What wonder, if in this state of things one half of our settled ministers in all denominations are unsettled in their minds, and waiting for "a call!" What wonder if the doors of vacant churches are besieged by an army of candidates, composed not only of young men who are openly looking for their first charge, but largely of old soldiers, some of whom by unworthy devices conceal the fact of their candidacy! Surely, if we need a civil service reform in the State, there is no less need of a pastoral service reform in the Church. And this reform, to be effective, must begin at the denominationalism which fills the land with feeble churches and half-supported ministers, and wastes in sectarian rivalries what ought to go to the evangelizing of the world.

The first and most important step towards the correction of any evil is to see and acknowledge its existence; and the second is like unto it, — an earnest desire for a better state of things. The unity of Christendom — a unity that the world can see, and be convinced by it that the Father has sent His only begotten Son — is to-day a longing in the heart and a prayer on the lips of multitudes of Christians. We hail every expression of such desire as a prophecy of its fulfilment, according to others the same sincerity we claim for ourselves. We do not sympathize with those who view with squint suspicion the proposals for reunion by the American Episcopal Church indorsed by the Lambeth Conference; and while we cannot accept the terms proposed, in their present form, as sufficient and practicable, we do heartily embrace and respond to their spirit. The reunion of Christendom is a sublime idea, an inspiring hope. It is not necessary to the indulgence of this hope to forecast the precise form of its fulfilment; and therefore we need not exclude from its embrace any of those throughout the world who profess the true religion. The best things in the world are not *made*, they *grow*. The unification of Christendom, as a whole or in part, cannot be accomplished by bargains and contracts between rival sects. Neither can it be effected by the absorption of one denomination under the distinctive forms of another. The *Romanist* may cry, "Lay aside your private judgment and submit to the infallible Pope;" the *Episcopalian* may say, "Come and be ordained by our bishops;" the *Baptist* may say, "Come and be immersed;" the *Presbyterian* may say, "We acknowledge the validity of your orders and sacraments, only accept our Calvinism, and we will be one;" and the *Methodist* may respond, "Give up your Calvinism, and accept our doctrine of free grace." But what do all these invitations amount to? They cannot be accepted. Men cannot and ought not to renounce their personal convictions of truth. If you should dissolve all Christian denominations to-day, it would create, not union, but anarchy. If you should renounce all creeds, the result would be, not a broader faith, but a confusion of tongues. Is there then no practicable way in which we may work towards the fulfilment of our hopes? Yes, certainly. We can hold to our distinctive forms, whether of discipline or of worship; but we can hold the form in subordination to the substance. We can hold our distinctive creeds until the time comes when they can be safely laid aside, meanwhile recognizing Christ, the Incarnate Word, as above all written words, human or Divine, the confession of faith in Him as above all creed subscriptions, and the Catholic Church, which is His Body, as above all Christian denominations. If these principles are accepted, not in word only, but in power, their dominance will show itself. There are three directions in which they may work themselves out gradually, but mightily, like the dawning of the day, — Recognition, Co-operation, and Federation.

1. *Recognition.* The Church of Rome is the only Christian denomination which officially claims to be *the* Church in any exclusive sense;[1] and this claim, coupled with her denial of any distinction between the Church as visible and invisible, necessarily precludes the church-standing, the Christian character, and the salvation of all who do not acknowledge her authority and participate in her sacraments. In this she is terribly logical and consistent. But what is to hinder any and all Protestant denominations from acknowledging each other individually and collectively as belonging to the Church of Christ, and treating each other accordingly? Theo-

[1] Some Episcopalians constantly speak of their own denomination as "the Church," and studiously avoid giving that name to any other denomination. The folly of this assumption is sufficiently declared by the title of their own Prayer-Book, which is "The Book of Common Prayer of the *Protestant Episcopal* Church *in* The United States of America." And the significance of this title is emphasized by the recent refusal of their Convention to strike out the words *Protestant Episcopal*. Whatever may be true of individuals, our Episcopal brethren as a body do not officially claim to be *the* Church in any exclusive sense; for which we are glad, for *their* sake more than for our own.

retically, and aside from the sectarian spirit of which we are all more or less guilty, there are only two obstacles in the way, — the mode of *baptism*, and the mode of *ordination* to the ministry.[1] But that these are not insuperable obstacles to mutual recognition, is evident; because upon the supposition that the validity of the sacraments depends upon the specific mode of their administration, and the authority of the ministry to administer them, and their consequent efficacy, depends upon a particular mode of ordination to the ministry, — it is not credible that Christ and His Apostles should fail to leave on record specific instructions which would prevent the possibility of mistake upon the subject. It may not be possible even for God to state an *abstract doctrine* in human language so that all human minds will apprehend it alike; but there is no such difficulty in the way of describing an act to be performed by human hands. If Christ was *immersed* Himself, and meant all His disciples to follow His example in this respect, and if immersion is essential to the validity

[1] It is a mistake to suppose that the causes of division and the obstacles of unity among Christians are mainly doctrinal. "It is clear, from the history of the Church, that diversity as to forms of church government or matters connected with worship and discipline, *more than differences about doctrine*, has been the cause of existing divisions in the Church. . . . Differences as to doctrine do not form such insuperable barriers to church union as diversity of opinion respecting ecclesiastical government. The creed of a church may be so general, embracing only the fundamental doctrines of the Gospel, such as can be professed with a good conscience by all true Christians, and thus ministers and members who differ widely within those limits may unite in one ecclesiastical organization. It is notorious that great differences of doctrine prevail in all large churches, as in the Church of England and in the Church of Scotland, and in this country in the Episcopal Church, and in less degree, perhaps, among Presbyterians" (Hodge, Church Polity, 95, 96).

of baptism, why did he not say so? Why is it not so written in explicit terms? If any one answers, "He *did* say so, and it *is* so written," we respond, "We cannot see it." And the fact that millions of the holiest and wisest men in all the Christian ages, whose candor and love of truth are beyond question, have not been able to see it, is proof conclusive that it is not there. The same observations apply to ordination to the ministry. If Paul and the other Apostles believed that no ordination is valid unless it be performed by the hands of a diocesan bishop, distinct from and superior in office to ordinary ministers, and that the succession of such ordinations is essential to the existence of the visible Church and to the efficacy of her sacraments, why did they not say so, and record the doctrine in explicit terms, for the instruction of all ages? The fact that men equally learned and honest differ on the subject, is proof conclusive that there is no such record. When our Episcopal brethren, in their overture for reunion, insist upon the *historic*, meaning the *diocesan*, episcopate as equally essential with the Holy Scriptures and the holy sacraments, we remind them that there is a *pre-historic* episcopate which is not diocesan, and that by their own acknowledgment what they call the historic episcopate is not explicitly enjoined in the Scriptures, which "contain all things necessary to salvation, and are the rule and ultimate standard of faith." Oh, is it not pitiful in the sight of God and angels that the mere mode of administering two outward ordinances, concerning which He has given no explicit instructions, should be magnified into partition-walls between His disciples for whom He prays that they all may be one! And the pity becomes more profound when we consider the fact that these two obstacles have not always and everywhere been regarded as insurmountable. It is only in this country that the Baptist denomination make their mode of baptism a warrant for "close communion." It is only since the days of Charles I. and his prime minister, Archbishop Laud, that the Episcopal denomination have refused to recognize the validity of other ordinations beside their own.

We shall be reminded that now and here these partition-walls are not so high as to prevent the different denominations from looking *over them*, and mutually recognizing each other as Christians. We admit this, and rejoice in the growing spirit of inter-denominational comity which is so characteristic of our times. But it is the unity of the visible Church that we are contending for. We long for church recognition as the only legitimate and permanent embodiment of Christian fellowship. Mutual recognition, aside from the organic life and work of the churches, performed as a holiday parade, and upon platforms erected for that special purpose, is little more than a confession of the evils of denominationalism; it does not apply any practical remedy. Sweet and pleasant in itself, it is only a sentiment, and unless it is embodied in deeds, it will evaporate in the words that express it. If it goes no farther, its practical effect is to disparage the Church and to alienate thinking men from her life and her work. What we need is such a mutual recognition as will lead to co-operation.

2. And this co-operation must be within, and not outside of, the visible Church. We do not undertake to forecast its methods, but we have a very distinct prevision of its results. *First* of all it will prevent the needless multiplication of churches, and the waste of Christian means and energies in particular localities.

Secondly, it will elevate the ministry, and cultivate a nobler type of Christian character, by laying aside petty rivalries and strifes about words and forms of worship whose only effect is the perversion of the hearers, and by insisting upon the great central facts and doctrines of Christianity. *Thirdly*, it will add immense resources and give a new impulse to the missionary work of the Church, which is the chief object of her existence, and it will give new efficacy to that work by presenting a united front and lifting up high above all sectarian colors the common banner of Christianity before the heathen world.

3. As both an expression and a practical means of promoting this recognition and co-operation, we are heartily in favor of *federation* between any and all denominations of Christians.

One thing seems clear, — that the unification of the Church cannot be accomplished by one denomination working upon another from without. Proselytism, whether by argument or persuasion, is a waste of time and strength. The converts made by such means are far fetched and little worth. Neither, again, can the denominations be unified by any power separate from and above them all. The wrecks of that experiment are scattered along the whole path of history. The time for world-empires, whether of the Church or the State, is past. The unity of the Church can be effected only by a vital power dwelling in every part and common to all. That power can be none other than the Holy Spirit. But the Spirit of God, in nature and in grace, works by means. Cosmos, "the beautiful order," was not imposed upon, but evolved out of, Chaos. The Spirit,

> " with mighty wings outspread,
> Dovelike, sat brooding on the vast abyss,
> And made *it* pregnant."

The earth and the waters brought forth abundantly. The unification of Christian denominations must be attained by bringing out into clearer recognition and adjusting to new relations that which is already in them. The first stage in the process is the practical acknowledgment that the things in which they agree, whether in doctrine, discipline, or worship, are not only more important in their bearing, but more and greater in themselves, than the things in which they differ.

The conviction of this truth comes home to every candid mind in the careful study of the creeds of Christendom. But the thought of theologians and scholars needs to be embodied in a visible form, in order to be apprehended by the popular mind. What more simple or safe embodiment of the idea can be invented than the federation of Christian denominations? The possibilities of such federation are unlimited. It does not involve the surrender of sectarian peculiarities, but simply the subordination of them for a time to that which is confessedly higher and more important. Under any plan which may be adopted it will have this great advantage, that practice will go hand in hand with theory, and the experiment reach no farther than experience shall warrant. Beginning on a small scale, and embracing at first only the subdivisions of sects holding the same system of doctrine and order, and separated by distinctions as small as the difference between a psalm and a hymn, or between the sound of a pitch-pipe and the swell of an organ, who shall say that it will not enlarge its circumference and intensify its assimilating power until it includes the Christian world in its embrace? It is easy to sit in the seat of the polemic, surmising difficulties and predicting failure; but it is far nobler to hope for and hasten unto the blessed time when out of many folds there shall be one flock and one Shepherd. The greatest living poet sang in his youth of a political millennium, —

"When the war-drums throb no longer, and the battle-flags are furled
In the parliament of men, the federation of the world;"

and though the vision has not yet come to pass, who will say there has been no progress towards its fulfilment? Behind and above all the kingdoms of the world is the kingdom of our Lord and His Christ. Of the increase of His government and peace there shall be no end. Who shall say how near may be the time when the isles which wait for His law shall hail the light of His coming, and the troubled sea, moaning on every shore, shall hear and be hushed at the stillness of His voice? And above all, who will refuse to do what he can to prepare the way of the Lord; to exalt every valley; to make low every mountain; to gather out the stones, and make smooth the rough places in the highway of our God? I am a Presbyterian, not only by birth, but by conviction, and yield to no man in loyalty to the denomination in whose service my life has been spent, and in whose bosom I hope to die. But I do not expect to be a Presbyterian, nor anything of the kind, in heaven. And as my sun grows larger and more mellow towards its setting, I would gladly exchange everything that is not essentially Christian for a few of the days of heaven on earth in the unity and peace of the Church of God which He hath purchased with His own blood.

LECTURE IV.

THE CHURCH MEMBERSHIP OF INFANTS.

CHURCH membership is the birthright of all who are born of Christian parents. This Christian birthright is recognized and confirmed in the baptism of infants. We say "the baptism of infants," not "infant" baptism; because the latter phrase sanctions the popular error that there are two kinds of baptism, and that the ordinance as administered to infants is not, in the full sense of the word, a sacrament, but only a ceremony of consecration. We hold with Paul that there "is one Lord, one faith, one baptism" (Eph. iv. 5), — one in the correspondence between the outward sign and the inward meaning; one because it is not to be repeated, since regeneration, which it signifies and seals, can be experienced only once; and one in the sense that it is indivisible, and cannot be lawfully administered except in the fulness of its significance, and to those who are fully qualified to receive it. Whatever right the Church may have to institute new ceremonies, she has no right to institute new sacraments, nor in anywise to alter or to modify the meaning of those Christ has ordained for all time. If the baptism of infants does not signify and seal "regeneration and engrafting into Christ," in the same sense and to the same extent as in the case of adults, we have no right to administer it to infants. The practice of the Church is utterly indefensible upon any other ground. "Baptism is to be administered but once, with water, to be a sign and seal of our regeneration and engrafting into Christ, and that even to infants."[1]

For similar reasons we reject also the phrase, "believer's baptism," on which the opponents of the baptism of infants so strenuously insist. If they quote the words of Christ, " he that *believeth* and is baptized shall be saved," we remind them that the salvation promised is as plainly conditioned upon believing as baptism is. Are they prepared to adopt the phrase, " believer's salvation," as covering the whole purpose of God in redemption? What then becomes of infants dying in infancy? Does God bestow the reality upon those to whom He refuses the sign? Our Baptist brethren — blessed be their inconsistency! — believe in the salvation of infants as strenuously as we do. By this heart-faith, which is infinitely better than their exegesis or their logic, they accord to those who cannot consciously believe or profess their faith, all that is symbolized by baptism; for surely they will not affirm that an infant can be saved without regeneration, — and yet, by an epithet which has no warrant in Scripture, they exclude these subjects of salvation from the outward ordinance. They dare not insist on believer's salvation, but they hold exclusively to believer's baptism. Surely the salvation is unspeakably greater than the baptism, which is only its outward sign and seal. The same Jesus who said, "Except a man be born of water and the Spirit, he cannot enter into the kingdom of God," took infants into His arms and said, "Of such *is* the kingdom of God."

I. Before presenting the argument for the Church membership of infants and their consequent right to the sacrament of baptism, it may be well briefly to review

[1] Larger Catechism, Q. 177.

the history of the doctrine. From the days of the Apostles to the time of the Reformation, and through the Reformation period to the rise of the Baptist denomination in England, there is not in all Christian history or literature a line or a word of objection to the baptism of infants, *upon grounds with which Evangelical Christians in our day can have a particle of sympathy.*

In the beginning of the sixteenth century the Anabaptists of Germany, whose political and theological excesses brought such disrepute upon the Reformation under Luther, and against whom the great Reformer labored with voice and pen, no less zealously than against the errors of Rome, opposed the baptism of infants upon the ground that they are by nature holy, and need neither regeneration nor the outward sign of it.[1]

In the beginning of the twelfth century there was a small and ephemeral sect among the Waldenses who rejected the baptism of infants. Their leader and founder, Peter de Bruis, was addicted to that method of exegesis which consists in taking passages of Scripture addressed to a particular class of persons, and applying

---

[1] In the tenth article of the Formula of Concord, we have a list of "Anabaptist articles which cannot be endured in the Church." Among these are the following: "That Christ did not assume His flesh and blood from the Virgin Mary, but brought them from heaven; that Christ is not true God, but merely superior to other saints, because He has received more gifts of the Holy Spirit than any other holy man; that our righteousness before God does not consist in the merits of Christ alone; that infants not baptized are not sinners before God, but pure and innocent, and in this their innocence, when they have not as yet the use of reason, may without baptism (of which in the opinion of the Anabaptists they have no need) attain unto salvation" (Schaff's Creeds of Christendom, iii. 174).

them indiscriminately to all. He insisted that according to the precepts of Christ and His Apostles none can be saved but those who deny themselves, and take up the cross, and work out their own salvation with fear and trembling. From this he inferred that infants cannot be saved, and therefore ought not to be baptized. Certainly, if we grant his premises, his conclusions are irresistible. But who now will grant his premises? The sect he founded had but a brief existence, and in the Waldensian Confession (1655) there is not a trace of his opinions.

Going back in church history, we do not find another recorded word against the universal practice of baptizing infants till we come to the writings of Tertullian. This eccentric and fanatical Father was born A. D. 160, and died not later than A. D. 240. He was a distinguished leader of the sect known in ecclesiastical history as Montanists, and an eloquent advocate of their ascetic views and practices. Though married himself, he denounced marriage as inconsistent with the highest development of Christian life and character. In a treatise dedicated with grim humor to his wife, while combating the love of offspring as a plea for marriage, he speaks of "the bitter, bitter pleasure of children," and calls them "a burden perilous to faith.". He asks: "Why did the Lord foretell a woe to them that are with child, and to them that give suck, except because He testifies that in that day of disencumbrance the encumbrances of children will be an inconvenience." He exclaims with bitter irony: "Let us marry daily, and in the midst of our marrying let us be overtaken, like Sodom and Gomorrha, by that day of fear." By the day of disencumbrance and the day of fear he seems to mean the second coming of Christ, which he believed to be near at hand, for he declares that "the unmarried at the first trump of the angel will spring forth disencumbered, will freely bear to the end whatever pressure and persecution, with no burdensome fruit of marriage heaving in the womb, none in the bosom." [1]

Tertullian is the author of the earliest extant treatise on Baptism. In this he earnestly advises against the administration of the sacrament to infants. His advice is based upon the assumption that baptism of itself washes away sins, and that sin committed after baptism is mortal, inasmuch as the cleansing ordinance cannot be repeated. For the same reason he recommends its postponement in the case of adults. He says: "If any understand the weighty import of baptism, they will fear its reception more than its delay." [2]

Now, without considering the grounds of his objections, it is sufficient for our purpose to observe that Tertullian's arguments fully assume the prevalence of the baptism of infants in the Christian Church at the commencement of the third century. Many writers trace the evidences of the practice back to a much earlier date, to the writings of Irenæus, the disciple of Polycarp, the disciple of John the Apostle; of Justin Martyr, at the beginning of the second century; and even of Clement of Rome and Hermas, who wrote in the last days of the Apostles. [3]

But we do not care to insist upon this evidence. We are willing to fortify the historic argument at the narrow place where the first battery is erected against it. The fact and the mode of the attack concedes to us the,

[1] Ante-Nicene Library: Tertullian's Works, i. 285.
[2] Tertullian's Works, i. 254.
[3] See Wall's History of Infant Baptism, and Bingham's Antiquities of the Christian Church.

whole territory between this point and the times of the Apostles. Tertullian virtually admits that the practice of the whole Church is and has been against him. He does not assert nor insinuate that this practice is an innovation. He makes no appeal from the usage of the Catholic Church to the authority of Christ and His Apostles, which he certainly would have done if there had been any ground for such an appeal. He pleads for the privilege of postponing baptism in the case of adults as well as of infants. "His arguments," says Bingham, "tend not only to exclude infants, but all persons that are unmarried or in widowhood, for fear of temptation, — which are rules which no one beside himself ever thought of, much less were they confirmed by any church practice." "His whole argument," says Dr. Schaff, "rests upon false premises, which were not admitted by the Church. His protest fell without an echo." The universal prevalence of the baptism of infants, from the beginning of the third century onward, is proved by the clearest and most abundant evidence. Nor is there any lack of testimony as to the Divine origin and authority of the practice. Origen, who was contemporary with Tertullian, declares that the Church "derived an order from the Apostles to baptize infants," and that "according to the custom of the Church, baptism is administered to infants, who would not need the grace of baptism if there was nothing in them that needed forgiveness and mercy."[1]

Cyprian, in his Epistle to Fidus, affirms that in the Council of Carthage, A. D. 253, the sixty-six bishops or pastors present unanimously agreed that it is not necessary to postpone baptism till the eighth day, which was

[1] Our quotations from Origen, Chrysostom, Augustine, and Pelagius are taken from Wall's "History of Infant Baptism."

the time fixed by the Mosaic law for circumcision, but that it might be administered at any time after birth, — which gives us a clear proof not only of the prevalence of the practice, but of the universal opinion in the Church that baptism, under the New Testament dispensation, takes the place of circumcision under the Old Testament.[1] Chrysostom, towards the close of the fourth century, says: " Our circumcision — I mean baptism — comes without pain, and procures for us a thousand benefits, and fills us with the grace of the Spirit; and it has no fixed time, as circumcision had; but one that is in the beginning of his age, or one in the middle of it, or one that is in old age, may receive this circumcision without hands." Augustine, in the beginning of the fifth century, says: "The whole Church practises infant baptism; it was not instituted by councils, but was always in use." In his controversy with the Pelagians concerning Original Sin, which they denied, he dwells severely upon their inconsistency in baptizing infants, showing that the sacrament can have no meaning as applied to those who are not by nature sinful. He says: " The Pelagians grant that infants must be baptized, not being able to resist the authority of the whole Church, which was doubtless delivered by our Lord and His Apostles." Other defenders of the orthodox faith were not as fair to the Pelagians as Augustine was. Pelagius himself complains of their misrepresentations. He says: "Men *slander* me by the charge that I deny baptism to infants. I never *heard* of any one, not the most impious heretic, who denied baptism to infants." Now, who can impeach the testimony of Pelagius on this point? If the practice of baptizing infants was so prevalent in the Church in his day that

[1] Ante-Nicene Library: Cyprian's Works, i. 196.

he never heard of any one who denied it, surely this is a phenomenon which demands an explanation. How shall we account for it? Augustine and Origen declare that the practice was founded on the example and precepts of the Apostles. And in their day, though the Church was full of controversies, and men were no more bound then than they are now by prescriptive authority, this explanation was never questioned. If men now deny the explanation of the Fathers, this does not destroy the facts, which still remain to be explained. The burden of proof is on them. They are bound to show where and how the practice of baptizing infants arose, and above all to account for the fact that it was universally accepted by the Church without opposition or protest. It is no sufficient answer to this reasonable demand to make general and sweeping charges of unsoundness against the Fathers, and to remind us that a great many corruptions crept into the Church during the first four centuries. We admit, of course, that many of the Fathers erred concerning the faith, and that soon after the days of the Apostles the Church began to adopt many unscriptural practices. We admit also, for we have abundant evidence of the fact, that many of these errors in opinion and practice had reference to the doctrine and administration of baptism. But all this does not touch the question before us, which is, how the Church could have passed from the baptism of none but adults to the universal practice of baptizing infants, without any recorded controversy upon the subject, and without leaving any historic traces of the change.[1]

[1] When men so learned and so candid as Augustine and Pelagius, though earnestly opposed to each other in doctrinal opinions, agree in declaring that they never heard of any one who claimed to be a

II. To the historic argument thus briefly recited, the most common and plausible answer is an appeal to *the alleged silence of Scripture*. We are told that the testimony of the Fathers is of no account. We are challenged to produce a single text of Scripture in which the baptism of infants is enjoined or permitted, or a single example of such an administration of the ordinance recorded in the Bible.

Even if we admit to its fullest extent the alleged silence of Scripture, which we are far from doing, this argument is more specious than sound. It has this fatal defect, that it proves too much. There are many things about which the Bible says nothing, which all Christians believe and insist upon.

Marriage is admitted by all Christians to be a Divine institution. Church and State guard it as the foundation of society, and both insist that in order to constitute a lawful marriage there must be, not only an agreement between the parties, but a *ceremony*, the essence of which is a verbal contract in the presence of at least one witness. No two persons are regarded as lawfully married simply because they have agreed to live together as man and wife, nor is there a church in Christendom to whose communion persons sustaining such a relation to each other would be admitted. But where is the express Scripture warrant for this requirement? There is not

Christian, either orthodox or heretic, who did not maintain and practise the baptism of infants; to suppose, in the face of such testimony, that the practice crept in as an unwarranted innovation between their time and that of the Apostles, without the smallest intimation of the change having ever reached their ears, — is, of all incredible suppositions, one of the most incredible. He who can believe this must, it appears to me, be prepared to make a sacrifice of all historic evidence at the shrine of blind and deaf prejudice. — *Miller on Infant Baptism, Presbyterian Tracts,* i. 28.

a specific text nor a recorded instance in the whole Bible to sustain it. No form of ceremony is prescribed, no example of the performance of such a ceremony is reported, there is not in all Scripture an explicit declaration that any ceremony whatever is necessary. Will the opponents of the baptism of infants carry out their favorite method of reasoning to its logical conclusion, and insist that, because the Scriptures are silent upon the subject, marriage ceremonies are unscriptural and wrong, and ministers exercise usurped prerogatives in performing them?

All Christians who observe the Lord's Supper agree that it is to be administered to all who make a credible profession of Christ's name and join themselves to His people. But where is there a single passage of Scripture which says that *women* are to be admitted to the Lord's table? Where is the passage in the New Testament which expressly declares that any women ever did participate in the communion in the days of the Apostles? It cannot be found. Will the opponents of the baptism of infants be consistent with themselves and make the silence of the Scripture a plea in bar against the admission of women to the Lord's Supper? They will doubtless answer that women are redeemed by Christ, they are capable of salvation, they have the qualifications for communion, and having received the benefits signified and sealed by this sacrament, they are entitled also to the outward sign and seal. All of which is equally true of the right of infants to baptism. If the silence of Scripture does not exclude women from the one sacrament, neither does it exclude infants from the other, even if the silence were the same in both cases, which we are very far from admitting.

Most Christians rejoice to believe that infants, dying

in infancy, are saved through the mercy of God in Christ, notwithstanding they are incapable of exercising and confessing faith in Christ, which is the only expressed condition of salvation. But where is the text which says this in so many words? It is an inference which we accept as fully warranted by Scripture. But where is the explicit statement of this doctrine? An "able minister of the letter which killeth" (2 Cor. iii. 6) can easily construct a Scripture argument to prove that no infant can be saved. He that believeth and is baptized shall be saved; no infant can *believe* and be baptized: therefore no infant can be saved. But "the Spirit, which maketh alive," recognizes that Christ in the words quoted does not lay down the exclusive condition of salvation for all mankind, but only for those who are capable of hearing and believing; and infers from His silence — a silence which is broken, however, by many still small voices, and from the knowledge of His character and mission — that there is salvation also for those who are incapable of believing. The fact is, that no Christian, Roman Catholic or Protestant, restricts his faith or practice by that which is expressly set down in Scripture. It is not the orthodox doctrine that the Scriptures record in words all things necessary for God's glory and man's salvation. The Catholic truth on this point is clearly stated in the Westminster Confession of Faith (chap. i. sect. 6): "The whole counsel of God concerning all things necessary for His own glory and man's salvation, faith, and life, is *either* expressly set down in Scripture, *or by good and necessary consequence may be deduced therefrom.*" The Scripture warrant for the baptism of infants is not so much direct as it is inferential. But it is not the less strong on that account. It underlies a multitude of facts; it is involved in exceeding great and precious promises, which are still moving on to their fulfilment; it is circumstantial to doctrines which are fundamental to the whole system of revealed truth; it is rooted in the Gospel which was "preached aforetime to Abraham," and in the whole structure and design of Apostolic Christianity, by which "the blessing of Abraham has come upon the Gentiles through Jesus Christ" (Gal. iii. 8, 14); it rests not upon any one part of the Bible, but upon the Bible taken as a whole; it is in the very *warp* of the Scriptures.

III. The whole controversy concerning the church membership and baptism of infants hinges upon the more profound question *of the perpetuity and identity of the Church as a Divine institution in the world.* We hold that the Church of God is one and the same in all ages, being built upon the foundation of the Prophets as well as of the Apostles. God did not begin to build under the Old Testament, and then throw the work away and begin over again under the New. Judaism and Christianity are not different, much less hostile, religions. There is an organic and vital connection between the Old and the New Testament Scriptures; and as they constitute in their oneness the Word of God, which liveth and abideth forever, so the people of God under both dispensations constitute one and the same Church. The proof of this lies on the very surface of the Scriptures. The *titles* of the Church run through the whole sacred history, and are used in the same sense by Prophets and Apostles. The *Kahal* of the Old Testament is synonymous with the *Ecclesia* of the New. The *Church* of God is the *kingdom* of God. In His parables, the Saviour constantly speaks of the kingdom of God in such connections and under such imagery as to show that He is describing an external and visible organization,—the very same kingdom which is described in such glowing terms by Isaiah, and to which such precious promises of perpetuity and glory are made by all the Prophets. This Church or kingdom is not a series of scattered and isolated democracies, but one visible organization under a royal and Divine dominion. Its membership, even under the Old Testament dispensation, was not confined to the natural descendants of Abraham. Any Gentile might join it by complying with certain prescribed conditions. Hence at the day of Pentecost "there were dwelling at Jerusalem devout men *out of every nation under heaven*, both *Jews and proselytes*" (Acts ii. 5, 10). And while the converts to Christianity continued with one accord in the temple, claiming their privileges and performing their duties as defined under the old dispensation, and without any consciousness of being separated from the Church of their fathers, "the Lord added to the Church daily such as should be saved."[1]

Not only the titles but the *mission and functions* of the Church are the same under both dispensations, and could be fulfilled only by her perpetuity. "She is the pillar and ground of the truth" (1 Tim. iii. 15). To her are "committed the oracles of God" (Rom. iii. 2). If the New Testament Church is not the development and perpetuation of the Old Testament

---

[1] The abolition of those restrictions which were suited to a preparatory state fitted her for universality; but that which fitted her for universality could in no sense whatever be her annihilation. The Jews were not cut off till after the Gentiles were taken in; and the excision of the Jews was no more the extermination of the visible Church than the lopping off of the diseased branches is the felling of the tree. — MASON: *Essays on the Church of God* (Works, ii. 276).

Church, then the Old Testament Scriptures are not committed to her, and are no part of her rule of faith and practice, and the whole Scriptures have never been committed to any church for their preservation and exposition.

Moreover, *the promises* made to the visible Church and kingdom of God, many of which are yet unfulfilled, necessarily involve her perpetuity and identity. Take, for example, the words of Isaiah (lx. 3–5): " The Gentiles shall come to thy light, and kings to the brightness of thy rising. . . . The abundance of the sea shall be converted unto thee, the forces of the Gentiles shall be converted unto thee." These and similar promises were made, not to the Jews as a nation, not to the Jewish commonwealth, but they were made to the Church of God, embodied and covered under these temporal conditions. Christ gives us the summary of all these Old Testament promises to the Church when He tells us "they shall come from the east and from the west, from the north and from the south, and sit down with Abraham, Isaac, and Jacob in the kingdom of God."

The whole history of the new dispensation shows that the Church is one and the same. Christ Himself was circumcised, and received the baptism of John, and "fulfilled all righteousness" as a birthright member of the kingdom of God under the old economy. And while He was still a regular attendant upon the temple and an observer of the Feasts, He said, "tell it to the Church," as a rule of discipline for all time. He ate the passover the same night in which He instituted the Lord's Supper, thus showing the identity of the two sacraments, which Paul recognizes when he says, " Christ our Passover is sacrificed for us; let us keep the feast with the unleavened bread of sincerity and truth " (1

Cor. v. 7). Christianity appeared to both Jew and Gentile, and achieved its earliest and most signal triumph under the aspect of a new development of the same old religion. The Gospel was first proclaimed in the synagogues, and appealed for its vindication to the Old Testament Scriptures. The great Apostle of the Gentiles constantly insisted upon this vital connection between the Old and the New. Before Agrippa and the assembled Romans he declared, "I stand and am judged for the hope of the promise made of God unto our fathers" (Acts xxvi. 6). Appealing to the Jews, who rejected the Gospel and prided themselves on adhering to the law, he says, "We are the circumcision, which worship God in the spirit, and rejoice in Christ Jesus" (Phil. iii. 3). In the eleventh chapter of the Epistle to the Romans, the Apostle compares the Church of God to the olive-tree, from which some of the natural branches (the Jews) were broken off, and into which the wild olive-tree (the Gentiles) were grafted. But he cautions the Gentile Christians against being puffed up by the mercy which had been shown to them. "And if some of the branches be broken off, and thou, being a wild olive, wert grafted in among them, and with them partakest of the root and fatness of the olive-tree, boast not against the branches; thou bearest not the root, but the root thee." The tree remains the same, though the branches are changed, and the root and fatness of it support and nourish those who are grafted into it. "The ancient theocracy is merged in the kingdom of Christ. The latter is but an enlargement and elevation of the former. The Church of God is the same in all ages and under all dispensations. It is the society of the true people of God, together with their children. The olive-tree is one, though the branches are numerous, and sometimes changed."[1]

It follows from the perpetuity and identity of the Church that whatever privileges were granted and whatever promises were made to her under the old dispensation, remain in full force until they are either explicitly repealed or exhaustively fulfilled.

IV. The promises and privileges given to her and constituting her endowment and inheritance in all ages are summed up in *the covenant with Abraham, which is the perpetual charter of the Church.*

The idea of a covenant between God and men, whether in the broad sense of a Divine arrangement or in the more specific sense of a promise suspended upon a condition, is one of the seed-thoughts of the Bible. Abraham stands in the same relation to the redeemed that Noah sustains to the whole human race; and the covenant with Abraham is the revelation and the promise of redemption, just as the covenant with Noah was the revelation of the Divine purpose and plan of Providence over the world. To regard Abraham as a Jew or as one of the children of Israel is to misapprehend his relation to the people of God in all ages, and to miss the true scope and meaning of the promises which were made to him as the father of all the faithful. He was a Gentile, called out from the world and made the covenant head of the Holy Catholic Church. The original promise concerning the seed of the woman was localized in his family, and afterwards in the family of Jacob in preference to that of Esau, and still further restricted to the tribe of Judah, the father of the Jews, and still further to the house and lineage of David, the theocratic representative of the Messiah; but all these re-

[1] Dr. Hodge, Commentary on Romans, xi. 17-24.

strictions were outward and temporary, they did not abrogate the original promise, nor restrict the universality of its meaning. Abraham and Israel and Judah and David, with all they specifically represented, were but trustees to whom the keeping of the promise was committed until, in the fulness of time, the glory of Israel should become a light to lighten the Gentiles.

The Abrahamic covenant in its universality and permanence must be distinguished from the national covenant made at Mount Sinai with the children of Israel and the mixed multitude who constituted "the church in the wilderness" (Acts vii. 38). This Sinaitic covenant was superseded and done away with by the bringing in of "the better covenant established upon better promises" (Heb. viii. 6, 9). But this better covenant was new only in respect to that which it superseded. In itself it was the fulfilment of the same old promise, which the law, including all that was peculiar to the Sinaitic covenant, could not disannul (Gal. iii. 17). The covenant with Abraham, which was made four hundred years before the giving of the law on Sinai, is the earliest and the most permanent embodiment and publication of the covenant of grace. This is evident from its express terms, whether we consider its duration, its subjects, or its substance.

As to its duration, it is an *everlasting covenant*. " I will establish My covenant between Me and thee, and thy seed after thee for an everlasting covenant" (Gen. xvii. 7). [1]

---

[1] Some commentators take the word "everlasting" as applied to the possession of the land, in an accommodated sense, to signify its possession during the continuance of the Mosaic dispensation. But we cannot bring our mind to accept this interpretation. Besides seeming forced and unnatural, it does not appear to be sustained by

As to its *subjects*, the Abrahamic covenant *includes all the nations of the earth*. It was not made with Abraham as the progenitor of the Jews, but as "the father of many nations;" and this is further explained by the declaration, "In thee and in thy seed shall all the nations of the earth be blessed." The seed of Abraham is synonymous and identical with the "seed of the woman," in the specific application of the expression, to the "one seed which is Christ" (Gal. iii. 19), and in its broader application to all Christ's redeemed people in every age and land.

Abraham never was and never can be the father of

the facts. The children of Israel did not have the land of Canaan for an everlasting or continuous possession even from the days of Moses to the coming of Christ. The only period during which they were in undisputed possession was the reign of David and Solomon; and surely that cannot be fairly considered an everlasting possession even in the accommodated sense of the word. We are shut up to the conclusion that the unfulfilled promise is yet to be made good in one of two ways: (1) by the actual return and permanent settlement of Abraham's natural descendants in the land wherein he was a stranger and pilgrim; or, (2) by the final ingathering of the whole Church of God, which is the spiritual seed of Abraham, into that heavenly and better country for which the patriarchs longed even while they dwelt in the earthly Canaan (Heb. xi. 9–16).

"Now, if the whole land of Canaan was promised to this posterity, which was to increase into a multitude of nations, it is perfectly evident that the sum and substance of the promise was not exhausted by the gift of the land whose boundaries are described in Gen. xv. 18–21, as a possession to the nation of Israel, but that the extension of the idea of the lineal posterity, 'Israel after the flesh' to the spiritual posterity 'Israel after the spirit,' requires the expansion of the idea and extent of the earthly Canaan, whose boundaries reach as widely as the multitude of nations having Abraham as father; and therefore Abraham received the promise that he should be 'heir of the world'" (Rom. iv. 13). — Delitzsch on Pentateuch, i. 225.

many nations in any lineal and literal sense. His natural seed never was and is not now as the stars of heaven and as the dust of the earth for number. The children of Israel, with the Edomites and Ishmaelites added, never numbered a hundredth part of the population of the earth. Besides, if we look at the terms of the covenant, we shall see that Ishmael and the sons of Keturah were expressly excluded from the process by which the seed of Abraham was to become innumerable. He was to become a multitude of nations through Sarah and the son of his old age; and the promise, so far as its fulfilment was to be accomplished through his natural descendants, was still further restricted in the family of Isaac by the exclusion of Esau; so that if Abraham is to become the father of many nations, according to the terms of the covenant, it must be through Jacob. But the twelve sons of Jacob and their descendants constituted only one nation, with whom God entered into the legal and national covenant of Sinai. Was the law against the promises of God? Did that legal and national covenant with the Israelites do away with the better covenant established upon better promises, made with Abraham four hundred years before? By no means. These successive restrictions were designed to keep alive the promise during the age of preparation, and to secure its ultimate expansion in the fulness of time. In Christ, the Son of Man and the Son of God, the spiritual posterity of Abraham embraces all nations; Abraham is "the father of all who believe" and "the heir of the world" (Rom. iv. 11, 13).

It is evident, not only from the perpetuity and universality of the Abrahamic covenant, but also from the *substance* of its promises, that it was a covenant of grace and salvation. It was the Gospel in its germ. Its central promise and innermost meaning was salvation through Christ. It summed up and provided for the fulfilment of all the gracious intimations of redemption which had been given to man since the fall; and from it, as from a Divine seed, all subsequent revelations of grace and truth are unfolded. From the beginning it opened the door for the admission of all nations to the fellowship of God and His people. Its holy sign and seal were by Divine command applied not only to Abraham and his children, but to all who were in his house, — to the stranger and *his* children. And this door was kept open and carefully guarded under the Sinaitic covenant. Not only the lineal descendants of Abraham, but proselytes from every land, might come with their children into fellowship with the God of Israel, who was even then declared to be the God of the whole earth.[1]

The exposition of the Abrahamic covenant in the Epistles to the Romans, the Galatians, and the Hebrews, demonstrates conclusively that it is a revelation of the covenant of grace, and identical with the Gospel. The Apostle repudiates and resents the imputation that he is advocating a new religion, or setting up a new church, or proclaiming the fulfilment of any other promises than those "unto which are twelve tribes instantly serving God day and night hope to come" (Acts xxvi. 17). He affirms that "the Gospel was preached aforetime unto Abraham," and that the covenant with him "was confirmed before of God *in Christ*" (Gal. iii. 8, 17); that "Christ is the *minister of the circumcision* for the truth

---

[1] The exclusiveness of the Jews in the later periods of their national history, grew not out of the sacred trust committed to them for the benefit of mankind, but out of their own political pride, whereby they perverted that trust and made void the law of God by their traditions.

of God, to confirm the promises made unto the fathers" (Rom. xv. 8); that "He has redeemed us from the curse of the law, that *the blessing of Abraham* might come upon the Gentiles" (Gal. iii. 13, 14); that the literal are not the true children of Abraham according to the terms of the covenant, "for he is not a Jew who is one outwardly," "neither because they are the seed of Abraham are they all children, but the children of promise are counted for the seed," "for the promise that he should be heir of the world was not to Abraham or to his seed through the law, but through the righteousness of faith" (Rom. ii. 28; ix. 7; iv. 13). "And if ye be Christ's, then are ye Abraham's seed, and heirs according to the promise" (Gal. iii. 29).

These three grand features of the Abrahamic covenant, — its everlastingness, its universality, and its graciousness, — demonstrate that every promise made to the father of the faithful, and every principle which entered into the organization of the church in his house, holds good and is in full force at the present day; that the relation established between Jehovah and the true children of Abraham "to be a God unto thee and to thy seed after thee" can never be dissolved; that the Abrahamic covenant is the perpetual charter of the Church.

V. The covenant with Abraham includes as its most essential and distinctive feature on its human side *the church-membership of infants.* The promise is, "I will be a God to thee and to thy seed after thee." And to show that this promise pertains to the seed of believers from their birth, the sign and seal of the covenant under the Old Testament dispensation was fixed by Divine command upon both the natural and adopted children of Abraham in their infancy, that God's "Covenant might be in their flesh for an everlasting covenant."

They were circumcised, not to bring them into the Church, but because they were born into the Church by virtue of the covenant relation of their parents to God. Otherwise there is no force nor meaning in the threatening, " The uncircumcised man-child shall be cut off from his people; he hath broken my covenant" (Gen. xvii. 14). How could he be *cut off* if he were not already in organic and vital connection with God's people? How could he *break* God's covenant if he were not born an heir to its privileges and a subject to its obligations? No one who admits that there was any Church of God under the Old Testament dispensation will deny that the infant children of all who belonged to it, whether Jews or proselytes, were recognized and treated as birthright members. It was just this that constituted the difference and the advance in the revelation of grace which was made to Abraham beyond what was made to the patriarchs before him. It was just this that marked a new era in the progressive history of redemption. It was just this that emphasized and gave a permanent significance to Abraham's calling out of the world, and made him and his house the germ of the Church which is to exist throughout all ages, till the plan and work of redemption are complete in the glory of the Church triumphant. God had believing people and worshippers in the world before Abraham, but no organized and visible Church. And broad and deep at the foundation of that Church is laid the great principle that the family is its unit, and that the children of believers are included in the covenant with their parents as birthright members of that Church.

VI. As the Abrahamic covenant in its graciousness and universality is an everlasting covenant, and as the Church under the New Testament is identical with the

Church under the Old Testament, so also *baptism is identical with circumcision.* It is the seal of the same covenant; it recognizes and confirms the same relation to God; it is expressly declared in Scripture to mean the same thing; and therefore, by good and necessary consequence, it is to be applied to the same subjects.

The everlasting promise is: "I will be a God to you, and to your seed after you."

To what other promise does Peter point, on the day of Pentecost, when he says: " *The* promise is to you and to your children" (Acts ii. 39)? And what is his design in this reference but to assure the Jews and proselytes whom he is addressing that by joining the fellowship of Christ's disciples they would not forfeit any of the blessings covenanted to Abraham and to his seed? He enforces upon the adults, to whom he is speaking, the exhortation to repent and be baptized, by the powerful motive that their children would have a right and title to the same covenant promises, the seal of which they would themselves receive in their baptism.

Circumcision and baptism are identical in their symbolic meaning. They both signify the inward and spiritual grace of regeneration. "For he is not a Jew who is one outwardly, neither is that circumcision which is outward in the flesh; but he is a Jew who is one inwardly, and circumcision is that of the heart in the spirit, and not in the letter" (Rom. ii. 28). "In like manner," says Calvin, "may we in the present day refute the vanity of those who in baptism seek nothing but water. That man trifles, or rather is delirious, who would stop short at the element of water and the external observance, and not allow his mind to rise to the spiritual mystery."[1]

---

[1] Calvin's Institutes, book 4, chap. xvi. 14.

What that spiritual mystery is, Paul explicitly declares in Col. ii. 11: "We are circumcised with the circumcision *made without hands*, the putting off of the body of sins of the flesh by the *circumcision of Christ*, being buried with him *in baptism.*" And again, he affirms that baptism is the seal of the Abrahamic covenant (in Gal. iii. 27, 29). "For as many as have been baptized into Christ are Abraham's seed and heirs according to the promise."

Now, if baptism is *the circumcision of Christ* and *the seal of the Abrahamic covenant;* if it signifies the same thing and seals the same promises under the new dispensation that circumcision did under the old, — it follows irresistibly, in the absence of any express restriction to the contrary, that it is to be applied to the same classes of persons and upon the same conditions; that is, to adult proselytes who profess their faith, and to the children of believers. The only change is in the outward form of the ordinance; its signification and its subjects are left unchanged. If the State of New Jersey, by Act of Legislature or in a constitutional convention of the people, should alter the form of its seal, saying nothing about the uses to which it should hereafter be applied, that would neither invalidate any document which has been ratified by the old seal, nor prevent the new one from being applied to similar State papers in the future. The argument for the baptism of infants is thus put into a nutshell. Infants were circumcised under the old dispensation; circumcision signifies and seals the same thing with baptism: therefore infants are to be baptized. We retort upon those who demand a more explicit Scripture warrant, in so many words, for the baptism of infants, by demanding of them an explicit warrant for excluding them from the ordinance. The burden of proof lies on them, not on us. The covenant made with Abraham still stands, and is enlarged, in fact, according to its original design and promise, so as to include "those which were afar off, even as many as the Lord our God shall call." "Though it be but a man's covenant, yet, if it be confirmed, no man disannulleth or addeth thereto" (Gal. iii. 15). And the most explicit condition upon which the blessings promised in this covenant are suspended is the command that every child of believing parents, whether of the natural or the adopted seed of Abraham, shall receive the appointed sign and seal. Now, show us the chapter and verse of the New Testament where Christ, or one of His Apostles, has declared or intimated that infants are no longer to be regarded and treated as members of the Church of God, heirs of the covenant promises, and recipients of its appointed seal.

VII. In the light of these scriptural facts and principles we interpret *the Saviour's great commission*. He was "a minister of the circumcision for the truth of God to confirm the promises made unto the fathers" (Rom. xv. 8). "He hath redeemed us from the curse of the law, that the blessing of Abraham might come upon the Gentiles" (Gal. iii. 13, 14). When, after His sacrificial death and triumphant resurrection, He said to His disciples, "Go ye therefore and teach all nations, baptizing them in the name of the Father, and of the Son, and of the Holy Ghost, teaching them to observe whatsoever I have commanded you," He did not repudiate His mission to the seed of Abraham, nor annul the covenant relation between God and His people, but only announced the predestined and promised enlargement of its scope as including all nations; He did not abolish the seal of the covenant, but only changed its outward form; and above all, He did not restrict the subjects to whom that seal should be applied, but only declared in explicit terms that the enlargement which had been prefigured in the old law of proselytism was now complete. One of the most important rules in the interpretation of any Scripture precept is to put ourselves in the place of those to whom it was originally addressed. Its meaning is not to be determined by the words alone, but by the circumstances in which they were spoken, by the state of mind to which they were addressed, and by all the preceding history whereby the understanding of them would be influenced. This rule is always observed in the interpretation of human law. A new statute is interpreted in the light of the old. Whatever of the old is not repealed, either expressly or by necessary implication, stands in all its original force. And when, after the lapse of years, doubts arise as to these implications, the solution is sought for in the question how they who were first required to obey the law would naturally understand it. There is no difficulty in applying these simple rules to the interpretation of the great commission. They to whom it was addressed were Jews, members of the Church under the old dispensation, and fully imbued with its spirit. The idea of the church-membership of infants, and the application of the seal of the covenant to them, were as familiar to the minds of the Apostles as the idea of God's existence. They could not possibly infer from anything Christ had commanded or taught that this fundamental principle was to be repealed. Certainly nothing in the great commission gives the least intimation of such a change. Nor is there any intimation that such a change was in fact accomplished, in all the subsequent discussions between the Apostle of the Gentiles and the Jewish converts who were still zealous for the law of Moses.

The emphasis of the great commission was on "all nations." Henceforth they were not to confine their proselyting labors, as they had hitherto done, to the lost sheep of the house of Israel. Their new field was the world. Now, suppose the command had been, "Go, disciple, or proselyte, all nations, *circumcising* them in the name of the Father, and of the Son, and of the Holy Ghost:" would there have been the least doubt in their minds as to whether the children of believing parents ought to receive the seal of the covenant? Certainly not. Their lifelong training and their whole habits of mind would have led them to take for granted that the children were to be included with their parents just as they always had been. In the absence of all instruction to the contrary, why should they not, for the same reasons, include children with those whom they were commanded to baptize? What possible reason can be assigned for excluding them from baptism, which will not apply with equal force as an argument against their circumcision? And so, on the other hand, what argument could have been used in favor of the *circumcision* of children, in case that word had been used in the great commission, which did not then and does not now apply in favor of the baptism of children? The enlargement of the field in which the Apostles were to perform their proselyting labors, and the alteration in the outward form of the sign to be applied to those who were proselyted, could not suggest, much less require, any change in the subjects to whom, or the conditions upon which, that sign was to be applied. This would hold good even if baptism, whether of adults or of infants, were an entirely new thing, a ceremony invented by Christ, and first announced to the Apostles in the great commission. But the fact is, that while Christ instituted baptism as a sacrament of the New Testament, the use of water in religious ceremonies as a symbol of purification was common to many nations, and was as familiar to the Jews as the eating of bread and the drinking of wine, which the Saviour consecrated into the symbols of His body and blood.[1]

VIII. The recorded fact that *the Apostles baptized households*, in immediate connection with the professed faith of one or both the parents, ought to be interpreted in the light of the facts and principles we have just applied to interpretation of the great commission. It

---

[1] The learned Dr. Lightfoot has demonstrated that it was the universal custom of the Jews in Christ's day, and for ages before, not only to circumcise, but also to baptize the infant children of heathens brought as proselytes into the Jewish Church.

"Hence, also, the reason appears why the New Testament does not prescribe by some more accurate rule who the persons are to be baptized. The Anabaptists object, 'it is not commanded to baptize infants;' to whom I answer, it is not forbidden to baptize infants, therefore they are to be baptized. And the reason is plain. For when Pedobaptism in the Jewish Church was so well known, usual, and frequent in the admission of proselytes, there was no need to strengthen it by any precept when baptism was now passed into an evangelical sacrament. For Christ took baptism into His hands and into evangelical use as He found it, this only added, that He might promote it to a worthier end and to a larger use. The whole nation knew well enough that little children used to be baptized, and there was no need of a precept for that which had ever by common use prevailed. On the other hand, there *was need of a plain and open prohibition* against the baptism of infants if our Saviour would not have them baptized. For since it was most common in foregoing ages, if Christ had been minded to have that custom abolished, He would have openly forbidden it. Therefore, His silence and the silence of the Scripture on this matter confirms Pedobaptism, and continueth it to all ages" (Lightfoot's Works, ii. 59).

is easy to *say* that there were no children in the families of Cornelius, of Lydia, of the Philippian jailer, and of Stephanus; and it is no less easy to assert that these four are the only instances in which households, as such, were baptized by an Apostle. But without impeaching the sincerity of those who make these assertions, we venture to say that they never would have been made except under the stress of necessity to sustain a foregone conclusion. The thing to be proved is assumed in the premises. Infants are not to be baptized, therefore the Apostles baptized no more than four households, and in them there were no infants. In the absence of explicit statements, the decision of both questions must turn upon the balance of probability. Since we know that Peter and Paul baptized four households; and since there is nothing whatever in the record of these cases to indicate that they were exceptional; and since the baptism of households is in full accord with the principles of the Abrahamic covenant, the precepts of the Mosaic law, and the practice of the Jews in the treatment of proselytes; and since none of these principles, precepts, or practices were repealed or reprobated by Christ, — the strong probability, amounting to a moral certainty, is that Paul and all the Apostles were in the habit of baptizing households upon the professed faith of parents.

And so also, we think, there is a probability, amounting to a moral certainty, that there were children in the households whose baptism is recorded. The natural probability in the case is confirmed by the form of the record. Why should these households be lumped together, instead of recording the names of the individuals baptized? Paul declares that at Corinth he had "baptized Crispus and Gaius and the *household* of Stephanus"

(1 Cor. i. 14–16). Now, if that household consisted exclusively of adults, why not give *their* names, as well as the names of Crispus and Gaius? If each one of them was a believer, having a personal standing in the church, not through the household covenant, but by virtue of a personal profession of faith and a personal relation to Christ, what could justify the Apostle in ignoring their individuality and embracing them all under the head of Stephanus? It seems to be a moral certainty that the members of that household were children under age, for whom the father stood as the federal head.

The form of the record in the case of the Philippian jailer greatly strengthens this opinion. To the question, "What must I do to be saved?" Paul answers, "Believe on the Lord Jesus Christ, and thou shalt be saved, and thy house." This certainly establishes a *connection* between the jailer's faith and the salvation of his house. The one *in some sense* secures the other, whatever secondary means may be employed to realize that security. To make the Apostle's words mean nothing more than the truism that the same terms of salvation were offered to the jailer and to the adult members of his family, is to put a platitude into his mouth utterly foreign to his use of language. He might as well have said, "Believe on the Lord Jesus Christ, and thou shalt be saved, *and the Roman emperor.*" The connection between the faith of the father and the salvation of his house is real and influential; it is something more than the common conditions upon which he and other men might obtain salvation. "Believe on the Lord Jesus Christ, and *thy house shall be saved.*" This seems to us to be the plain meaning of the words. Nor is this connection nullified by the recorded fact that the Apostle "spake the word of the Lord to him and to all that were in his house." The validity of God's promises does not depend upon our ability to understand them. He speaks to His children, as we do to ours, many things which are as yet beyond their comprehension. Neither, again, is the connection explained by the power of the father's example, for that example had no time to exert an intelligent influence upon the household previous to their baptism,—"he was baptized, he and all his straightway." The whole record, when regarded simply as an account of the conversion and baptism of a company of adults, is strange and incongruous. But how plain and consistent with itself and with other Scriptures it becomes, when we read between the lines the everlasting principles of the Abrahamic covenant, of which baptism is the seal!

IX. *The incarnation of Christ in its relation to infancy* is a theme upon which the Scriptures say little, but suggest much. Is there no connection between His coming in the flesh and the salvation of that vast multitude, probably the majority of the human race, who die before they are capable of exercising faith in Him? Is there no doctrinal significance and no saving efficacy in the fact that He assumed our nature in the form of an infant born of a woman, rather than in the form of a man created like Adam? They who reject the baptism of infants are bound by logical consistency to answer these questions in the negative. The ablest advocates of their views do not hesitate to declare that "the Gospel has nothing to do with infants," that "the salvation of the Gospel is as much confined to believers as baptism is," and that "we know nothing of the means by which God receives infants, nor have we any business with it."[1] All of which is undeniably true, if you first allow them

[1] Carson on Baptism, p. 173.

to give a narrow definition to the Gospel by which they beg the whole question at issue. If the Gospel, as they assume, is nothing more than the proclamation of the terms on which God will save adults who are capable of believing in Christ, then, of course, the Gospel has nothing to do with the salvation of infants, and its ordinances have no respect to them. But we cannot accept a definition which thus hands over our little ones to uncovenanted mercies. As we understand it, the Gospel is much more and better than the proclamation of the terms on which God will save those who are capable of believing; it is the declaration of His infinite love to a fallen world, the revelation of the way by which He seeks and saves that which was lost. We deny that any one, infant or adult, is regenerated by the proclamation of the Gospel. We are born again by the Holy Spirit, whose influences, the purchase of Christ's death and intercession, are not confined to words nor to any outward means, but, like the wind which bloweth where it listeth, works when and where and how He wills. How beautiful and how profound in their grasp of the true meaning of the Gospel are the words of Irenæus, the disciple of Polycarp, the disciple of the Apostle John: "Christ came to redeem all to Himself, all who through Him are regenerated to God, infants, little children, boys, young men and old. Hence He passed through every age, and for infants He became an infant, sanctifying the infants; among the little children He became a little child, sanctifying those who belong to this age, at the same time setting them an example of piety, of well-doing, and of obedience. Among the young men He became a young man, that He might set them an example and sanctify them to the Lord."

The belief that all who die in infancy are saved

through Christ, which is now wellnigh universal among Protestant Christians, is not based upon any new revelation, but upon a clearer and broader apprehension of the old. It is the true import of the Gospel that "Where sin abounded, there grace did much more abound;" that "As sin hath reigned unto death, even so might grace reign through righteousness unto eternal life by Jesus Christ" (Rom. v. 20, 21). And how can grace "abound more exceedingly" than sin does, if infants are not included in the Gospel salvation? And what then did Christ mean when He took infants in His arms and declared, Of such is the kingdom of God? We believe that the satisfaction which He, as the seed of the woman and the Saviour of the world, rendered to God's broken law, takes away the guilt and condemnation of Adam's sin from the whole human race. "Behold the Lamb of God, which taketh away *the sin* of the world" (John i. 16). The multitude of the redeemed, which no man can number, will include not only all believers, but all who have not "sinned after the similitude of Adam's transgression;" that is to say, all who die in infancy. To limit Christ's seed, the travail of His soul which He saw and was satisfied, to those whom we can see and from whom we can hear the confession of their faith, is to bound the vision and the purpose of Christ by our finite senses. The only restrictions we are authorized to put upon redeeming grace are those which God Himself has expressly imposed. We may not exclude any whom He has not excluded. He has excluded those who hear the Gospel and believe not; but He has not excluded any infants. Here the silence of the Scriptures is profoundly significant, and it is exactly analogous, as it is co-extensive, with their silence in regard to the baptism of infants. Their baptism and their salvation rest upon the same broad foundations. The silence in both cases is underlaid and pervaded by a multitude of good and necessary inferences, and re-echoes with the sweetest utterances of the still small voice of God. It is a silence and an infinitude like that which we feel on the seashore, where the waves that murmur and break at our feet are as nothing to the fulness which stretches in our thoughts beyond the bounds of our horizon.

> "There's a wideness in God's mercy
> Like the wideness of the sea."

And as we believe that mercy is covenanted to our infant offspring, we do not hesitate to apply to them its outward sign and seal by baptizing them into the name of the Father, and of the Son, and of the Holy Ghost.[1]

X. *Why then do we not baptize all infants?*

If Christ's incarnation, in the form of a child born of a woman, has a special significance and efficacy in its relation to childhood, and if all who "have not sinned after the similitude of Adam's transgression" are in-

---

[1] God having appointed baptism as the sign and seal of regeneration, unto whom He denies it, He denies the grace signified by it. If therefore God denies the sign unto the infant seed of believers, it must be because He denies the grace of it; and then all the children of believing parents dying in infancy must, without hope, be eternally damned. I do not say all must be so who are not baptized, but all must be so *whom God would not have baptized*. But this is contrary to the goodness and love of God, the nature and promises of the covenant, the testimony of Christ receiving them to the kingdom of God, the faith of godly parents, and the belief of the Church in all ages. It follows hence unavoidably that infants who die in their infancy have the grace of regeneration, and consequently as good a right unto baptism as believers themselves. — OWEN: *Works*, xvi. 260.

cluded among the redeemed, why do we restrict baptism to the children of believers? The answer to this question is threefold: *First*, because baptism is not in any case the efficient cause of salvation; it does not produce, it only signifies and seals, our regeneration and engrafting into Christ. *Secondly*, because the efficacy of baptism, as a means of salvation, is not experienced by those who die in infancy, but only by those who live to maturity. An infant dying unbaptized is just as safe in Christ as though it had received the sacramental seal. *Thirdly*, because God has expressly conditioned the baptism of infants, even as He has conditioned the baptism of adults. But these conditions, depending in both cases upon duties prescribed to those who are capable of performing them, do not of themselves exclude any from a participation in the sacrament. God does not *deny* baptism to *any* infant. This is true in the same sense that He does not deny salvation to any adult. Paul declares that "God our Saviour will have *all men* to be saved, and to come to the knowledge of the truth" (1 Tim. ii. 4). And Peter says: "He is not willing that any should perish, but that all should come to repentance" (2 Peter iii. 9). We take these declarations in their plain and full meaning. We do not whittle them away in order to dovetail them into other Scripture statements. At the same time we recognize the fact that God has prescribed certain conditions upon which alone men can be saved. *We* may not limit the Holy One of Israel in the exercise of His saving grace, but He may and does limit Himself. "He so loved the world" (that is, all mankind) "that He gave His only begotten Son, that *whosoever believeth Him* should not perish, but have everlasting life." If in such declarations He seems to our finite apprehension to contradict Himself, we may safely leave Him to solve the difficulty. Meantime, it is enough for us to know that He has laid upon His Church the obligation to go and disciple and baptize all nations.

In the same way, and with no greater apparent contradiction, He will have all infants to be baptized. He does not deny the sign and seal of His saving grace to any, even as He does not exclude any from salvation; but at the same time He has restricted the universal application of baptism to infants by the express condition that parents must themselves profess to believe and covenant to bring up their children in the faith and obedience of the Gospel. This condition is expressed in the explicit terms of the Abrahamic covenant, in the command of Christ to proselyte all nations as the prerequisite to the baptism of themselves and their little ones, and in the example of the Apostle in baptizing the households of believers. The minister has no discretion in this matter. His office is purely ministerial and declarative. He is to baptize only the children of those who are within the pale of the visible Church and in covenant with God, just as the priest under the old dispensation was to circumcise only those whose parents, whether by birthright or adoption, stood in the same Divine relationship. And the reasons for this restriction are obvious. The efficacy of baptism as a means of salvation is realized through the fidelity of those who are parties to the covenant. Ministers have no right to aid or encourage parents in making vows which there is no reasonable ground to believe they intend to fulfil. All God's purposes of salvation include the means as well as the end. There is no such thing revealed in Scripture as an absolute and unconditional decree of eternal life, to be executed irrespective of Christian character and the means by which that character is to be wrought out. A Christian education, in the case of those who live to years of maturity, is the normal and permanent agency by which salvation is to be secured. Instruction and regeneration in adult years are exceptional, and belong to the infancy and formative period of the Church rather than to her maturity. As she approaches nearer to her millennial glory, and performs more fully her Divine commission, she will realize more and more the fulfilment of the promise, "All thy children shall be taught of the Lord" (Is. liv. 13). The miserable superstition which looks upon baptism as the *christening* or *Christianizing* of a child, and the still more degrading notion which regards it as the formal and ceremonial *giving of a name*, have their roots in ignorance and indifference to the true meaning of God's solemn ordinance, and go very far to explain the lamentable fact that so many children of the Church repudiate their obligations and sell their birthright for a mess of pottage.

XI. *What profit is there in the baptism of infants?* This is substantially the question that Paul discussed in regard to circumcision (in Rom. iii. 1, 2), and we may answer it as he did, — "Much every way." If, as we have shown, the baptism of our children is warranted and required by the example of the Apostles, by the conduct and words of Christ recognizing children as members of His Church, by the express conditions of the Abrahamic covenant, which is the perpetual charter of the Church, and by the identity of circumcision with baptism as the sign and seal of that covenant; then our obligation in this matter rests upon something infinitely higher and better than our apprehensions of the good which may result from our obedience.

But we are very far from resting our answer to the question under discussion upon prescriptive authority. We are encouraged to embrace our privilege and perform our duty by antecedent probability and by ascertained facts.

By the baptism of our little ones into the name of the Father, the Son, and the Holy Ghost, we recognize and lay hold upon the covenant promises which are to believers and their children, and accept God's pledge that if we do our duty in the performance of our vows, His blessing will follow. We put a visible mark of distinction upon the child, separating it from the pagan and unbelieving world, and acknowledging it as a birthright member of the Church of God. We put ourselves under covenant bonds to behave ourselves before our children, and to mould their character, not as "pagans suckled in a creed outworn," but as the children of God and heirs of His promises; and we endow our lips with an argument of Divine persuasiveness when, at the earliest dawn of intelligence, mingled with the sweet story of old, we whisper into the souls of our children the assurance that they are the lambs of Christ's flock, and bear His mark. We believe that no Christian parent, whose example and teaching were consistent, ever made such an appeal to the tender soul of a child without evoking a quick and abiding response. It does not invalidate these reasons to observe that the carelessness and neglect of parents so often make them of no effect. It is easy to pick out individual instances, where children seem to have been trained according to the baptismal covenant, and yet have become reprobate concerning the faith; and then, generalizing from these exceptional instances, to ask unbelievingly, What profit is there in the baptism of infants? We believe that the comparative number of such sad cases is greatly exaggerated; that it is unwarrantably increased in our estimation by counting all as unregenerate and unconverted who have not passed through a prescribed process of religious experience and "joined the church;" and that if we knew the secret history of the worst cases, and could trace out on the one hand the fatal defects in their Christian education, and on the other hand the instances in which Divine grace triumphs in those who, like Saul of Tarsus, are "born out of due season," the sad catalogue would be largely decreased, even if it were not entirely obliterated.

The patent facts on the other side of this question, the innumerable instances in which the baptism of infants and their education in accordance therewith have brought forth immediate and apparent fruits, are full of glory to God and joy to us. The whole history of Christianity abounds with them.

We pray and look for a grand revival on this subject, which will largely increase the ministry with the best material, and give a new impulse to all the enterprises of the Church. Not the least of the blessed fruits of such a revival, indeed the very root of its influence, will be its effect upon Christian parents. It is true that they are bound to bring up their children for God and His Church, whether they make a covenant promise to do so or not. And so also every man is bound to live a Christian life, whether he professes his faith and obedience to Christ or not. Such professions do not create, they only acknowledge, our obligations. But is there no inherent propriety, no tribute of honor to God, no stimulus and no comfort to ourselves in such acknowledgments? A king who ascends the throne of his ancestors, a chief magistrate who assumes the presidency of a great people to which he has been elected, is bound by the very inheritance or assumption of the office to discharge its duties faithfully. But is there no fitness and no moral power in the coronation or inauguration oath? The most solemn office which any man or woman can inherit or assume, is the office of training an immortal soul. It is the type and the germ of all governmental authority; it is the image of the Divine. God has no higher or more tender title than Our Father. To regard children as the unfortunate accidents of marriage is bestial. To look upon them as an encumbrance to faith is heathenish. Marriage is the Divinely appointed means for propagating the Church. The parental office is greatly magnified by the fact that our children are begotten by us, and receive from us by heredity untold influences for good or for evil. If the assumption of any office on earth ought to be signalized by a solemn inauguration, this ought to be. The craving for such a ceremony is a parental instinct. God recognized it and wrought it into the foundations of the Church in the Abrahamic covenant. To cast it out of the Church is to tarnish her historic glory and to diminish her power; to root it out of the parental heart is to destroy one of its finest susceptibilities to the religion of the Bible.

We do not believe in any human, much less in any ceremonial or mechanical, salvation. "By grace are ye saved." "It is not of him that willeth, nor of him that runneth, but of God, that showeth mercy." But this is the Divine side of redemption, with which we have nothing to do but to believe and adore. On the human side the means are just as much ordained as the end. We must "give diligence to make our calling and election sure." We must "work out our salvation with fear and trembling, *because* God works in us to will and to do of His own good pleasure." And the same is true of the salvation of our little ones. God, like a tender human mother, prepares for His true children before they are born. The cradle is made ready before they are laid in it. He does not leave them, like the ostrich, to be hatched in the desert and fed upon sand. Christians do not come from His moulding hand like Adam, full formed; they are begotten and nourished, and grow as babes to the full stature of men. Christian nurture, beginning in infancy, inheriting traditional influences, and surrounded at the first dawn of consciousness by a religious atmosphere, is the normal and Divine method for propagating the Church. Of this method the baptism of infants is the visible exponent and the mutual pledge between God and His believing people. "To be unbaptized, therefore, is a grievous injury and reproach, and one which no parent can innocently entail upon a child."[1]

[1] Hodge's Theology, iii. 579.

LECTURE V.

ORDINATION TO THE MINISTRY.

ALL the great Protestant denominations — Lutherans, Episcopalians, Methodists, Baptists, Congregationalists, and Presbyterians — declare in their confessions and insist in their polity that the Christian ministry is of Divine appointment and essential to the existence of the visible Church. And the great body of their adherents regard the ministry, not as a profession co-ordinate with worldly callings, but as a sacred office, whose functions are performed in some sense by a Divine authority, of which ordination is the symbol and seal. There is not a local church in any of these denominations which would receive as its pastor a man who would declare that he is not called of God to his work; and there are few, if any, who would acknowledge as their minister one whose call of God has not been ratified in some formal way by the Church. Here, then, is common ground. The agreement is generic, and wrought into the conscious life of the Church. Under the unifying influences and blessed hope of this agreement let us discuss our specific differences in an irenical spirit. What is ordination? What are the Scriptural forms under which it is to be administered? Who have the right to administer these forms? These three questions cover the whole ground.

I. Ordination is "the public solemn attestation of the judgment of the Church that the candidate is called of God to the ministry of reconciliation, which attestation authorizes his entrance upon the public discharge of his duties."[1] This definition is broad and simple, and though it is not as comprehensive as some would desire, we think it will be accepted, so far as it goes, by all who believe that ordination to the ministry is a Divine ordinance.

All Christians who believe that the ministry is a Divine institution believe also that men are called of God individually to fill the sacred office. This call is the work of the Holy Spirit in the heart. It must precede and is the Divine warrant for the investiture of the man with his office. Ordination does not constitute the call nor confer the essential qualifications for the office; it assumes and ratifies both. In this all Protestants agree. It is taught with special emphasis in the Episcopal ordinal. The candidate must declare, before the hands of the bishop can be laid upon him, that he thinks and trusts that he is "truly called according to the will of our Lord Jesus Christ, and inwardly moved by the Holy Ghost to take upon him this office." "The Church at all times," says Haddan, "and our branch of the Church in terms so strong that men sometimes demur to them, has required the inward call as well as the outward appointment."[2]

Now, this inward Divine call to the ministry is given to men in two ways, — the one immediate, miraculous, and extraordinary; the other mediate, gracious, and ordinary. The immediate and miraculous call attests itself in the heart of the recipient, and is attested to others by supernatural signs. In such cases there is no need of any formal ordination. The mode of the call and

[1] Hodge's Polity of the Church, p. 144.
[2] Haddan, Apostolic Succession, p. 52.

the infallible proofs which accompany its announcement leave nothing to be submitted to the judgment of the Church. To those who present such evidences of their commission it need only be said, " We know that thou art a teacher come from God, for no man can do these miracles which thou doest except God be with him." Hence the Apostles were not ordained in the technical sense of the word. They were *appointed* to office, and miraculously endowed by Christ Himself. They were commissioned to organize the Church under its New Testament form, and it was neither necessary nor practicable to submit their claims to its judgment. The case of Paul is an apparent, but only an apparent, exception to this remark, as we shall show hereafter. We desire now to emphasize the observation that *the Apostles were not ordained*. Where it is said in the Authorized Version "He *ordained* twelve whom He called apostles" (Mark iii. 14), the word in the original is ἐποίησεν, which the Revised Version correctly renders "*He appointed.*" Ordination, in the technical sense, is appropriate only to those whose call to the ministry is through the ordinary operations of the Holy Spirit, unaccompanied by any direct revelation, and unattested by any miraculous signs. In such cases a man is not competent to judge for himself, nor can he enforce his judgment upon others. He believes and professes that he is called of God; but the credibility of that profession is to be submitted to the impartial judgment of others, just as a private person's profession of faith in Christ is to be examined and approved before he can be recognized as a member of the visible Church. And just as "baptism is the sign and seal of our regeneration and engrafting into Christ, and that even to infants," so also ordination is the sign and seal of a man's

Divine call to the ministry. It is not the Divine call, but the *ratification* of it. It does not confer the essential qualifications and the Divine authority of the office. This is the Romish doctrine, which all Protestant confessions repudiate, and none more explicitly than the Episcopal ordinal. If the man has not the natural ability and the human learning necessary for his work, and, above all, if he has not the call of the Holy Spirit in his heart, the hands of the ordainers can no more confer these things upon him than the sprinkling of consecrated water on the person of the baptized can regenerate the soul. But, then, it does not follow from this that the mere formal authority to enter upon his work is all that one who is called of God receives in his ordination. All Divine ordinances include in the words and the fact of their institution a promise of special Divine blessings to those who rightly use them. Ordination is not a sacrament according to our definition of the word. Nevertheless, as the sacraments become "effectual means of salvation by the blessing of Christ and the working of the Holy Spirit in them that by faith receive them," so we believe that ordination is in the same way an effectual means of preparing the minister of Christ for the work to which he is called.[1] God honors His own ordinance; in the very act of ordination, in answer to prayer, and with the laying on of hands, He bestows not only the formal investiture of

[1] We are constrained to differ on this point from many Presbyterian writers, who in their zeal for orthodoxy lean backward. Thus Dr. Smythe, in his "Presbytery and Prelacy," p. 171, says: "Ordination is nothing more than induction to the sacred office. It is not the medium of any communicated character, official authority, or actual grace. No such meaning or interpretation is sanctioned by the Word of God, and it is therefore superstitious." This is good dogmatism, but poor exegesis.

the office, but the inward and spiritual grace needful for the performance of its duties. What is there unreasonable, unscriptural, or contrary to Christian experience in this belief? To denounce it as a superstition, to reject it with a sneer at the alleged impossibility of Divine grace coming to us through the laying on of hands by sinful men like ourselves, is the very essence of rationalism in the evil sense of the word. It limits the Almighty to methods which we think we can understand and explain, it empties the sacraments of all Divine efficacy, and in its logical conclusions shuts out everything supernatural from the economy of Divine grace. In regard to what is conferred in ordination, the case of Timothy is not exceptional, but typical. Paul exhorts him not to " neglect the gift that is in thee which was given thee by prophecy with the laying on of the hands of the presbytery " (1 Tim. iv. 14). And again, "that thou stir up the gift of God which is in thee by the putting on of my hands" (2 Tim. i. 6). What is the χάρισμα τοῦ Θεοῦ which was bestowed upon Timothy in his ordination? We must believe that it was something more and better than the external authority for entering upon his office, something in addition to and confirmatory of his prophetic appointment to the ministry; for it was *in him* as a personal possession and experience. Moreover, it was something to be *stirred up* and increased by use. He could not stir up his Divine call nor his official authority; these were fixed facts, incapable of increase or diminution. The only thing to which the Apostle's words can be applied without doing violence to the laws of language is the special grace of God for the performance of his official duties, given to him in the act of ordination. Is it going beyond the recorded facts to call this charism "the grace of orders" in the same sense that the benefits received in baptism and the Lord's Supper may be called "sacramental grace"? While we avoid the popish error which links God's spiritual gifts mechanically with the mere performance of outward ceremonies, we should be equally careful to avoid the greater, because the more unbelieving, heresy, which makes the performance of His appointed ordinances a mere outward form, and divorces them from His efficacious blessing upon those who rightly use them.

Into the question whether any one who believes himself to be called to and qualified for the work of the ministry may enter upon it without being ordained, we will not enter at length. The doctrine which sanctions such irregularities is new in the Presbyterian Church, and even among Congregationalists. The Westminster standards expressly declare that every minister of the Word must be "lawfully ordained." The history of the Church is against it, and we fail to see any warrant for it in Scripture, or in the present needs of the Church and the world. If a man claims to have a direct and extraordinary call from God to preach or to administer the sacraments, let him show his credentials, as Prophets and Apostles did, by miraculous signs. If he cannot do this, let him submit his claims and qualifications to the judgment of his brethren. The refusal to do so is a mark, not of superior piety, but of extraordinary presumption.[1]

[1] For a full discussion of this subject, and a complete answer to the arguments in favor of lay evangelism as they are used in our day, we refer our readers to the "Jus Divinum Evangelici Ministerii," a treatise published by the Provincial Synod of London in 1654. The learned authors of this remarkable book declare the opinion that men, who suppose themselves called and qualified, may enter upon the work of the ministry on their own responsibility, is

II. In regard to the outward form of ordination there is much confusion in the minds of ordinary readers of the New Testament, owing to the fact that our translators have rendered several Greek words of various signification by the one English word "ordain." The Revised Version does not entirely correct this infelicity. We cannot enter into a critical discussion of all the Scripture passages which bear upon our subject, nor can we review the conflicting theories founded upon them. It will be sufficient to state our conclusions. The essential elements of the act of ordination are *prayer and the laying on of hands, with the avowed intention of setting apart the candidate to the work of the ministry as one who, after due examination, is believed to be called of God to that office.* Fasting is no part of the ceremony. It may or may not precede or follow, in the same way that a sermon may or may not be preached on the occasion. As a part of the ordaining act, the fast would necessarily be a very brief one, and hardly worthy of the name. To construe the one passage where fasting is mentioned as having preceded the praying and laying on of hands (Acts xiii. 2, 3) into the theory that fasting is an essential part of ordination, is to generalize upon a very small induction of facts. In this case the

"a highway to all disorder and confusion," an "inlet to errors and heresies," and is "insufferable in a well-ordered Christian community." These are the views of the men who framed our Presbyterian standards and fought the battle for evangelical truth and Christian liberty against formalism and spiritual tyranny. The movements of our time, by which such views are repudiated and denounced, have no right to the exclusive title of "evangelistic." So far as they produce any permanent results, their tendency and effect are to educate the masses away from the house of God and from His ordinances, and to aggravate the evils they are zealously, but not wisely, intended to cure.

fasting was begun before there was any intention to ordain any one. Moreover, it is doubtful whether this was a case of ordination to the ministry at all, while in other cases in regard to which there is no question fasting is not mentioned.

Though prayer and the laying on of hands are essential parts of the ordaining act, it does not follow that every ceremony in which one or both of these is employed is an ordination to the ministry. This is sufficiently obvious in regard to prayer; why should it not be equally obvious in regard to the laying on of hands? This ceremony was used in the Primitive Church on various occasions and for various purposes. It was often no more than an expressive gesture accompanying a benediction. When Christ laid His hands on the children and blessed them, He certainly did not ordain them to the ministry. Neither did the Apostles ordain every one on whom they laid hands. The significant act was in many cases the outward sign of conferring the miraculous gifts of the Holy Ghost. In others it was the external form under which a miracle was wrought. Why, then, should it be hastily inferred that Ananias' laying hands on Saul (Acts ix. 17), had anything to do with his appointment to the apostleship? It is not called an ordination, and the record does not warrant our connecting it with anything but the restoration of the Apostle's sight. The passage in Acts xiii. 1–5, to which we have just referred, is more difficult. If, as many think, it describes Paul's ordination to the apostleship, his case was exceptional; he is the only Apostle who was formally ordained. And the exception can be accounted for only on the ground that his former attitude toward the Church required a special authentication of his call to himself and others. But it is not easy to see what additional force his own open vision of the risen Saviour, his direct appointment as a chosen vessel to carry Christ's name to the Gentiles, and his power to work miracles, could derive from the laying on of the hands of prophets and teachers. We prefer the interpretation which makes this setting apart of Paul and Barnabas not an ordination to the apostleship or to any office in the Church, but their consecration to a missionary work which was so important in itself, and marked such a distinct epoch in the history of Christianity, as to warrant the use of the form of ordination. This is the view adopted by Haddan and other High-Church Episcopal writers.

Election by the people of a particular church to the pastoral office is no part of ordination to the Christian ministry; still less is ordination a mere adjunct following and consummating such an election. At this point there is a vital distinction between the Presbyterian and the Independent theory, growing necessarily out of the two views as to the constitution of the visible Church.[1]

[1] According to the Independent theory, "besides particular *churches*, there is not instituted by Christ any church more extensive and catholic, entrusted with power for the administration of His ordinances, or the execution of any authority in His name." From which it follows that "the essence of the call of a pastor, teacher, or elder into office consists in the election of the church, together with his acceptance of it and separation by fasting and prayer; and those who are so chosen, though not set apart by imposition of hands, are rightly constituted ministers of Christ, in whose name and authority they exercise the ministry to them so committed." (See Savoy Declaration, Schaff's Creeds of Christendom, iii. 371, 375; also John Owen's Nature of a Gospel Church, Works, vol. xvi.) The Westminster Confession, on the other hand, declares that "*the* visible *Church* is also catholic or universal under the Gospel," and that "to *this catholic, visible Church* Christ hath given the ministry,

According to our theory, men are not ordained to the pastoral office in a particular congregation, nor to the ministry of any denomination of Christians, but to the ministry of the Word and sacraments in the visible Catholic Church. Election to the pastoral office is simply one of the evidences by which a man's fitness for the work of the ministry is certified; it is no more a part of his ordination than his examination in Greek or Hebrew. It is one thing to make a gold ring, and another to appropriate it to a bride's finger. It is one thing to make a man a minister in the Church of Christ, and another to install him pastor over a particular flock.[1]

Scripture examples do not sustain the position that election by the people is any part of ordination. All that the one hundred and twenty disciples did in Acts i. was to appoint two and set them before the Lord. Indeed, it is by no means certain the people did this. "They" in verse 24 most naturally refers to the Apostles. But it was God who *chose* Matthias, by means of the lot; there was no ordination in his case. "The lot fell upon Matthias; and he was numbered with the eleven Apostles." In the case of the deacons in Acts vi. the people looked out seven men of honest report, and the Apostles "prayed, and laid their hands on them," thus

oracles, and ordinances of God for the gathering and perfecting of the saints in this life unto the end of the world" (Conf. of Faith, chap. xxv. 2, 3).

[1] Presbyters are not by ordination confined unto places, but unto functions. They who theoretically hold the contrary do not act out their own doctrine. They do not ordain a man over again every time he changes his pastoral charge. They change their location many times without being re-ordained. All this, I presume, they would not do if their persuasion were as strict as their words pretend. — HOOKER: *Ecc. Polity*, book v. 80.

ordaining them to their office. Nor is there in any other Scripture example the least intimation that popular election is either of the essence or any part of the form of ordination. If the theory of Independency could be sustained, it would logically follow that a man ordained to the ministry is a minister only in that particular charge to which he is chosen, and is not authorized to exercise his office in any other place or among any other people, and that he would cease to be a minister at all as soon as the people's call and his own acceptance of it were reversed by the dissolution of his pastoral relation. But this is contrary to all Scriptures, as well as to all Christian usage. God has *set* ministers in the same Church with Apostles and Prophets (1 Cor. xii. 28). They are called "ministers of God," "ministers of Christ," "ministers of the New Testament," "ambassadors of Christ." To make either their investiture or their tenure of office dependent upon the changing preferences and whims of a particular congregation, is utterly to destroy their relation to Christ and to His universal Church. And besides all this, the theory that election by the people is essential either to the calling or ordination of a minister, if consistently carried out, would prevent the extension of the Church to heathen lands. The whole work of missions, from the days of Paul and Barnabas till now, is a standing protest against it. The practice of our Independent brethren is in this respect better than their creed. They ordain home and foreign missionaries without popular election.

III. We come now to the vexed question, Who have a right to ordain?

We need spend little time to show that this right does not belong to private church members, individually or collectively. No local congregation of believers is authorized to ordain its own minister. We admit, of course, as do the highest of High Churchmen, that all church power is conferred upon and resides in the whole body of the Church. We do not believe in any hierarchy aside from the royal priesthood of believers. But it does not follow from this that church power is to be exercised by the people indiscriminately.[1]

Both the examples and the precepts of the Scriptures teach plainly that ministers are to be ordained by men already in the sacred office. All the instructions on the subject in the New Testament are contained in the Pastoral Epistles, which are addressed, not to churches, but to their office-bearers. The common-sense of mankind as shown in civil affairs is against the reasoning which infers the right of the people to ordain, from the admitted fact that all church power resides in the body of the Church. According to the American theory of government all political power resides in the people, and is to be exercised for their benefit; and this is virtually the theory of the British Constitution as illustrated in its history since the expulsion of the Stuarts. But it does not follow that every citizen, or every society or assembly of citizens, can take on themselves at pleasure the administration of the government, or even the inauguration of one whom they have chosen to office. The citizens of a New England town have no right to administer the oath of office to the town constable.

[1] The powers to bind and to loose, to preach the Word and administer the sacraments, reside in the whole body, and are to be exercised for the benefit of the whole body; but they are delegated to Christian ministers as the organs and representatives of the body, — for which reason, though the powers belong essentially to them, it does not follow that all have a right to exercise them. — GOULBURN: *Holy Catholic Church*, p. 151.

Assuming that ordination to the ministry is to be performed by those already in office, it remains to decide what officers possess this right. On this question the whole Protestant world is divided, the Episcopal denomination standing on one side, and all other denominations on the other. The question is one of vital importance. It underlies the integrity of the visible Church, the validity of its sacraments, and the Divine authority of its ministers. It comes home to the conscience of every one who claims to be a minister of Christ and a steward of the mysteries of God. It behooves him to know whether he is a usurper of the sacred office, or whether he is lawfully ordained to it according to the design and ordinance of the Supreme Head of the Church. Let us endeavor distinctly to understand the issue, — to strip it of all extraneous questions, and consider it in its naked simplicity. So far as Presbyterians are concerned, if we may take our standards as a fair expression of our views, there is no dispute with our Episcopal brethren — (1) In regard to the existence of the visible Church as a Divine and perpetual institution in the world; nor as to the duty of all Christians to labor and pray for its visible unity; nor as to the sin of schism or unnecessary divisions. (2) Neither is there any dispute between us about the infallible inspiration and plenary authority of the Apostles as Christ's agents in the organization and establishment of the Church; nor about the fact that in fulfilment of Christ's promise there has been an unbroken succession from the Apostles of an order of men called and authorized to rule the Church, preach the Word, and administer the sacraments; nor about the necessity of ordination by prayer and the laying on of hands as the formal conference and seal of ministerial authority.

(3) Neither do we differ in regard to the nature and efficacy of the sacraments, to be administered only by ministers of the Word lawfully ordained, as the outward signs, seals, and conveyance of inward and spiritual grace. Doubtless there are many in the Presbyterian Church who hold the mere remembrance theory of the Lord's Supper, and regard baptism as only an outward form of consecration. And so also there are in the Episcopal Church all shades of opinion, from the baldest Zwinglianism to the *opus operatum* and mechanical theory of Romanism. But the Presbyterian and Episcopal *standards* are at one on this subject. There is just as much of the doctrine of sacramental grace in the one as in the other. They both teach that the sacraments are "effectual means of salvation," that the Lord's Supper is "the communion of the body and blood of Christ," and that baptism is "the sign and seal of regeneration and engrafting into Christ, and that even to infants."

(4) Nor do we differ as to the authority of the Church, in the exercise of a wise discretion, and in conformity to the circumstances of different times and countries, to institute rites and ceremonies, provided nothing is done contrary to Scripture, and nothing aside from Scripture is insisted on as necessary to salvation; nor as to the right of the Church under the same conditions to confer special functions upon her office-bearers, as human expedients for her government, such as the duties assigned to synodical missionaries and superintendents, moderators of ecclesiastical assemblies, whether temporary or permanent, and overseers of large dioceses or districts of the Church, including more than one congregation. What then is the contention between us? It relates simply to the question who have the right to ordain

men to the Christian ministry. They say it belongs exclusively to diocesan bishops, who, as a distinct order, are the official successors of the Apostles. We say it belongs to presbyters, who are the only bishops recognized in the New Testament. This is the core of the whole controversy.[1]

[1] In this discussion we should guard ourselves against the "fatal imposture and force of words." Writers on both sides of this controversy use words in a double sense. This is the case with the phrase "apostolic succession," which may mean either a succession *of* Apostles, or a succession of ministers *from* the Apostles. In the former sense we reject, but in the latter sense we believe in, apostolic succession. The same is true of the word "bishop." We have no difficulty in accepting Cyprian's favorite maxim: " Ecclesia est in episcopo," when we couple it with the no less authoritative saying of Jerome: "Idem ergo presbyter qui est episcopus;" "presbyter" and "bishop" being the generic and synonymous terms by which the Scripture describes the authority Christ has instituted in His Church for her edification. In the same way we could adopt such statements as these: "That the ministry is derived from Christ, and is perpetuated through *episcopal* ordination;" that "the Apostles ordained a *bishop* over each newly erected church;" that "the order of bishops is essential to the outward being of the Church" (Blunt's Annotated Prayer-Book, p. 150). It would not be fair, however, for us to make such statements without qualification, because we use the word "bishop" in its Scripture sense of "overseer," and as synonymous with "presbyter;" whereas our Episcopal friends use the same word under the imposed and non-scriptural sense of *diocesan* bishop, as descriptive of an order of officers entirely distinct from presbyters. We admit, of course, that the Apostles were bishops, because the greater includes the less, and the exercise of all church power was vested in them. Peter and John expressly call themselves presbyters, elders, or bishops, — in the Scripture sense of the words. But we deny that "the apostolate was in *substance* an episcopate;" the episcopal functions of the Apostles were a very small part of their office. We deny that "their miraculous powers belonged to their persons and were separable from their office;" the powers to work miracles were part of their endowments for their official work, as their commission expressly declares; they were, as

It is admitted on both sides (as Mr. Gore contends in his recent work on "The Church and the Ministry") "that Christ in founding His Church founded also a ministry in the Church in the person of His Apostles; that these Apostles had a *temporary function* in their capacity as founders under Christ, and as witnesses of His resurrection; and that underlying this temporary function was another, — a pastorate of souls and a stewardship of Divine mysteries, which was intended to become perpetual."[1]

In all this Dr. Witherow, the latest writer on the other side, fully agrees. He shows conclusively that the ministry was not derived from the Church, but from Christ;[2] that this ministry included both temporary and permanent agencies; that the apostleship includes all minor offices in itself;[3] the Apostles were the first

Paul calls them, "the *signs* of an Apostle." There is the same ambiguity in the word "apostle." It is sometimes used in Scripture to designate the office of the Twelve, and sometimes applied in its etymological meaning to any one *sent* to perform a particular duty. Thus Epaphroditus, whom the Philippian Church sent to Paul in prison, is called ὑμῶν ἀπόστολον, which is rendered in our English version "your messenger" (Phil. ii. 25). So also in 2 Cor. viii. 23, those whom Paul sent to the church at Corinth are called ἀπόστολοι ἐκκλησιῶν, which our translators have properly rendered "messengers of the churches."

In the "Didache," or "Teaching of the Twelve Apostles," the word "apostle" is used simply to describe a *travelling missionary*, who was forbidden to remain more than two days in one place. And in this we have a clear proof that at the time the Didache was written, there were no successors of the *Apostles* in the technical sense of the name, and no office in the Church corresponding to the modern *diocesan* bishop.

[1] Gore on the Church and the Ministry, p. 69.
[2] Witherow's Form of the Christian Temple, p. 12.
[3] Under the head of temporary agencies we include not only Apostles, Prophets, and Evangelists, but the various spiritual gifts

ministers of Christ; and all other ministers are, in fact, their successors in all those functions of their office which were intended to be perpetual. If this were all that is meant by "apostolic succession," we should have no difficulty in adopting either the doctrine or its name. But Mr. Gore and those whom he represents incorporate with it two assumptions, for which there is no warrant in Scripture, and no proof in recorded facts either in the New Testament or in the earliest Christian writings. *First*, they assume that the Twelve Apostles were the Divinely appointed "*Depositaries*" of all official grace in the Church; and *secondly*, that from them, as from a sacred fountain, the grace of office, without which no ministerial act is valid, can be transmitted only through diocesan bishops descending in regular succession from the Apostles, and possessing the exclusive right and power of ordination. This is what is meant by "the historic episcopate," which the Episcopal Church co-ordinates with the Holy Scriptures and with the administration of the sacraments, in their overture for the reunion of Christendom.[1] We give them full credit for sincerity, and freely admit that if

or charisms, with which so many of the first Christians were endowed. The presence of these men and the supernatural gifts, of which they were possessed in such variety and abundance, constitute the distinctive characteristic of the Church in the New Testament age. . . .

In the discharge of the Divine commission, with which they were entrusted, the Apostles preached Christianity to Jew and Gentile, planted churches, and guided and governed the churches which they set up. In doing so they discharged all the duties which ordinary ministers perform. — *Ibid.*, pp. 13, 17.

[1] These proposals, as revised by the Lambeth Conference, are as follows: "That in the opinion of this Conference the following articles supply a basis on which approach may be, by God's blessing,

their claim could be sustained by Scripture, which "contains all things necessary to salvation," we should be bound joyfully to accept their proposals. But before the tribunal of God's Word we dare not do so. And our hesitation is greatly confirmed by the admissions and contradictions of their own best writers in their interpretation of Scripture on this subject.

We have no disposition to dispute about words, still less would we take advantage of any inconsistency in the use of them by our Episcopal brethren. It is not always easy to understand them. But we are warranted in saying that none of them advocate a succession of Apostles in the *full meaning of the title.* Thus even Blunt, though he affirms that the "apostolate was *in substance* an episcopate," admits immediately afterwards that "their extraordinary powers and the *apostolate itself* ceased with the death of the Apostles."[1] We might ask, If the apostolate ceased, did not the substance of it cease also? But the learned annotator comes back again to his original position that the substance of the apostolate is an episcopate. He affirms that "the Apostles ordained a bishop over each newly organized church; and these chief pastors or bishops inherited the

---

made towards Home Reunion: (1) The Holy Scriptures of the Old and New Testament, as containing all things necessary to salvation and as being the rule and ultimate standard of faith. (2) The Apostles' Creed as the baptismal symbol, and the Nicene Creed as the sufficient statement, of Christian faith. (3) The two sacraments ordained by Christ Himself, — Baptism and the Supper of the Lord, — ministered with unfailing use of Christ's Words of Institution, and of the Elements ordained by Him. (4) The Historic Episcopate, locally adapted in the methods of its administration to the varying needs of the nations and peoples called of God into the unity of His Church."

[1] Annotated Prayer-Book, p. 530.

powers of ordination, government, and church censures, which were the ordinary parts of the apostolic office." Now, this statement just as it stands is good Presbyterian doctrine, provided the word "bishop" is used in its Scripture sense as interchangeable with "presbyter." But this is not the author's meaning. By "bishops" he means an order of men distinct from and superior to presbyters, inheriting from the Apostles, by right of official succession, the exclusive possession of the power of ordination and government in the Church. And this is the head and front of the contention between us. Here we join issue in the question of fact.

Is it not remarkable, and a strong presumption against the Episcopal theory, that the power of ordination is never once mentioned in the instructions Christ gave to the Apostles, never once asserted by the Apostles themselves, and that not one clear and indisputable instance of its exercise by Apostles alone is mentioned in Scripture? If they were, in the intention of Christ and in their own consciousness of their position, the head of a long succession of ordainers, a succession on whose integrity depends the very existence of the visible Church, the validity of the sacraments and the right of men to administer them, is it credible that the chief thing for which this succession was established should never be mentioned by Christ or by themselves?

This, however, is only a negative argument. The Saviour and His Apostles may have said and done many things not recorded in Scripture. We are willing and anxious to accept all facts, whether recorded in Scripture or in other histories, and all good and necessary inferences from them. There are only two grounds on which the claims of diocesan episcopacy can be sustained: (1) a succession, in fact, of an order of men superior in office to presbyters, having the exclusive right to ordain, *established by the Apostles themselves;* or (2) the *custom of the Church,* introduced after the death of the Apostles and without their sanction. Most Episcopal writers strangely confound these two grounds, and play fast and loose between them. If, indeed, the custom could be traced back to the days of the Apostles, the inference would be irresistible that it has their sanction. But if there is any interval, however short, between their death and its establishment, its Divine and binding authority is gone. An interval of *one* year breaks the chain as effectually as though it were a thousand years. The testimony of the Fathers is contradictory. Jerome is in open conflict with Cyril. If our opponents may reject the witness of the one, we have the same right to reject the witness of the other.[1]

It is admitted on all hands that if we leave out the Apostles, the only two classes of permanent church officers mentioned in Scripture are bishops and deacons (Phil. i. 1). If by bishops be meant only *diocesan* bishops, then there were no presbyters. If both diocesan bishops and presbyters are included under the one title, then bishops and presbyters are not two distinct orders.[2]

---

[1] It is not pretended that there is any explicit patristic testimony for the existence of diocesan episcopacy until at least a century after the death of the Apostles. The apostolic Fathers bring little aid and comfort to our opponents. The recently discovered "Teaching of the Twelve Apostles" and the Epistles of Clement do not help them. The New Testament is the only extant book which tells us historically what was done in the Church in the lifetime of the Apostles. See Appendix, Lecture V. (A).

[2] Our Episcopal friends stand at this point between Scylla and Charybdis. But let us not exult over them, for we stand on a similar position in regard to ruling elders. While they claim three orders in the ministry, we claim three orders of church officers.

It is admitted by all candid writers on the subject that the words "presbyter" and "bishop," as used in the New Testament, are synonymous and interchangeable.[1] Some of the ablest Episcopal writers candidly acknowledge this.[2] "The one thing needful," says Mr. Haddan, than whom we know of no abler or more consistent advocate on his side of the question, "to make the truth clear, is simply the straightforward acceptance of what is manifestly the plain usage of the New Testament; namely, the employment of ἐπίσκοπος and πρε-

"The ordinary and perpetual officers of the Church are bishops or pastors, the representatives of the people usually styled ruling elders and deacons" (Form of Government, iii. 2).

But to justify this enumeration we must make ruling elders a subordinate class in the one order of presbyters, or else we must admit that their office rests upon the custom of the Church under the general Scripture description of helps and governments (1 Cor. xii. 28). If the distinction between presbyters and diocesan bishops is based upon the same broad ground, we have no dispute with those who insist upon it. They only distinguish upward, while we distinguish downward.

[1] This presbyter-bishop of the New Testament is found in all ages of the Church and in all lands. Herein is the true historic succession of the ministry in the unbroken chain of these ordained presbyters. Herein is the world-wide government which is carried on through them. This is the one form of church government that bears the mark of catholicity, that is *semper, ubique, et ab omnibus.* — DR. BRIGGS: *Whither,* p. 230.

[2] On this point Bishop Lightfoot is very explicit. "It is a fact now generally recognized by theologians of all shades of opinion that in the language of the New Testament the same officer in the Church is called indifferently 'bishop' (ἐπίσκοπος) and 'elder,' or 'presbyter' (πρεσβύτερος)." After elaborately proving this, he adds: "Nor is it only in the apostolic writings that this identity is found. Saint Clement of Rome wrote probably in the last decade of the first century, and in his language the terms are still convertible" (Lightfoot on Epistle to Philippians, p. 95). See also Gore on the Church and the Ministry, p. 136.

σβύτερος as equivalent terms.¹ The same author further admits that to make the presbytery who laid hands on Timothy an assembly of diocesan bishops, or to insist that the Ephesian elders, whom Paul declared to be bishops by the appointment of the Holy Ghost, were bishops in the Episcopal sense of the word, "are desperate devices."² We fully agree with this author that there is no Scripture authority for the office of diocesan bishop, unless it can be shown that it is the perpetuation of the apostolate. Diocesan bishops are either successors of the Apostles as apostles in their peculiar functions, or else their authority rests solely on the custom of the Church, without scriptural or apostolic sanction.³

¹ Haddan on Apostolic Succession, p. 74.
² Ibid., p. 75.
³ When the end for which any office is instituted is accomplished, and the mode by which men have been inducted into it is no longer in use, and the attestations of its authority can no longer be produced, the conclusion that the office itself has ceased to exist is irresistible. The application of these simple tests to the question, whether the Apostles *as such* have any successors, is easy. The Apostles all received their appointment directly. The original twelve were neither chosen nor ordained by men; Christ *made* them apostles. Paul claims in this respect to be on an equality with the others. " Paul, an apostle, not of men, neither by man, but by Jesus Christ" (Gal. i. 1). "The lot fell upon Matthias; and he was numbered with the eleven Apostles" (Acts i. 26). There was no human election or ordination in his case; it was an essential if not the chief design of the Apostles' peculiar office that they should be eye-witnesses of the resurrection. This is the avowed end for which Matthias was chosen. To qualify Paul for the same office the risen Saviour appeared to him on the way to Damascus; and hence, when he would vindicate his title to the apostleship, he says, " Am I not an apostle? Have I not seen the Lord Jesus Christ?" (1 Cor. ix. 1.) It was an essential qualification of the Apostles for their distinctive office that they should be endowed with power to

The best representative of Episcopacy, and the most generally accepted authority in its defence, is Richard Hooker. To this day he retains the respect of all parties in the Episcopal Church. We freely accord to him the title of "judicious," and have an unbounded admiration for his exposition of that law whose seat is the bosom of God, and whose voice is the harmony of the world. His whole argument on the question before us is summed up in the following passage: —

"The form of regiment established by the Apostles at first was that the laity or people should be subject unto a college of ecclesiastical persons which were in every city established for that purpose. These in their writings they term, sometimes presbyters, sometimes bishops. *To take one church out of a number for a pattern of what the rest were,* the pres-

work miracles. Hence Paul says, "Truly the signs of an apostle were wrought among you" (2 Cor. xii. 12). Now, we submit that it is a manifest absurdity to say that men who have not received the direct appointment of an apostle, and are not qualified to perform the specific work of an apostle, and are not able to show the signs of an apostle, are invested by Divine right with the apostolic office.

Dr. Lightfoot, Bishop of Durham, in the essay on the Christian Ministry appended to his Commentary on Philippians, says: "The opinion hazarded by Theodoret and adopted by many later writers, that the same officers in the Church who were first called apostles came afterward to be designated as bishops, *is baseless.* . . . The Apostle, like the Prophet or the Evangelist, held no *local* office. He was essentially, as his name denotes, a missionary moving about from place to place. . . . It is not therefore to the apostle that we must look for the prototype of the bishop."

"When I see bishops, immediately sent of God, infallibly assisted by the Holy Ghost, travelling to the remotest kingdom to preach the Gospel in their own language to the infidel nations, and confirming their doctrine by undoubted miracles, I shall believe them to be the Apostles' true successors in the apostolic office" (John Owen's Plea for Scripture Ordination, p. 56).

byters of Ephesus, as it is in the history of their departure from the Apostle Paul at Miletum, are said to have wept abundantly all,—which speech doth show them to have been many. And by the Apostle's exhortation it may appear that they had not each his several flock to feed, but were in common appointed to feed that one flock, the Church at Ephesus, for which cause the phrase of his speech is this, *attendite gregi*, 'look all to that one flock over which the Holy Ghost hath made you bishops.' These persons ecclesiastical being termed as then presbyters and bishops both, were all subject unto Paul, as to an higher governor appointed of God to be over them. But forasmuch as the Apostles could not themselves be present in all churches, and as Saint Paul foretold the presbyters at Ephesus that there 'would rise up from among their own selves men speaking perverse things to draw disciples after them,' there did grow in short time among the governors of each church those emulations, strifes, and contentions whereof there *could be no sufficient remedy provided, except, according unto the order of Jerusalem already begun*, some one was endued with episcopal authority over the rest, *which one, being resident, might keep them in order*, and have pre-eminence or principality in those things wherein the equality of many agents was the cause of disorder and trouble. This one president or governor among the rest had his known authority established a long time before that settled difference of name and title took place, whereby such alone were called bishops. And therefore, in the book of Saint John's Revelation, they are entitled 'angels.'"[1]

Now this is the best that even Hooker can do; and subsequent writers on the same side have only reiterated his arguments with the variations of the kaleidoscope. The first thing that must strike a candid reader of this passage is the *circularity* of its reasoning. It draws absolute conclusions from premises which are at

[1] Hooker, Ecc. Pol., book vii. chap. v. sect. 1, 2.

best but probable, and then it doubles back the conclusions to strengthen the premises. The author agrees at the outset to stake the whole question of the Scripture authority for diocesan bishops upon the case of Timothy and the church at Ephesus. This is candid and fair; if Timothy was not a diocesan bishop and a successor of the Apostles, resident at Ephesus, there are none such in Scripture. But the argument has not proceeded two steps before James is lugged in with the bald assertion, as though it needed no proof, that the order of diocesan episcopacy was already established in his person in Jerusalem before Timothy's time. Why, then, did not our author begin at Jerusalem? If the episcopacy of James is so indisputable that it can be adduced without proof to establish an antecedent probability that Timothy was made diocesan at Ephesus, why not rest the whole discussion upon James and the church at Jerusalem? Any one who reads the record in Acts xv. will see that it is less available for diocesan episcopacy than what we know of Timothy. A chain is no stronger than its weakest link, and this first link is very weak. We admit, of course, that James and all the other Apostles, whether in Jerusalem or anywhere else, had all the authority that has ever been claimed for diocesan bishops; but how does this prove that they transmitted this authority to a succession of such bishops?

Again, our author asserts that the *only remedy* for schismatical contentions among presbyters is their subordination to bishops superior in rank and authority to themselves. But where is the proof of this? Not in the New Testament; such a remedy for schism is nowhere mentioned. Not in history; for, as a matter of fact, the establishment of diocesan episcopacy has not brought peace and unity. There are to-day, to say nothing of the past, in the bosom of the Episcopal Church diversities of doctrine and practice quite as broad, and controversies quite as bitter, and the speaking of things quite as perverse, as any that prevail among other denominations of Christians. Moreover, there is a fatal superfluity in this argument of the "only remedy," — it proves too much. It constantly points and urges toward Rome. For if the only remedy for contention among presbyters is a diocesan bishop, what remedy is there for strife among bishops, whom all history proves to be men of like passions, but archbishops; and what cure for the strife of archbishops but patriarchs; and who shall keep the patriarchs in order, but the pope? This plea of the "only remedy" runs through and unifies the whole system of the Romish hierarchy; if it is good in its first application, it is equally good in the last. And thus, as Milton says, it is "the stirrup by which Antichrist mounts into the saddle."[1]

But to our mind the conclusive proof that this is not the only remedy, and not a Divinely appointed remedy at all, is the consideration that Paul did not apply it in his treatment of recorded cases. Take, for example, the desperate case of the church at Corinth. It is nothing to the purpose to say that Paul was the bishop of that church, and kept the presbyters in order by his authority, because the Apostle was not *resident* at Corinth, and manifestly did not fulfil the conditions upon which the efficacy of the remedy depends, according to Hooker's statement. In the Epistles to the Corinthians, which are full of rebuke against division and strife, there is not a word about bishops.[2] In the case of Ephesus, of

[1] An Apology for Smectymnuus.
[2] In the year 96, after the death of Paul, Clement of Rome wrote

which we have an explicit account, the remedy prescribed by Paul is entirely inconsistent with the present or prospective existence of any higher order than presbyters in the permanent ministry of the Church.

The Apostle meets the elders of that church at Miletus. He informs them that after his departure contentions and strifes would arise among them, which in his absence could not be controlled by his authority. Now, if ever, is the time to apply, or at least to prescribe, the "only remedy." Timothy, his supposed successor in office, was present (Acts xx. 4). Does the Apostle point to him and say, "Here is my successor in office, appointed to rule over you as the only remedy for schismatical contentions?" No! but he says to the presbyters in the presence of Timothy, "Take heed to yourselves and to the flock over which *the Holy Ghost has made you bishops.*" So the Revised New Testament honestly renders the passage, substituting the word "bishop" for "overseers," which was the weak evasion of King James's translators. Now is this conceivable upon the supposition that Timothy was at this very time diocesan of the church at Ephesus? What! lay the whole episcopal function upon the presbyters in the presence of their own bishop, and declare that this is the appointment of the Holy Ghost? If it be answered that Timothy was made sole bishop of Ephesus at some time after this interview, this starts a fresh crop of questions and difficulties. Where is the proof

his epistle to the church at Corinth. It is evident from this epistle that at the time it was written there were no officers in the church at Corinth but deacons and presbyters, whom Clement also calls "bishops." This demonstrates that the episcopal office, as something distinct from that of presbyters, was not ordained by the Apostle at Corinth. The same is clearly shown by the epistle of Polycarp in regard to the church at Philippi.

that Timothy was *ever* made bishop at Ephesus? The subscription to the Second Epistle to Timothy — made by an unknown hand at an uncertain time (which the Revised Version properly expunges) — and the testimony of Eusebius in the third century, are nothing to the purpose. Hooker quotes them; but even omitting the distinction between a Scripture and a diocesan bishop, we cannot accept them as of any value in this argument, for our inquest is for *Scripture* proof. The words in 1 Tim. i. 3, "As I besought thee to abide still at Ephesus, when I went into Macedonia, that thou mightest charge some that they teach no other doctrine," certainly do not imply that Timothy was ordained to the office of supreme bishop in Ephesus. And even if they did, it is evident that he did not hold any such office at the time when Paul, in his presence, told the elders that the Holy Ghost had made *them* bishops over that flock. It is equally plain that this was not the occasion when Paul besought him to abide in Ephesus, for the Apostle was now going to Jerusalem, and not into Macedonia. And it is further evident, from the record itself, that the Apostle was not in Ephesus at any period subsequent to this interview with the elders at Miletus. On this point his own words are conclusive. He says: "Behold, I know that ye all, among whom I have gone preaching the kingdom of God, *shall see my face no more*" (Acts xx. 25). He *knew* it. Was he mistaken in what he so confidently asserted? Would he have affirmed this so positively if, indeed, it had been, as some presume to say, only an "expectation" and "a human inference from the danger which he knew to be before him"?[1] We cannot think so.[2] Paul was

[1] Conybeare and Howson, Life and Epistles of Paul, ii. 241.
[2] "Some suppose that this was merely an opinion or surmise of

never at Ephesus again. His beseeching Timothy to remain there must be referred to some previous departure, when he went, not to Jerusalem, but into Macedonia, and must be interpreted in consistency with the fact that in his last interview with the presbyters of that church he declared that the Holy Ghost had made *them* bishops over that flock. To assert without proof that this appointment of the Holy Ghost was afterward revoked as an insufficient remedy for the evils which Paul foresaw and to which he applied it, is a purely gratuitous assumption. Nor are these facts in any way modified by the Epistle to the Ephesians, written, as all the critics agree, by Paul subsequently to the interview at Miletus. In that epistle Timothy's name is not mentioned. Is this consistent with the supposition that he was sole bishop there? Can any intelligent Episcopalian conceive of an inspired apostle, or any one who believes in diocesan Episcopacy and understands the courtesies which prevail among gentlemen, writing a letter of religious instruction to the diocese of Long Island, without even mentioning the name of his honored head, Bishop Littlejohn?

From Timothy and the church at Ephesus Hooker makes a wide step and a long link in his chain of reasoning to the angels of the seven churches of Asia.

Paul, without Divine communication or direction; but this idea was expressed in verse 22 by the phrase, '*not knowing* the things which shall befall me there,' *i. e.*, in Jerusalem, — and it surely cannot be assumed that 'knowing' and 'not knowing' mean precisely the same thing. If 'not knowing' there denotes that it was hidden from him and remained uncertain, then 'I know' must mean that it had been revealed in some way, and was certain. To attach the same sense to directly opposite expressions, in the same context and in reference to the same subject, is to nullify the use of language." — *Alexander on the Acts, in loco.*

Let us admit at once that by the angels are meant, not the churches themselves, as many commentators plausibly contend, but individual men and presiding officers. Does this prove that they were diocesan bishops? What, seven diocesan bishops in the little province of Asia, and each of them having only one church in his diocese! Why, they appear to us to be nothing more than pastors and permanent moderators of parochial presbyteries.

We are compelled, therefore, as many of the most eminent bishops and scholars of the Episcopal Church have been, to adopt Jerome's account of the historic origin and prevalence of episcopacy.

"As, therefore, presbyters do know that *the custom of the Church* makes them subject to the bishop which is set over them, so let bishops know that *custom*, rather than the truth of any ordinance of the Lord's, maketh them greater than the rest, and that with common advice they ought to govern the Church."[1]

But now suppose we admit, for the sake of the argument, that diocesan bishops are of Divine appointment, and that the apostolic office is perpetuated in them: does it follow that they have the *exclusive right* to

[1] Jerome on the Epistle to Titus, quoted by Hooker, Ecc. Pol., book vii. 5, 8.

Hooker labors hard to reconcile this testimony with the doctrine of *jure divino* episcopacy. But that he does not succeed to the satisfaction of the most zealous Episcopalians is evident from the fact that many of their later writers take the opposite course, and impeach the credibility of Jerome as a witness. Thus Haddan says: "The sweeping implications of Jerome in the teeth of the practice of the universal Church only *throw discredit upon himself, as dealing in over-wide statements*" (Apostolic Succession, p. 120). This is setting us a very bad example of disrespect for the testimony of the Fathers.

ordain men to the Christian ministry? By no means. This is a separate doctrine, and requires a distinct proof. How meagre and inconclusive is the alleged proof, appears in the fact that the passage of Scripture most frequently and dogmatically insisted upon as conveying such power is the saying of Christ: "As My Father hath sent Me, so send I you." "This," says Mr. Blunt, "is the great charter bestowing the exclusive power of ordination upon bishops."[1] But surely there must be a large reading between the lines to see any such exclusive power in this charter. The learned author might as well say it bestows upon the Apostles the exclusive power to preach the Gospel or administer the sacraments. The fact is that it simply asserts their Divine mission, without specifying any of the purposes for which they were sent. The whole reasoning is in a vicious circle. It begins with the promise of demonstration, and ends with begging the question. The only sources from which we can ascertain what the Apostles were empowered to do, are the instructions given to them by our Lord, their own claims as to their authority, and the inspired record of their doings. In their recorded instructions there is not one word about ordination; so far as the New Testament informs us, they never claimed the power of ordination as belonging exclusively to themselves; while they performed the duties of the apostolate, the exercise of this power was not confined exclusively to them; and therefore, even if we admit that the apostolic office is perpetuated in the Church, there is no Scripture ground for including the power of ordination among its peculiar functions.

Admitting that Timothy and Titus were diocesan bishops, and, as such, successors of the Apostles, there

[1] Annotated Prayer-Book, p. 543.

is nothing to show that they had the exclusive right to ordain in their respective dioceses. The avowed purpose for which Timothy was left in Ephesus was not to ordain, but to "charge some that they teach no other doctrine" than what Paul had taught. The injunction to "lay hands suddenly on no man," admitting that this refers to ordination to the ministry, might be addressed to any presbyter, upon the supposition that presbyters had the right to ordain, and therefore is no proof that presbyters were excluded from the exercise of that right. The words addressed to Titus, "For this cause left I thee in Crete, that thou shouldst set in order the things that are wanting, and ordain elders in every city" (Tit. i. 5), are entirely consistent with the theory that Titus was presiding elder or moderator of presbytery in Crete, and possessed the power of ordination in common with the other members of the body over which he presided. It is consistent also with the theory held by many that he was a temporary agent or representative of Paul, performing a special work in the organization of the church in Crete, and that the authority with which he was clothed ceased when that work was done.[1] Inasmuch as he is never called an apostle, and there is no record of his appointment to that office, the exercise of the right to ordain does not prove that he *was* an apostle; it rather proves that the power of

[1] Hooker says: "The Apostles sometimes gave their episcopal powers unto others, to exercise as agents only in their stead, and as it were by commission from them. Thus Titus and thus Timothy at *the first*, though *afterwards* endued with apostolical power of their own" (Ecc. Pol., book vii. chap. iv.). But where is the proof that they were afterwards endued with apostolical power of their own? "It appeareth," says our author, "in those subscriptions which are set upon the Epistle to Titus and the second to Timothy, and by Eusebius in his Ecclesiastical History." These subscriptions,

ordination was conferred upon those who were *not* apostles.

These views are abundantly confirmed by all the examples of ordination found in the New Testament.

If the transaction recorded in Acts (xiii. 1-3) was an ordination to office, it is conclusive against the Episcopal theory, because, while one of the ordained was the Apostle to the Gentiles, the ordainers were simply "prophets and teachers;" and if they might ordain an apostle and those miraculously called to office, much more might they do the same for presbyters and those whose call is in the ordinary way.

If, on the other hand, we agree with Haddan and other High-Church Episcopal writers that the separation of Barnabas and Saul for the work to which the Holy Ghost had called them was not an ordination in the technical sense, but only an extraordinary solemnity upon an extraordinary occasion,[1] — and we think this is the true interpretation — this does not affect the force and application of the example as against the Episcopal theory, for the form of that extraordinary solemnity was the form of ordination. They who had the right to use these acts of the ordination ceremony upon an extraordinary occasion and upon extraordinary subjects, had *a fortiori* the right to use them upon ordinary occasions and upon such ordinary subjects as a presbyter.

besides being uninspired additions of uncertain date and authorship, do not affirm that Titus and Timothy were apostles or *diocesan* bishops, but simply bishops, which we all admit. The testimony of Eusebius can hardly be accepted as a Scripture proof " It is the conception of a later age which represents Timothy as bishop of Ephesus, and Titus as bishop of Crete. Saint Paul's own language implies that the position they held was temporary" (Bishop Lightfoot, on the Christian Ministry, p. 199).

[1] Haddan on Apostolic Succession, p. 84.

He who is authorized to sprinkle water upon a child in the name of the Father, the Son, and the Holy Ghost, has the right to administer the sacrament of baptism. The right to participate by the laying on of hands in an ordination service implies and includes the power to ordain.

And this brings us to the crucial case, — the ordination of Timothy. There is no question that he was ordained in the fullest sense of the word, and that the ceremony is described in these two passages: "Neglect not the gift that is in thee, which was given thee by prophecy, with the laying on of the hands of the presbytery" (1 Tim. iv. 14); "Wherefore I put thee in remembrance that thou stir up the gift of God which is in thee by the putting on of my hands" (2 Tim. i. 6). These two statements describe the same transaction,[1] and they can be reconciled only by admitting that the Apostle and the presbytery were equal participants in Timothy's ordination, and had equal authority to perform the ceremony. In the one passage the Apostle does not mention himself at all; it was done by the hands of the presbytery. In the other the presbytery is not mentioned; it was done by the hands of the Apostle. Each statement is complete in itself as a record of the transaction. What is the legitimate inference? That the hands of the presbytery and the hands of the Apostle were, in regard to the power of ordina-

[1] We are aware that this is a disputed point, and that even as good a commentator as Bishop Ellicott favors the opinion that the first passage describes Timothy's ordination as a presbyter, which is supposed to have taken place at Lystra, while the second passage describes his consecration as a bishop, which is alleged to have been done at Ephesus. This interpretation is quite as good for our argument as the other. But it rests upon mere conjecture, and is not generally accepted, even by Episcopal writers.

tion, interchangeable. Paul acted as the presiding officer of presbytery, and yet as one of the presbyters, with whom he held the ordaining power in common; for he, with Peter and John, was also an elder. How is the force of this inference contravened? The witnesses are not agreed. One says that by the "presbytery" is not meant the college of presbyters, but the abstract office which was potentially and by eminent domain in the Apostles. But the word πρεσβυτέριον is never used in this abstract sense; and besides, how was it possible for an *office* to lay *hands* on Timothy? Another says the first passage ought to be reconstructed thus: "Neglect not the gift that is in thee by the *prophecy of presbytery* with the laying on of hands, — *i. e.*, the Apostles' hands." So Bengel renders it. According to this interpretation the presbytery took no part whatever in the ordination. This method not only does violence to the grammatical structure of this passage, but makes all Scripture a nose of wax in the hand of destructive criticism. So far as we know, no respectable defender of episcopacy has adopted it. Another makes the presbytery a college of diocesan bishops, which Haddan calls a "desperate device." But desperate as it is, Blunt claims for it the highest patristic authority, and the testimony of "all the best commentators, ancient and modern."[1] And he adds: "The utmost that can be claimed for the passage is that priests *sometimes* imposed their hands, together with an apostle or bishop." But why "sometimes"? If it was lawful once under apostolic sanction, why not always? And why may we not reverse the statement, and say the Apostles *some-*

[1] Annotated Prayer-Book, p. 543. By this sweeping assumption he excludes Alford, Ellicott, Wordsworth, and a host more of Episcopal writers from the category of the "best commentators."

150   THE MINISTRY AND SACRAMENTS.

times imposed their hands with the presbytery? The one assumption is just as valid as the other.[1] It seems to us that the only consistent conclusion from these Scripture records, and the only theory which can explain the subsequent history of the Church, is that which recognizes diocesan Episcopacy as a growth, and not an original and positive institution. Whether such growth proceeded from germinal principles within the Church, or was grafted on it from without; and whether it was justified by the changed conditions of the Church after the Apostles' death, — are questions aside from this discussion. In the days of the Apostles "presbyter" and

---

[1] Some Episcopal writers insist strongly upon the alleged distinction between the prepositions employed in the two passages under consideration. The gift that was in Timothy is said to be imparted *by* (διά) the laying on of the Apostles' hands, and *with* (μετά) the laying on of the hands of the presbytery. This is supposed to indicate that the imposition of the Apostles' hands was the *instrumental cause* of the Divine charism, while the imposition of the hands of the presbytery was simply an *accompaniment* which added nothing to the efficacy of the ordination. (See Blunt's Annotated Prayer-Book, p. 543; Hobart's Festivals and Fasts, p. 25; Haddan on Apostolic Succession, p. 84.) This distinction is purely imaginary, and would never have been invented but for the necessity of the argument. The two prepositions are constantly used in the New Testament interchangeably. "Many signs and wonders were done by (διά) the Apostles" (Acts ii. 43). "And when Paul and Barnabas were come, and gathered the church together, they rehearsed all that the Lord had done *with* (μετά) them" (Acts xiv. 27). Besides, the distinction, even if it were valid, proves too much for those who use it. If the laying on of the hands of the presbyters in the case of Timothy were simply an *accompaniment*, and not an essential part of the ordination, why do they quote Paul's injunction to Timothy, "Lay hands suddenly on no man," as a proof that Timothy had power to ordain, and was therefore a bishop? According to their own reasoning, Timothy might "lay hands on," and yet exercise no ordaining power, and therefore be no bishop.

"bishop" were interchangeable names for the same class of church officers, who received from the Apostles and shared with them the right to ordain others to the Christian ministry. They kept and exercised this right for a considerable time. But after the death of the Apostles and the expiration of their peculiar office, when the number of presbyters had greatly increased, one was chosen in each city or district, as president over the rest, who imposed hands in ordination as the head and representative of the presbytery. Out of this arrangement grew by degrees the superior dignity and exclusive authority of bishops, who increased in power and pride with the increasing corruptions of the Church, until they not only laid their hands, as ecclesiastical superiors, on the heads of presbyters, but set their feet, as temporal rulers, on the necks of princes. This is the theory of Jerome, adopted by Calvin and by many of the most eminent scholars and bishops of the Church of England. It is reasserted and illustrated with great ability by Mr. Hatch. He affirms that "the episcopate grew, by the force of circumstances, in the order of Providence, to satisfy a felt want." He professes to find "adequate causes not only for the existence of a president (among presbyters), but also for his supremacy without resorting to *what is not a known fact*, but only a counter-hypothesis, — the hypothesis of a special institution." For this view he claims the support of Jerome, whom he calls "the earliest and greatest of ecclesiastical antiquaries."[1]

[1] Bampton Lectures for 1880, p. 98. The same theory is maintained by Bishop Lightfoot. "At the close of the apostolic age the traces of the episcopate are few and indistinct. . . . If 'bishop' was at first used as a synonym for 'presbyter,' and afterwards came to designate the higher officer under whom the presbyter served, the episcopate, properly so called, would seem to have been developed from the

The doctrine that the power to ordain belongs exclusively and by Divine right to diocesan bishops, and its necessary corollary that non-episcopal ordination is null and void, is new even in the Episcopal Church. It is not taught in the Thirty-nine Articles. The English Reformers never asserted it in theory or in practice.[1] There is no trace of it in the writings of Cranmer, Parker, Grindal, and Whitgift, the first four Protestant Archbishops of Canterbury. If, as some maintain, it was asserted by Bancroft, the fifth primate, it is certain that he did not undertake to enforce it; for in the consecration of the Scottish bishops he insisted and persuaded his colleagues that the non-episcopal ordination they had received as presbyters was lawful and sufficient.[2]

We have the testimony of Burnett that in the attempt to establish episcopacy in Scotland " the bishops never required the Presbyterian ministers there to take episcopal ordination, but only to come and act with them in Church judicatories."[3]

Bishop Hall, who wrote the first formal treatise in defence of the Divine right of episcopacy, which he dedicated to Charles I. in 1639, acknowledges the validity of non-episcopal ordination, and declares that he knows of more than one, ordained without a bishop, who had enjoyed promotions and livings in the Church

subordinate office. In other words, the episcopate was formed, not out of the apostolic order by localization, but out of the presbyterial by elevation; and the title which originally was common to all, came at length to be appropriated to the chief among them " (Lightfoot, The Christian Ministry, p. 196).

[1] See Keble's Preface to Hooker's Ecc. Polity, p. 30.
[2] Archbishop Spottiswoode's History of the Church of Scotland, iii. 209.
[3] Burnett's Vindication of the Church of Scotland, p. 84 (London, 1696).

of England, "without any exception against the lawfulness of their calling."[1] Blunt, in his "Annotated Prayer-Book," admits that up to the days of the Commonwealth non-episcopal ordination was recognized as valid in the Church of England. He gives a list of those who obtained preferment without episcopal ordination, and loftily says: "They show the manner in which the Church of England was sagaciously leavened with foreign Protestantism by those *who wished to reduce it to the same abject level.*"[2]

The first systematic attempt to enforce exclusive episcopal ordination was made by Laud, the sixth Archbishop of Canterbury, whose zeal for the Mitre and the Crown, which he regarded as inseparable, was like the wrath of Achilles, — "the direful spring of woes unnumbered." The high-handed tyranny and bloody cruelty of that attempt were among the chief causes of the revolution which brought both the king and his ecclesiastical prime-minister to the scaffold. But the seed sowed by Laud did not perish at his death. In the violent reaction of the Restoration both his political and his ecclesiastical theories were dominant; and the party in power made full use of their oppor-

[1] Hall's Works, ix. 536.
[2] See Annotated Prayer-Book, p. 30. For further and abundant proof that Presbyterian ordination was recognized in the Church of England up to the time of Charles I., our readers are referred to Dr. Fisher's article in the "New Englander" for 1874, to Dr. Hodge's "Church Polity," to Goode's "Non-Episcopal Orders," to vol. i. of Schaff's "Creeds of Christendom," to the excellent article of Dr. R. B. Welch on "Christian Unity and the Historic Episcopate," in the "Presbyterian Review" for July, 1889, and to the recent lecture of Dr. Fisher on "The Validity of Non-Episcopal Ordination," published by Charles Scribner's Sons. The historic proof on this point is abundant and conclusive.

tunity to avenge their own wrongs and to enforce their doctrines. The solemn promises of Charles II. to those without whose aid he never could have attained to the throne of his fathers were ruthlessly broken. The Presbyterians and moderate Episcopalians were betrayed and trampled on. By the Act of Uniformity, in 1662, episcopal ordination was made essential not only to preferment in the Church of England, but to the performance of any ministerial function in the land; and the Act was enforced with relentless cruelty. "The clergy made war on schism with such vigor that they had little leisure to make war on vice."[1] Such men as Howe and Baxter were imprisoned for preaching contrary to Act of Parliament. Two thousand of the best ministers of the land were expelled from their benefices. The effect of this was not merely the loss of their services and the extinction for the time of their evangelical spirit in the Church, but it was the final overthrow of the party which from the beginning had tried to bring the Church of England into closer fellowship with all the Reformed Churches, and into more complete harmony with the religious instincts of the nation. "The Church of England stood from that moment isolated and alone among all the churches of the Christian world."[2]

This separation was effected in 1662 by the introduction into the preface of the Ordinal of the following sentence, as it now stands in the Episcopal Prayer-Book in England and in this country: "No man shall be accounted or taken to be a lawful bishop, priest, or deacon in this Church, or suffered to execute any of the said functions, except he be called, tried, and admitted thereto according to the form hereafter following, or hath had episcopal consecration or ordination."

[1] Macaulay's History, i. 165.
[2] Green's History of the English People, iv. 364.

What is the implication of this law in regard to non-episcopal ordination? Does it involve the opinion and warrant the inference that those who have not been ordained by a diocesan bishop have no Divine right to exercise any of the functions of a minister in the Church of Christ? We think it certainly does. They who are called High Churchmen candidly say so. We can readily understand them, and can respect both their candor and their consistency, whatever we may think of their opinions and of the attitude they feel compelled to assume. The history of the law and the uniform practice of the Episcopal Church in England and America since it was adopted confirms the High Church interpretation. The Episcopal Church receives priests from the Greek and Roman Catholic churches as having already received a valid ordination, while she uniformly re-ordains ministers coming to her from other Protestant denominations.

But surely Episcopalians do not regard this as a *re-ordination*. The lowest of Low Churchmen, we venture to say, would not admit that they ordain over again those who have already received a lawful and valid ordination. The Church of England and her daughter in this country " hold no other orders lawful than those ministered by bishops, and she acts on that principle as her law. How can she avoid condemning as unlawful, and that not in England, but everywhere, all other orders non-episcopal?"[1] This is both frank and logical. While the law of the Episcopal Church, as interpreted by her uniform practice, continues what it is; while no man who has not been episcopally ordained is admitted to her ministry, nor even allowed *occasionally* to minister in her pulpits and in her celebration of the sacraments, — it is

[1] Haddan's Apostolic Succession, p. 175.

neither consistent nor candid to contend that the Episcopal Church does not condemn the ordination of other denominations as null and void. Nor is the force of this inference at all impaired by insisting, as some do, upon the peculiar phraseology of the law, which says, "No man shall be accounted or taken to be a lawful bishop, priest, or deacon in *this Church* . . . except he has had episcopal consecration or ordination." Was the expression, "this Church" intended to separate, and does it in fact separate, the Episcopal Church in the matter of its orders from the corporate life and the Divine mission of the visible Church of Christ? Was it intended to affirm that episcopal ordination confers upon those who receive it authority to preach the Word and administer the sacraments *only within the bounds of the Episcopal denomination?* No Churchman, High or Low, would admit this. They all hold, as we do, that ordination makes a man a minister of the visible Church of Christ, and gives him a commission as broad as that of the Apostles to preach the Gospel and administer the sacraments to every creature. If, therefore, non-episcopal ordination does not confer the right to perform ministerial functions within the bounds of "this Church," it does not confer the right to perform such functions anywhere. It is but a weak evasion to tell us that they recognize our ordination as valid in the Presbyterian denomination; for it is not a human right conferred and limited by a voluntary association of men that we are discussing, but a Divine right conferred by the Supreme Head of the Church. The question before us is whether they recognize our ordination as valid *in the visible Church of Christ.* For their own sake we answer this question in the negative. We are not willing to believe that they account us true ministers of Christ and stewards of the mysteries of God, and yet presume, in defiance of Christ's commission to us, to say, "You may preach and administer the sacraments anywhere else, but we cannot allow you to perform any function of the ministry in 'this Church.'" This would be the very essence of sectarianism and schism. We dare not accuse them of such disloyalty to the doctrine of the Church, and to Christ, her living Head.

But it is asked, as though the question carried with it a complete vindication of their position, so far, at least, as we have any right to complain of it, "Does not the Presbyterian Church exclude from her pulpits and the administration of the sacraments some who claim to be ministers of Christ?" Yes, certainly, we exclude some who *claim* to be ministers of Christ; but we exclude none *whose claims we recognize as valid*. We dare not put a sectarian fence around our pulpit or our communion-table. They belong, not to us, but to Christ. In the matter of ordination we recognize the obvious distinction between validity and regularity. We think the substance of this or of any Divine ordinance may remain, even when, through want of explicit instruction from God, or of clear apprehension on the part of men, the form of it has been changed. We recognize ordination by a diocesan bishop as *valid*, though we regard it as *irregular*; and there is not a presbytery in the world who would for a moment entertain the proposal to re-ordain an Episcopal minister.

"Why, then," say some of our Episcopal brethren, "since you acknowledge the validity of our ordination, will you not heal the schism between us by taking orders at the hands of our bishops?" This proposition has been made, and we believe that it is made, not in any spirit of proselytism, but in good faith, and with an earnest desire for the unity of the visible Church. But there are three obstacles in the way of its acceptance: (1) We cannot consent to be ordained twice; (2) we cannot admit the assumption on which the necessity for episcopal ordination is based; (3) even if we could plead guilty ourselves, we cannot admit that multitudes of Christ's ministers, who, without such ordination, have made full proof of their ministry and gone to their reward, were usurpers in the sacred office. So long as this remains the only condition of mutual recognition, the case seems hopeless. And while this obstacle stands, alliances and conventions outside of the Church, kind words and acts of courtesy carefully separated from ministerial functions, and from the communion of the body of Christ, however sweet and pleasant in themselves, are utterly inadequate to the case; and when we consider the great interests at issue, they seem like "vanity and a striving after wind" (Eccles. i. 14, Revised Version).

If the Episcopal Church could come back to the spirit and practice of her earlier, and in this respect her better, days, and acknowledge non-episcopal ordination as valid, though in her judgment irregular, this would put us upon an equal footing; it would tend to remove prejudice, and silence evil speaking on all sides; it would perhaps put an end to that supercilious and irritating assumption which makes "*this* Church" synonymous with "*the* Church;" and so it would create an atmosphere of mutual confidence and respect in which the unity of the Church would grow like the lily, and cast forth roots as Lebanon. Zealous Episcopalians will probably resent the bare suggestion of such a concession on their part. Some, like Dr. Blunt, will look upon it as a renewed attempt of foreign Protestantism to bring them down "to the same abject level." But vehement protests, though they express the sincere conviction and desire of individuals, are not always true prophecies of what great bodies of people will do. Extreme opinions are never the most stable. Stranger changes than the one suggested have swept over even the Episcopal Church. When Bancroft, or Hall, or Laud first preached the doctrine of exclusive *jure divino* episcopacy, there was little prospect of its being dominant and established by law in the Church of England. And yet in half a century its triumph was complete, and that, too, through what seemed for a time to be its utter overthrow. And so, the recent attempt to reconcile the Church of England with Rome and the Greek Church having failed, the desire for visible, catholic unity, coupled with the Protestant instincts of the English people, may make such utterances as those of Bishop Wordsworth,[1] in his charge to the clergy of his diocese, and of Bishop Lightfoot, in his essay on the Christian Ministry, the seeds of another great movement leading to better and more permanent results. We

[1] In dealing with this question we must not allow ourselves to be carried away by any merely mechanical or imperfect view of what is called apostolic succession, or, in other words, of the continuity of the ministry and of the Church itself. That continuity consists in doctrine at least as much as in order; and it may be claimed upon the former ground by all bodies that accept the articles of the Christian creed. More than this, it may be reasonably doubted whether orthodox non-Episcopalian bodies have not done more to maintain the true apostolic succession as explained and insisted on by Irenæus and Tertullian than the Church of Rome has done, which has gone far, by alterations and additions, to corrupt the simplicity, not only of the apostolic doctrine, but of the apostolic ministry; whereas the only true and perfect continuity consists, as I have said, in having retained or recovered both. — BISHOP WORDSWORTH: *Address to Clergy*, 1885.

know that the doctrine of exclusive episcopal ordination was enacted into a law for political quite as much as for ecclesiastical purposes. The dominant opinion in the days of the Restoration was that prelacy and kingship must stand or fall together. "No bishop, no king," was always the battle-cry and the pass-word of the Stuarts and their adherents in Church and State. But the history of this country has demonstrated, what all Protestant denominations admit, that both Church and State can stand alone, and each fulfil its own functions better for the separation. The recognition of this truth, together with their sincere desire for unity, may yet modify the attitude of the Episcopal body towards other denominations, by making them realize that they are dissenters from us as much as we are dissenters from them. The political complications of past centuries, which identified questions of Church government and modes of worship with the conflicts between civil liberty and tyranny, have passed away, and their traditional animosities are dying out for lack of fuel. There is no reason for perpetuating the old disputes between Cavalier and Roundhead, between the fierce and bloody intolerance of Laud and the Stuarts on the one hand, and the no less fierce resistance of the Solemn League and Covenant on the other. Thanks to Puritan and Covenanter, that contest has ended in the triumph of liberty for us all. The banners of that great war are rotting away in ecclesiastical museums, and it is time for its battle-cries to die out in the Church.

These observations are made in no spirit of unfriendliness towards the Episcopal Church in England and in this country. We have no sympathy with the ignorant and indiscriminate denunciation of her government and forms of worship as inconsistent with vital piety, or as having a kinship with the errors of Romanism. We recognize her historically and in the present as one of the grand bulwarks of genuine Protestantism. We have a sincere admiration for the decency and order of her worship, and a profound gratitude, as every Christian scholar must have, for the rich biblical literature she has given and is still giving to the world. We observe with unmixed pleasure her increasing zeal for missions and for preaching the Gospel to the poor at home, and the demonstration she is giving that her liturgical forms and her maintenance of church authority are not inconsistent with evangelistic fervor and success.

And because we thus regard her we desire to see her laying aside every weight, taking up every stumbling-block, and casting off every prejudice which narrows her sympathies and hinders her progress towards the triumph of the Gospel and the unity of the body of Christ. Nor do we assume that she alone needs to adjust herself to the good time coming, that the stumbling-blocks are all in her way, or that the shells of traditional prejudice cling only to her limbs. The Presbyterian Church is equally liable to changes, and by no means exempt from the need of them. Are they not now passing over and through us? Is not the atmosphere of our Church different from what it was a generation ago? While there is no less zeal for essential truth, we know and feel that there is far more toleration for non-essential differences in opinions and in forms of worship. We do not sympathize with those who are alarmed and troubled by these things, for we regard them, not as the changing colors of the autumn leaves that prophesy decay, but rather as the tender hues and budding fertility of the spring, which predict and produce the coming harvest.

LECTURE VI.

THE LORD'S SUPPER.

THERE is in our day a wide-spread defection from the doctrine of the sacraments as taught in all the creeds of the Reformation. This departure is not only nor chiefly towards Rome. The drift is much stronger in the direction of a vague formalism, which makes the holy ordinances instituted by Christ mere outward signs, having no Divinely appointed connection with an inward and spiritual grace. "Low Churchmen" in all denominations vie with each other in making the sacraments simply memorials of Christ and badges of a Christian profession. They disjoin the sacraments from prayer and the Word of God, and deny that these holy ordinances are "effectual means of salvation." While they insist upon *Gospel* grace and the grace of prayer, "sacramental grace" is with them a mark of heresy and a term of reproach. Baptism is simply an outward form of consecration. The Lord's Supper is only a remembrancer, fitted to stir the feelings of the communicant, but conferring no Divine benefit which cannot be obtained by those who wilfully neglect its use.[1] Doubtless these

---

[1] "We believe there is scarcely any subject set forth in the confessions of the Reformed churches that is less attended to and less understood than this of the sacraments, and that many even of those who have subscribed these confessions rest satisfied with some confused notions on baptism and the Lord's Supper, while they have scarcely even a fragment of an idea of a sacramental principle or of

views are a reaction and a protest against errors lying in the opposite extreme; but they are not more tolerable on that account. The human soul cannot live on negations. There is great need of a sacramental revival among all denominations, and especially among Presbyterians. We ought to study our own Standards on this subject, and to compare them, in the light of Scripture, with the creeds of other denominations. Such investigation cannot fail to quicken our faith, enlarge our views, and remove many of the prejudices which have grown out of sectarian controversies.

All Christian teaching upon the Lord's Supper may be classified under four theories,— the *Roman Catholic*, the *Lutheran*, the *Zwinglian*, and the *Calvinistic*. These titles are not sharply definitive. The four theories have points of contact where they shade into each other. They have a common centre in Christ. They all agree that the sacrament is His appointment; that its design is expressed in His own words of institution; that its subject is Christ and His atoning sacrifice; that its continued observance is obligatory upon all Christians; that He is present whenever it is rightfully celebrated. And with the exception perhaps of the Zwinglian, they all agree that the Lord's Supper is an effectual means of grace and salvation. But they differ very widely as to the interpretation of Christ's words of institution, the

any general doctrine or theory on the subject" (Cunningham's Reformers and Theology of the Reformation, p. 239).

The reason why believers receive so little by their attendance on the Lord's Supper is that they expect so little. "They expect to have their affections somewhat stirred, and their faith somewhat strengthened; but they perhaps rarely expect to receive Christ, and to be filled with all the fulness of God. Yet Christ in offering Himself to us in this ordinance offers us all of God we are capable of receiving" (Hodge's Theology, iii. 624).

mode of His presence in the sacrament, the ground of its obligation or necessity, and the process and extent of its efficacy. The terms "Zwinglian" and "Calvinistic" are specially indefinite as descriptive of the theories to which they are applied.[1] In regard to the Lord's Supper, as well as other subjects, many things bear the venerable names of Zwingle and Calvin which they never taught. Still, they stand as the representatives of two sacramental theories which differ from each other quite as much as they both differ from the teaching of Luther and from the Romish doctrine.

The controversy on this whole subject did not begin with the Reformation.[2] The Romish doctrine, which was first authoritatively formulated by the Council of Trent in 1551, cannot be defended upon the ground of catholicity. Even before the Reformation it was never universally accepted. It is not taught in any of the ancient creeds. It was not affirmed by any ecumenical council for fifteen centuries after the birth of Christ. Into the question as to how far the Romish doctrine is sustained by the teaching of the Fathers of the first four or five

[1] Dr. Charles Hodge holds that "there were three distinct types of doctrine among the Reformed, — the Zwinglian, the Calvinistic, and *an intermediate form*, which ultimately became symbolical, being adopted in the authoritative Standards of the Church" (Theology, iii. 626). In this we venture to observe that Dr. Hodge differs from most orthodox writers upon the subject. But the question is one of classification and of names, and of no vital importance. We prefer to adhere to the common nomenclature. The doctrine of the Reformed confessions is, as most authorities agree, substantially that of Calvin, and not a compromise between his views and those of Zwingle.

[2] Gieseler sums up the history of the mediæval controversy on this subject as follows: "The ecclesiastical mode of speaking, that bread and wine in the Lord's Supper became by consecration the body and blood of Christ, may have been frequently understood of

centuries, we need not enter. It is not easy to form a consensus of the Fathers upon this or any other subject. They contradict each other in the interpretation of Scripture quite as much as modern commentators and theologians; and if their rhetorical language is to be taken literally, they constantly contradict themselves in regard to the Lord's Supper. And yet there are points of agreement, both negative and positive, in their testimony, which are fatal to the modern claims of the Church of Rome as to the catholicity of her doctrine. Dr. Schaff affirms [1] that there is no trace in all the ancient liturgies of the adoration of the consecrated elements, which follows transubstantiation as a logical necessity, and that in the whole patristic literature there are only four passages from which this doctrine can be inferred.

Harold Browne, Bishop of Ely, in his admirable lectures on the Thirty-nine Articles, after showing conclusively that the whole Primitive Church believed in the *real* presence of Christ in the Supper, says: "If there were no alternative but that the Fathers must have held either a *carnal* presence or none at all, then we must

a transformation of substance by the uneducated; but among the theologians of the West this misconception could not so readily find acceptance, in consequence of the clear explanations given by Augustine. When, therefore, Paschasius Radbert (in the beginning of the ninth century) expressly taught such a transformation, he met with considerable opposition. Still, the mystical and apparently pious doctrine, which was easier of apprehension and seemed to correspond better to the sacred words, obtained its advocates too; and it was easy to see that it only needed times of darkness such as soon followed to become general" (Gieseler's Ecclesiastical History, ii. 79). See also Freeman's Principles of Divine Service, ii. 6; Schaff's History of Christian Church, iv. 460; Schaff's Creeds of Christendom, ii. 130; Neander's Church History, iv. 335.

[1] History of Christian Church, iii. 501.

perforce believe that they were transubstantiationists." But he demonstrates another alternative, which has been acknowledged as possible even by eminent Romanist divines. By a long *catena* of patristic authorities he proves that the Fathers held to the spiritual presence of Christ and to the spiritual feeding of the soul upon His body and blood, and that "their writings contain abundant evidence that the doctrine of transubstantiation had not risen in their day." He concludes his argument with the following passage from Bishop Gardiner in his controversy with Cranmer: "The Catholic teaching is that the manner of Christ's presence in the sacrament is spiritual and supernatural, not corporal nor carnal, not sensible nor perceptible, but only spiritual, the how and manner whereof God knoweth."[1] The doctrine of the Church of Rome is thus defined in the Decrees of the Council of Trent: "By the consecration of the bread and wine a conversion is made of the whole substance of the bread into the substance of the body of our Lord, and of the whole substance of the wine into His blood, which conversion is by the Holy Catholic Church suitably and properly called transubstantiation." The best summary of the reasons for rejecting this doctrine[2] is found in the Thirty-nine Articles: "Transubstantiation cannot be proved by Holy Writ, but is repugnant to the plain meaning of Scripture, overthroweth the nature of a sacrament, and hath given occasion to many superstitions."[3] These four arguments are comprehensive and conclusive. Transubstantiation cannot be proved from Holy Writ, because the one passage adduced to support it admits of an easier interpretation, which brings

---

[1] Browne on the Thirty-nine Articles, p. 678.
[2] See Appendix, Lecture VI. (A).
[3] Article 28.

this one passage into harmony with the admitted interpretation of many similar texts;[1] it is repugnant to the plain meaning of Scripture, because an inspired Apostle, when repeating the words of the institution as he received them from the Lord, expressly declares that the sacred emblems, after consecration and at the very time when they are eaten and drunk by the communicant, are still bread and wine;[2] it overthrows the nature of a sacrament, even according to the Romish definition, by identifying the sign with the thing signified, thus destroying the sacramental relation between them;[3] it is

[1] Circumcision *is* the Lord's covenant, the Lamb *is* the Lord's passover, the ark of the covenaut *is* the face of God, that rock *was* Christ, I *am* the true vine, I *am* the door of the sheep. All Christians understand these statements as figurative. Roman Catholics are obliged to give a figurative meaning to the words, "This *cup* is the *New Testament* in My blood." There is no reason in the grammatical structure nor in the circumstances under which it was uttered to compel us to understand the words "this is My body" in its most literal sense.

[2] Cardinal Wiseman, in his fifth Lecture on the Eucharist, contends that if our Lord had meant to teach that the bread *represents* His body, He would have said, "This *bread* is My body;" "but He intentionally avoided calling it bread, and simply said 'this,' because when He spake, what He held in His hand was not bread, but His own body." The cardinal does not explain how, according to his views, the bread was transubstantiated *before* the words of consecration were fully uttered, neither does he account for the fact that Paul, when he is delivering what he had received of the Lord, expressly calls the elements *after* they are consecrated, and at the *very time* when they are received by the communicant, "this bread," and "this cup." "As oft as ye eat this bread and drink this cup," etc.; "Whoso cateth this bread and drinketh this cup," etc. (1 Cor. xi. 26, 27).

[3] The most holy Eucharist hath this, in common with the rest of the sacraments, that it is the *symbol* of a sacred thing, a visible form of an invisible grace. — *Decrees of Council of Trent*, Session 13, chap. 3.

the occasion of many superstitious, because it leads by logical necessity to the worship of the consecrated elements [1] and to the pretended repetition of Christ's offering [2] of Himself on the cross, and is therefore " most abominably injurious " to the one everlasting sacrifice for sins by which He has forever perfected them that are sanctified (Heb. x. 12–14).

There was a remarkable agreement among all the Reformers as to the doctrines of grace. The theology of Melanchthon and of Calvin, of Knox and of Cranmer,

[1] Wherefore there is no room left for doubt that all the faithful in Christ may, according to the custom ever received in the Catholic Church, render in veneration the worship in *latria*, which is due to the true God, to this most holy sacrament. — *Decrees of Council of Trent*, Session 13, chap. 5.

[2] "In the Divine sacrifice which is celebrated in the Mass the same Christ is contained and immolated, in an unbloody manner, who once offered Himself in a bloody manner on the altar of the cross. For the Victim is one and the same, the same now offering by the ministry of priests who then offered Himself on the cross, the manner of offering alone being different. 'If any one saith that the sacrifice of the Mass is only a sacrifice of praise and thanksgiving, but not a propitiatory sacrifice, and that it ought not to be offered for the living and for the dead, for sins, pains, satisfactions, and other necessities, let him be accursed'" (*Ibid.*, Session 22, chapters 2, 3). There is no valid objection to calling the Lord's Supper the "Eucharistic Sacrifice," — *i. e.*, the sacrifice of thanksgiving. Whether in its literal or its historic sense, the phrase does not signify a repetition, but only "the commemoration of Christ's one offering up of Himself upon the cross once for all, and a spiritual oblation of all possible praise unto God for the same" (Westminster Confession, xxxix. 2). Very different, however, is the teaching of some of the Anglican High Churchmen. Take the latest exposition of their views: "The holy Eucharist is a *perpetuation* of our Lord's *passion*. . . . The holy words of our Lord (in the institution of the Supper) then *had begun* that work which was to be accomplished by the unholy hands of others. It was commenced in the upper chamber, but consummated on the cross. And that which our Lord began to do by His own words when He was

was substantially the same.[1] How unutterable is the pity that this harmony in fundamentals could not have embraced all questions of Church government and worship! The bitter strife in regard to the sacraments, of which Luther and Zwingle were the recognized leaders, did more than all other causes to prevent the complete triumph of the Reformation. It is not for us to say which of them was most self-willed, or whether either is to be blamed for the evil results of the controversy. While neither can be properly called a theologian, they were both Christian heroes, having the courage of their convictions. But there is a real and profound difference in the views they adopted. For this reason all attempts to compromise their doctrines failed. The Reformed theologians labored hard to formulate a statement which both parties could adopt without a sacrifice of conscience. Calvin and Melanchthon exerted their utmost strength as peacemakers. Calvin especially, in his earnest desire to conciliate, went to the utmost verge of concession; so that while he is the most consistent of all the Reformed theologians, it is easy to quote fragments from his writings which make him appear at one time like a Lutheran, and at another like a Zwinglian. The Helvetic Confessions, the Formula of Concord, and the Consensus Tigurinus, are among the fruits of this effort to compromise. But they were simply flags of truce, not standards of permanent peace. They are not

upon the earth, He *still continues to do* through the ministry of His servants now that He has ascended into heaven" (Wilberforce's Doctrines of the Holy Eucharist, p. 44). We can see no difference between this and the Decree of the Council of Trent, except that it is more vaguely and feebly expressed.

[1] The Thirty-nine Articles are just as Calvinistic as the Westminster Confession. There is no doctrinal difference in the Standards of the Episcopal and Presbyterian churches.

to be compared in the explicitness of their teaching, nor in their living authority, with such symbols as the first Scotch Confession, the Thirty-nine Articles of the Church of England, and the Westminster Confession and Catechism, whose formative purpose was the positive statement of Scripture truth rather than the reconciliation of conflicting doctrines. Having failed in the attempt to compromise on the subject of the sacraments, the Lutherans and the Reformed separated permanently on this issue into two hostile camps, each retaining, however, in its own bosom some of the elements which it formally repudiated. In Germany the outward agreement was effected on political grounds by the pressure of the civil government, rather than by ecclesiastical authority and the force of reasoning. The Reformed Churches embraced and absorbed, but did not subdue, the Zwinglian element; and though there can be no question that the doctrine of the sacraments, taught in all the Reformed Confessions, whose influence has survived, is distinctively Calvinistic, the churches which adopt these Confessions have never been free from the prevalence of Zwinglian views. The Low and Broad Church parties in the Church of England are deeply imbued with them, and they have many advocates in the Presbyterian Church of Great Britain and America.

There is a popular impression that the Lutheran differs but little from the Romish doctrine of the sacraments. This impression is due either to ignorance or to prejudice. The Lutheran doctrine is essentially and explicitly Protestant in its rejection of transubstantiation and the errors which logically flow from it. It repudiates and condemns the worship of the consecrated elements, and the idea of the repetition in any sense of Christ's one everlasting sacrifice for sin. The term "consubstantiation," commonly applied to it, is a nickname, which is not found in any of the Lutheran symbols; and the ideas it conveys to ordinary readers are repudiated by Lutherans as strenuously as by ourselves. No intelligent Lutheran believes that the body and blood of Christ are literally *mixed up*, as Hooker says, with the bread and wine, or that they are locally confined to the elements in the sacrament, or that they are received and consumed with the mouth in the same way as the bread and wine. The Formula of Concord and many eminent Lutheran divines indignantly reject the notion of a physical eating with the teeth of Christ's body as "a malignant and blasphemous slander of the sacramentarians."[1]

The Lutheran doctrine not only repudiates transubstantiation, the worship of the consecrated elements, the repetition of Christ's sacrifice, and the carnal eating of His body and blood by the mouth of the communicant, — all of which gross conceptions are essential to the Romish doctrine, — but it rejects also the Romish notion that the sacrament of itself *contains* the grace which it signifies, and that its saving effects are independent of the faith of the recipient. At this point the Lutheran doctrine is a strong protest against the errors of the Church of Rome. How could it be otherwise, since it is Luther's doctrine? The saving efficacy and the absolute necessity of a personal faith in Christ was with him the very centre and stronghold of Christianity. In the beginning of his conflict with Rome, he declared "whatever be the case with the sacrament, faith must maintain its rights and honors." From this point he never swerved. "Non sacramentum, sed fides sacramenti, justificat," was one of his axioms. He also

[1] Schaff's Creeds, i. 317.

insisted that faith may receive, apart from the sacrament, the same thing as in the sacrament. "He never doubted, indeed, that the sacrament conveys a blessing; but he stands upon this, — that the Almighty God Himself can work nothing good in a man unless he believes."[1] Here, then, in its application to the vital question of a sinner's justification before God, Lutheranism is forever divorced from Romanism. This alone is a sufficient answer to the flippant assertion that consubstantiation is the same thing as transubstantiation under another name.

The statements of the Augsburg Confession,[2] both as to the sacraments in general and the Lord's Supper in particular, are capable of an interpretation entirely consistent with the teaching of the Reformed Confessions.[3]

It is in the explanations of the Augsburg Confession, in subsequent and apologetic symbols, especially in the Formula of Concord and the Saxon Visitation Articles, that the differences between the Lutheran and Reformed doctrine distinctly appear. These differences all centre in the question, What do *unbelievers* receive in the Lord's Supper? The Lutheran doctrine maintains that they receive *the same thing* with believers, though it produces opposite effects in the two cases: to the one it is an effectual means of salvation; while to the other

[1] Dorner's Hist. of Protestant Theology, i. 150.

[2] Of the Lord's Supper they teach that the true body and blood of Christ are truly present under the form of bread and wine, and are communicated to those that eat in the Lord's Supper and received by them; and they disapprove those that teach otherwise. Wherefore also the opposite doctrine is rejected. — SCHAFF: *Creeds*, iii. 13.

[3] The Lutheran definition of the sacraments agrees in all essential points with that of the Reformed Churches. — HODGE: *Theology*, iii. 488.

it is only a means of condemnation and spiritual death. According to the Reformed doctrine, unbelievers receive nothing but the outward and visible elements, while believers by faith receive and feed upon the body and blood of Christ.[1]

We cannot undertake accurately to define what Zwingle taught in regard to the sacraments, nor to harmonize the conflicting testimony of the learned in regard to it.[2] He does not seem to have been consistent with himself. His ardent mind was better qualified to pull down error than to build up the truth. Admitting all that has been said in explanation and defence of his teaching, it is evident that his doctrine fell far below the standard of the Reformed confessions. There is historic justice in applying the name "Zwinglian" to such statements in regard to the Lord's Supper as the following: —

1. That the bread and the wine of the Holy Communion are nothing but naked and bare signs, and that the ordinance itself is simply a commemoration of Christ's death, a badge of our Christian profession, and a pledge of mutual love among believers.

2. That the Lord's Supper is only a sign and seal of *pre-existing* grace in the communicant, and not a means or instrument by which more grace is bestowed upon those who worthily partake of it.

3. That Christ is present and operative for our salvation in the sacrament only in His Divine nature and in the *apprehension* of the believing communicant.

4. That the benefits received by the believer at the Lord's table are nothing more than the sacrificial virtue of the Saviour's death on the cross.

[1] See Appendix, Lecture VI. (B).
[2] Ibid. (C).

5. That the sacramental feeding of the believing soul on Christ, the eating of His flesh and the drinking of His blood in the Holy Supper, is identical with any and every exercise of faith in Him, and therefore can be done as well elsewhere as at the Lord's table.

6. That the necessity for the observance of the Lord's Supper is simply a necessity of precept, and not a necessity of means. In other words, that we are obliged to keep the feast of the Holy Communion only because Christ has commanded it, and not because we are to expect any *special* benefit from its observance.

Each of these statements will be fully discussed as we proceed. Meantime we cannot forbear to observe that we reject them not only because of their inconsistency with our doctrinal standards and with the teaching of Scripture, but because of the spirit which pervades them and the underlying assumptions on which they are based. Zwinglianism is essentially *rationalistic* in the evil sense of the word. Its chief effort is to explain away or reduce to a minimum the mystery of the Lord's Supper. It assumes that the theory which is most level to our comprehension, which brings the Holy Supper nearest to a common meal where Christians have sweet fellowship together, and makes it agree most with ordinary human experience, is for that reason nearest to the truth. We have heard Presbyterian ministers, in administering it, eulogizing the absolute simplicity, not only of its symbols, but of its whole design and efficacy, comparing it to the monument which recalls the memory of some great man, as though that explained its whole meaning and effect; and dwelling with minute particularity upon Christ's physical sufferings, as though our highest purpose in keeping the feast was to look on a pathetic picture and be moved by it.

We grow weary in our reading on the subject of the reiterated assertion that this or that view is incomprehensible, unreasonable, or contrary to common-sense; and the more so, because the same writers who use such arguments in regard to the Lord's Supper repudiate and denounce them when they are urged by others against the doctrine of the Trinity, the sovereignty of God, the incarnation, the atonement, the resurrection and exaltation of Christ, the vital union of believers with His glorified Person, and the wonder-working power of His Holy Spirit, — all of which revealed mysteries pervade and are embodied in the transcendent mystery of the Holy Communion.

Perhaps the ripest and the bitterest fruit of this rationalizing about the Lord's Supper may be found in Dean Stanley's "Christian Institutions." Adopting the idea of Renan, he makes the "Last Supper a continuation of those earlier feasts in which Christ had blessed and broken the bread and distributed the fishes on the hills of Galilee."[1] He can see no higher character in the communion of the first and second centuries than in the festive dinner of "a Greek club, where each brought, as to a common meal, his own contribution in a basket, and each helped himself from a common table."[2] He identifies the Lord's Supper with the love-feasts of the Early Church. He admits, indeed, that it was intended by its Founder to be "a glorification of the power of memory;" but in his account of what is thus to be remembered, he is careful to avoid any reference to Christ's death as the sacrifice for sin, and insists only upon His example and teaching as inculcating human charity. In proportion as the observance of this ordinance enables us "to move in unison" with the parables of the

[1] Christian Institutions, p. 41.   [2] Ibid., p. 46.

Prodigal Son, the Good Samaritan, and the Good Shepherd; with the Beatitudes on the Galilean mountains, the resignation in Gethsemane, and the courage on Calvary,—he affirms that "it is a true partaking of what the Gospels intended by the body of Christ."[1] He denies that the Lord's Supper is necessary for these ends, and insists that all who move in unison with these moral precepts and examples, "whether they be Christian in name or not, whether they have or have not partaken of the sacrament, have thus received Christ, because they have received that which was the essence of Christ, —His spirit of mercy and toleration."[2]

There is nothing new in these sentiments. But the strange thing is that a clergyman of high position in the Church of England, one accustomed to the public use of her solemn liturgies, should advocate such opinions; that he should claim for them the authority of "the clear-headed and intrepid Zwingle,"[3] and attempt to reconcile them with the Articles and Formularies of the Episcopal Church, by the vague assertion that "since the days of Elizabeth a strong Zwinglian atmosphere has pervaded the original theology of the Church of England, and been its prevailing hue."[4]

The Reformed, as distinguished from the Lutheran and the Zwinglian, doctrine of the Lord's Supper is called "Calvinistic," not because Calvin invented it, but because at the time of the Reformation he was its ablest and most influential expounder. He appealed from the teaching of Rome on the one hand, and from the doctrine of Zwingle on the other, not only to the Scriptures, but to the commentaries of the Fathers. In the chapter of the "Institutes" which treats of the Com-

[1] Christian Institutions, p. 121. [2] Ibid., p. 42.
[3] Ibid., p. 106. [4] Ibid., p. 109.

munion — one of the noblest pieces of writing in the records of the Reformation — he proves by quotations, especially from Augustine, that the Reformed doctrine is catholic and apostolic. He stands for the historic faith of the Church against both the inventions of Rome and the vagaries of those who broke away to an opposite extreme. There is no ground for doubting that the views he defended passed substantially into all the authoritative Confessions of the Reformation, and must be regarded as the orthodox doctrine of the Reformed.[1] That it is the doctrine of the Thirty-nine Articles and of the Westminster Confession, and that the Standards of the Episcopal and Presbyterian churches are in perfect accord upon this subject, no candid student will deny.[2] If there is any difference, it is in the fact that the latter teaches what are called "sacramentarian"[3] views rather more explicitly and in stronger terms than the former.

[1] Schaff's Creeds of Christendom, i. 376.

[2] The teaching of the Confession on the Lord's Supper is that of Cranmer, Latimer, Ridley, Hooker, Usher, and many others.... This teaching is as far removed from the "bare remembrance" theory, attributed to the early Swiss Reformers, as from the consubstantiation of Luther and the local or supra-local presence contended for by the Roman Catholics and Anglo-Catholics. — MITCHELL: *Lectures on the Westminster Assembly.*

The doctrine of the real spiritual presence is the doctrine of the English Church, and was the doctrine of Calvin and of many foreign Reformers. — *Browne on Thirty-nine Articles*, p. 678.

The peculiar views of Luther on the real presence and the ubiquity of Christ's body found no congenial soil in England. Cranmer abandoned them, and adopted, together with Ridley, the Calvinistic doctrine of a virtual presence and communication of Christ's body. — SCHAFF: *Creeds*, i. 601.

[3] The name "Sacramentarian" was applied by Luther to Zwingle and his followers, to convey the idea that they explained away and

The Reformed doctrine of the Lord's Supper is intimately connected with the two great mysteries of the incarnation and the personal union of believers with Christ. The Holy Communion has its profound roots in the one mystery, and its precious fruits in the other. Christ did not say, "This do in remembrance of *My death*." To make it simply a memorial of His sufferings on the cross is to belittle the ordinance, and presumptuously to restrict the meaning of the words of institution · "Do this in remembrance of *Me*." Christ Himself, in His Divine fulness, and not any part of His person or of His history, is the subject and the substance of the sacrament. His death as the sacrifice for sin, though it is the central point, is but a small part of the history of His relation to His redeemed people; and the importance and efficacy of this fact depend on what precedes and follows it. The cross of Jesus would be no more to us than the cross of the penitent thief, if He were not the Incarnate Son and Word of God, and if His cross were not inseparably connected with His resurrection and ascension to glory.

The sacrament is founded upon and leads us to His one indivisible Person, which is the reservoir of all Divine fulness for our salvation. He is not, and cannot be, divided. His human nature never had, and never can have, any existence separate from His Deity. He was conceived by the Holy Ghost, and was the Son of God from the moment of His conception. His human soul and His human body were separated for three days,

reduced to nothing the value of the sacraments; while Zwingle, throwing back the nickname, protested that it might be applied with more propriety to those who made great mysteries of the sacraments. — CUNNINGHAM: *Reformers and Theology of the Reformation*, p. 236.

when the one descended to Hades,[1] and the other lay in the tomb; but neither was parted for a moment from His Divine nature. Moreover, since the incarnation Christ's Divine nature does not exert any saving power, nor bestow any gracious gift upon men, except in and through His human nature. The Son of God was from the beginning the living Word of the Father, the life and the light of men; and now since the Word became Flesh, it is the *Son of Man* who has power on earth to forgive sins, and is exalted a Prince and a Saviour to give repentance and remission. By its union with the Divine nature the humanity of Christ is infinitely exalted. It was so even on earth; the touch of His finger was life-giving, and there was virtue in the hem of His garment. The light of God which transfigured Him on the mount came from within. It follows from this that wherever Christ is, there is His human as well as His Divine nature. His human nature is virtually omnipresent, because it is inseparably and forever united to the Divine.

The incarnation of the Son of God accomplishes its chief purpose in the personal union of the believer with Him. This union is a great mystery (Eph. vi. 32). But its mystery is no hindrance to our faith in its reality nor to our experimental knowledge of its blessedness. The Scriptures in which it is asserted are numerous, varied, and explicit. The sixth chapter of John, the farewell address of Christ, and the intercessory prayer are full of it. We are one with Him, even as He is one with the Father, as the branch is one with the vine, as the husband is one with the wife, as the members are one with the body. The union is not only legal, but vital. He

[1] Thou wilt not leave my soul in hell, neither wilt thou suffer thine Holy One to see corruption. — *Acts* ii. 27, 31.

dwells in us, and we in Him; and "when He who is our life shall appear, then shall we also appear with Him in glory." It is trifling to set aside these Scripture statements as mere figures of speech. The figures fall short of the profound reality which they illustrate. It is no less trifling to resolve the mystery of this personal union with Christ into the indwelling of His Spirit in the souls of believers. It is accomplished *by* the indwelling of the Spirit, and therefore *additional* to it, and not identical with it. Our bodies as well as our souls are united to Christ, — our whole nature to His one Person. His saving work for us and in us will reach its consummation in the "redemption of our body."[1] When the Christian dies, he "sleeps in Jesus." "The souls of believers at death, being made perfect in holiness, pass immediately into glory; and their bodies, *being still united to Christ*, do rest in the grave till the resurrection."[2]

Now, both the everlasting unity of Christ's person and our personal union with Him are signified, exhibited, and brought home to our experience in the Lord's Supper. This is the chief end for which it was instituted. "It was designed to signify and effect our communion with Christ in His person, in His offices, and in their precious fruits."[3]

It is only by being made partakers of Christ Himself that we can partake of His benefits; and therefore the *res sacramenti*, the thing signified, sealed, and applied in the Holy Supper, is not merely the sacrificial virtue of His death, nor the benefits He procures for us by His sacrifice and intercession, but the personal Christ, once

[1] Romans viii. 23.
[2] Shorter Catechism.
[3] A. A. Hodge's Commentary on the Confession, p. 484.

crucified, now risen and glorified forever. He plainly asserts the necessity of this personal union with Himself in words[1] which, if they are not intended to describe the Lord's Supper, are certainly applicable to it; for Paul makes the application (in 1 Cor. x. 16) when he declares that the bread we break and the cup of blessing we bless is the communion (the κοινωνία, the actual participation) of the body and blood of Christ, — that is, of His Divine yet human person. "This I say, then, that in the mystery of the Supper, by the symbols of bread and wine, Christ, His body and blood, are truly exhibited to us; *first*, that we might become one body with Him; and *secondly*, that, being made partakers of His substance, we might feel the results of this fact in the participation of all His blessings."[2] In his commentary on the eleventh chapter of First Corinthians, Calvin asserts the same great truth still more strongly.[3]

In the light of the incarnation and the personal union of believers with Christ, we may undertake to answer certain questions which go to the root of the whole doctrine as to the design and efficacy of the Lord's Supper.

The *first* question relates to the real presence of Christ in the sacrament. In common language the idea of *presence* is usually restricted to local nearness and to discernment by the bodily senses. Yet even in

[1] John vi. 53–57.
[2] Calvin's Institutes, ii 564.
[3] Christ is obtained not only when we believe that He was made an offering for us, but when He dwells in us, when He is one with us, when we are members of His flesh (Eph. vi. 30), — when, in fine, we are *incorporated* with Him, so to speak, into one life and substance. For He does not simply present to us the *benefits* of His death and resurrection, but the very body in which He suffered and rose again. — *Calvin on* 1 *Cor. XI.*, 24–26.

common language a much wider conception of its meaning is often indicated. We say of another that he is present with us when we know that he is sitting behind a screen at the farther end of the same room, or in another room of the same house. Two hearers are present in the same audience without recognizing each other. We speak of the presence of the sun when it shines on us. A blind man would use the same language. Presence, therefore, even in common language, does not depend upon local nearness nor upon sense perception. One person is present with another wherever he reveals himself and makes his influence felt by the other; and even where such revelation is made and such influence exerted, though they are accepted and realized by some and not by others of the same company. On a bright day at a funeral the sun is as really present with the corpse as with the living mourners.

All Christians who believe in the Lord's Supper at all, believe also that Christ is present in it. The whole contention is about the mode of that presence. Many who admit its reality virtually deny it in their attempts to explain it, — those, for example, who make it a mere conception in the mind of believers. The Westminster Confession and Catechisms assert that "Christ's body and blood are present *to* the faith of the receiver no less truly than the elements themselves are *to* their outward senses." Their bodily senses do not produce, but only perceive, the presence of the elements. They are present to a blind man, though he does not see them. And so Faith perceives, but does not create nor secure, the presence of Christ's body and blood. It is as real to those who do not discern the Lord's body as to those who do.[1] While we fully agree, with Hooker, that they

[1] It seems impossible, with any show of reason, to assert that

who hold that Christ's body and blood are "externally seated in the very consecrated elements themselves," are driven either to incorporate Him with the sacramental elements or to transubstantiate their substance into His, we cannot accept the inference that "the real presence of Christ's most blessed body and blood is not to be sought for in the sacrament, but in the worthy receiver of the sacrament."[1] Surely there is a broad and tenable ground between seating Christ externally in the elements and confining Him to the thoughts and experiences of the communicants. The two extremes meet, and are equally objectionable in this point, that they limit and localize the Saviour's presence.[2]

No less objectionable is the theory which identifies Christ's presence in the sacrament with the omnipresence of the Divine nature. This, like the preceding notion, belongs to Zwinglianism in its lowest form, and cannot be reconciled to the Scripture doctrine of the person of Christ. The Romish Church is consistent with Scripture and with the teaching of all the Reformed Confessions when she insists that Christ's presence in the sacrament includes His human as well as His Divine nature, His body and blood as well as His Deity. But when she insists that this personal and real presence involves the

the *discernment* spoken of in 1 Cor. xi. 27-29 is the mere power of interpreting the signs as representatives of Christ's death, or that the guilt incurred is nothing more than the danger of abusing certain outward symbols. These expressions evidently point to a spiritual and awful sin, not of misusing and profaning outward symbols, but of misusing and profaning *Christ actually present in them.* — Bannerman *on the Church of Christ*, ii. 138.

[1] Ecc. Polity, ii. 84.
[2] The body of Christ in this holy sacrament is a thing external to ourselves, and in nowise dependent upon our perception, knowledge, or belief. — SCUDAMORE: *Notitia Eucharistica*, p. 558.

transubstantiation of the bread and wine *into* His Deity and humanity, we deny and protest against the assumption. We reject also the theory of a local presence in, with, or under the sacred symbols. Presence, as applied in Scripture and in our theology to the theanthropic person of Christ, has nothing to do with locality or limitation of any kind.[1] It refers to influence and manifestation. His whole human nature, body and soul, being forever united to His Divine nature, is virtually omnipresent; that is to say, its influence can be exerted and manifested anywhere, according to His Divine will. The ultimate source of such influence and manifestation, of course, is in His Divine nature; but they are exerted and put forth in and through His human nature.

This use of the word "presence" is perfectly consistent, as already shown, with the popular use of language. It is consistent also with Christ's own promises: "Lo, I am with you alway, even unto the end of the world." "Where two or three are gathered together in My name, there am I in the midst of them." To resolve such promises into the presence of the Holy Spirit, is to belittle and utterly to confuse them. Christ does not make a difference in His promises without a corresponding difference in the things to which they refer. His promised presence, though invisible and intangible, and

[1] That participation in the body of Christ which I affirm does not require a local presence, nor the descent of Christ, nor infinite extension, nor anything of that nature. His communicating Himself to us is effected through the secret virtue of the Holy Spirit, which cannot merely bring together, but join in one things which are separated by distance of place. In short, that He may be present with us He does not change His place, but communicates to us from heaven the virtue of His flesh as though it were present. — CALVIN: *Commentary on* 1 *Cor. XI.*, 23–26.

in that sense spiritual, is nevertheless personal, real, and objective; that is, outside and independent of our apprehensions of it. This spiritual but real presence of Christ is specially promised and covenanted to us in the Lord's Supper. The consecrated bread and wine are not merely the symbols of His body and blood, but the Divine seals of the covenant whereby Christ and all His benefits are not only represented, but applied to us; and therefore their use is the κοινωνία, the actual participation of Christ's body and blood by every believing communicant. "If they are 'seals' of the covenant, they must, of course, as a legal form of investiture, actually convey the grace represented to those to whom it belongs; as a deed conveys an estate, or the key, handed over in the presence of witnesses, the possession of a house from the owner to the renter. . . . It is the authoritative appointment of Christ that these signs, rightly used, shall truly represent and *convey* the grace they signify."[1] The grace signified is the fulness of the Godhead dwelling bodily in Christ (Col. ii. 9). His body and blood are specially mentioned and emphasized, because it is through His humanity that the Divine nature is brought into union with us and His Divine power made efficacious for our salvation, and also because it is in regard to His coming in the flesh, His sacrificial death, and His glorification as our representative that our faith most needs to be confirmed.

This will be more apparent in our answer to the *second* question, What does the believer receive in the

---

[1] Dr. A. A. Hodge, Commentary on the Westminster Confession, p. 449. The sacrament "is a help by which we may be engrafted into the body of Christ, or, already engrafted, may be more and more united to Him, until the union is completed in heaven" (Calvin's Institutes, book iv. chap. xvii. 33).

Lord's Supper? The unbeliever receives nothing but bread and wine. Here the Reformed doctrine differs radically from both the Romish and the Lutheran.[1] The unbelieving communicant is guilty of or concerning the body and blood of the Lord, not because he eats and drinks them *without faith*, but because, having no true faith, he does *not* eat and drink them at all.[2] They are present and offered to him as truly as to the believer; but he neither discerns nor receives them. He is guilty, not because he is personally unworthy, as all communicants are, but because he eats and drinks *unworthily*, in a way not suitable to the nature and design of the sacrament. The thing there signified, Christ truly exhibits and offers to all who sit down at that spiritual feast.[3] But just as the rain falling on the hard rock runs away because it cannot penetrate, so the unbelieving repel the grace of God, and prevent it from reaching them. "They bring death on themselves, not by *receiving* Christ unworthily, but by *rejecting* Him."[4]

But the believing communicant receives and appropriates that which the unbeliever ignores and rejects.

[1] Although ignorant and wicked men receive the outward elements in this sacrament, yet they receive not the thing signified thereby. — *Westminster Confession of Faith*, 29, 7.

[2] The wicked, and such as be void of lively faith, although they do carnally and visibly press with their teeth (as Augustine saith) the sacrament of the body and blood of Christ, yet in no wise are they partakers of Christ: but rather, to their condemnation, do eat and drink the *sign* or *sacrament* of so great a thing. — *Thirtynine Articles*, Art. 29.

[3] Christ's body and blood be offered by God unto all, yet they are received by such only as have the hand of faith to lay hold on Christ; and these, with the bread and wine, spiritually receive Christ, with all His saving graces. The wicked receive only the outward elements. — Usher: *Body of Divinity*, p. 399.

[4] Calvin, Institutes, book iv. ch. xvii. 33.

The bread and wine are called Christ's body and blood because our Lord, by holding forth these symbols, gives us at the same time that of which He has chosen them to be the signs and the seals; for Christ is not a deceiver, to mock us with empty representations. The reality is conjoined with the sign; or, in other words, we do not less truly become participants in Christ's body and blood in respect of their spiritual efficacy than we partake of the bread and wine.

It should be remembered, however, that the body and blood of Christ cannot be separated from Christ Himself, and that no saving benefit can be received from Him unless we are vitally united to His person. His body and blood represent His whole person and offices, His merits, the sacrificial virtue of His death, and all His benefits, both of grace and of glory. This is evident from His own words in John vi. 51–57; and this mode of speaking is adopted especially with reference to the Lord's Supper, because we cannot be made partakers of His Divine nature except in and through His humanity. "For the flesh of Christ is the conduit that conveys the graces of the Godhead and the graces of the Spirit of Christ into our souls, which otherwise than by His body we could not receive."[1] It is plainly the doctrine of the Standards of the Presbyterian Church that the believing communicant receives not only the *sacrificial virtue* of Christ's *death*, but Christ Himself in all the fulness of His Divine and human nature. "Sacraments are holy signs and seals to represent Christ *and* His benefits, and to confirm our interest in *Him*."[2] "Wherein *Christ and* the benefits of the New Covenant are represented sealed and applied to believers."[3]

[1] Isaac Ambrose's Looking to Jesus, p. 298.
[2] Confession, 27, 1.   [3] Shorter Catechism, 92.

In the Lord's Supper believers "are made partakers of His body and blood *with all His benefits*,"[1] "feed upon His body and blood, and have their union and communion with Him confirmed,"[2] "receive and apply unto themselves Christ crucified, and all the benefits of His death."[3] Our singing is often more orthodox than our preaching. Many a Zwinglian sacramental address has been contradicted, if not corrected, by such a hymn as this: —

> "Together with these symbols, Lord,
> Thy *blessed self* impart,
> And let Thy *holy flesh and blood*
> Feed the believing heart."

This leads us to a *third* question, — as to the mode of feeding on Christ, eating His flesh and drinking His blood in the Holy Supper. The great battle-ground of all sacramental discussions on this point is the discourse of Christ in the sixth chapter of John's Gospel. We cannot agree with those who deny all distinctive and transcendent meaning to that wonderful discourse, and make it only a highly figurative repetition of what Christ had already taught about the necessity of our believing in Him. The saying, "It is the spirit that quickeneth; the flesh profiteth nothing: the words that I speak unto you, they are spirit, and they are life,"[4] so often dogmatically quoted to sustain this view, seems to us to point in the opposite direction, and to indicate that the theme of the discourse is not so much faith in Christ, which He had frequently described in far simpler words, but that vital union with Himself, and that personal participation through His flesh in His eternal life, of which faith is only the instrumental cause.

[1] Shorter Catechism, 96. [2] Larger Catechism, 168.
[3] Larger Catechism, 170. [4] Verse 63.

This is a mystery unspeakably greater than our exercise of faith. It is co-ordinate with the incarnation itself. Whether the discourse refers directly and prophetically to the Lord's Supper or not, it certainly treats of the subject which is the inmost core of the holy sacrament; namely, the life which is hid with Christ in God, and nourished by feeding on Christ, which He declares to be the same thing as eating His flesh and drinking His blood.[1]

How the soul feeds on Christ's body and blood, is an open question among the Reformed Churches. It is agreed on all sides that the eating or feeding is by faith; but whether faith and eating are the same thing, is a disputed point. Do we feed on Christ, eat His flesh and drink His blood every time and wherever we believe on Him, or is this language applicable only to a *peculiar exercise of faith* in connection with the Lord's Supper? The Zurich and Helvetic Confessions maintain that "eating is believing, and believing is eating," and that "this eating takes place as often and whenever a man believes in Christ." Calvin admits that "eating is *by* faith, and that no other eating can be imagined. But,"

[1] John vi. 33–51, 56. "The mystery of our union with Christ, which in this discourse is expressed in words, is precisely the same which Jesus desired to express by an act in the Holy Supper" (Godet on John vi.). "It affords a key to interpret the sacramental phraseology applied to the Supper" (Bannerman on Church of Christ, ii., 139). "Jesus purposely framed His words so skilfully that they would apply in their strict literal sense to the enjoyment of Himself, and yet that afterwards the same words should by consequence be appropriate to express the most august mystery of the Holy Supper when that should be instituted" (Bengel, Commentary on John vi.).

"We are not at liberty to say that the discussion in John vi. was intended to be a commentary on the doctrine of the Lord's Supper. But the ordinance, for all that is blessed and real in its observance,

he adds, "there is this difference between their mode of speaking and mine: according to them, to eat is merely to believe; while I maintain that the flesh of Christ is eaten *by believing*, that eating is the *effect and fruit of faith*. This difference is little in words, but not in reality."

We fully agree with Calvin on this point. The distinction on which he insists is very important, as indicating a correct use of language. To say that because we eat *by* faith, therefore faith *is* eating, is about as logical as to maintain that whatever we do *by* our hand *is* our hand. Christ dwells in our hearts by faith; is this dwelling of Christ in us nothing more than our own faith? Doubtless faith itself is always and everywhere essentially the same. But it does many and various things. We have a catalogue of its heroes and a record of its achievements in the eleventh chapter of Hebrews. Does every Christian, as often as he believes, do all that was achieved by these ancient worthies? But Calvin's distinction between faith and the results achieved by it is still more important in its special application to the Lord's Supper. The doctrine that "faith is eating, and eating is faith," is the very essence of the Zwinglian theory. If "this eating takes place as often and whenever a man believes in Christ," then it follows necessarily that the Lord's Supper is simply a sign and remembrancer to assist our faith. A vine, or a door, or a flower of the field, when they remind us of the Saviour, and quicken our faith in Him, are just as

refers us to that sermon. The essential point in the sermon which we transfer to the Eucharist is, that in it we are called in a true, though spiritual sense, to eat and drink the body and blood of the Son of God" (Marshall Lang on the Last Supper of our Lord, p. 92).

truly the communion of His body and blood as the bread we break and the cup of blessing we bless in the Holy Supper. According to this theory, logically carried out, we have not seven, but seventy times seven sacraments, and the Lord's Supper is no more sacred, and has no more efficacy as a means of grace, than a thousand natural objects around us. We shrink back from such conclusions, and therefore reject the premises on which they rest. We believe there is a peculiar exercise of faith, suitable to the occasion and to the special manifestations of Christ in the Holy Sacrament, by which the believing soul feeds on Him. The teaching of the Zurich and Helvetic Confessions on this subject is peculiar to themselves. It is not found in any other of the Reformed Confessions. The Westminster Standards give no sanction to it. The earlier Scotch Confession and Catechism, which were superseded by those of the Westminster Assembly, are very explicit in repudiating the whole Zwinglian theory, including the point we are now considering. The views of the Westminster divines on all questions relating to the sacraments were thoroughly Calvinistic.

John Owen, the prince of all the Puritan theologians, strongly insists that both the manifestation of Christ and our participation of Him in the Lord's Supper "are expressed in such a manner as to demonstrate them to be peculiar, — such as are not to be obtained in any other way. . . . There is in it an eating and drinking of the body and blood of Christ, with a spiritual incorporation thence ensuing, which are peculiar to this ordinance. Herein is a *peculiar exercise of faith* and a peculiar participation of Christ."[1]

[1] Owen's Works, v. 8, 560.

LECTURE VII.

THE ADMINISTRATION OF THE SACRAMENTS.

ANY religion adapted to the constitution of human nature must have its external rites and ceremonies. The worship of God in spirit and in truth does not imply the absence of outward forms, but only the subordination of the form to the spirit, even as the body is subject to the soul. "That is not first which is spiritual, but that which is natural; and afterward that which is spiritual" (1 Cor. xv. 46). It was so in the creation, when God formed man of the dust of the ground and breathed into his nostrils the breath of life; and it is so in the *new* creation.

Man's dual nature has been recognized and provided for in all God's redemptive dealings with our fallen race. The Old Testament economy was full of natural symbolism addressed to the soul through the bodily senses. The burning bush, the pillar of fire and cloud, the ark of the covenant, the altar of sacrifice, and the whole ritual system made after the pattern showed to Moses in the holy mount, were the signs of God's presence and power among His people. Besides these outward signs, which have accomplished their temporary purpose, and been abolished by the development of the old dispensation into the new, there were two divinely appointed ceremonies which were not only the signs of God's presence, but the *seals* of His covenant with His people and the pledges of His immanent power in the

Church. Circumcision and the passover were not Levitical nor Jewish ceremonies, but seals of the righteousness which is by faith. Their form has been changed by the same authority that instituted them; but their substance, their significance, and their Divine efficacy continue.[1] Baptism is the circumcision of Christ (Col. ii. 11). The Lord's Supper is the feast which we keep because "Christ our passover is sacrificed for us" (1 Cor. v. 7). These two ordinances we call "the holy sacraments." It is useless to define the meaning or to justify the use of this name by an appeal to its etymology. The word *sacramentum* may be the correct Latin translation of the Greek μυστήριον, or "mystery," and the oath by which a Roman soldier bound himself to his commander and to his country may illustrate to some extent the allegiance we owe to the Captain of our salvation and to His Church; but all this is very far from determining the meaning or the use of baptism and the Lord's Sup-

---

[1] The sacraments of the Old Testament in regard to the spiritual things thereby signified and exhibited were for substance the same with those of the New. — *Westminster Confession*, chap. xxvii. 5.

Whatever therefore is now exhibited to us in the sacraments, the Jews formerly received in theirs; namely, Christ with His spiritual riches. The same efficacy which ours possess they experienced in theirs; namely, that they were seals of the Divine favor towards them in regard to the hope of eternal salvation. — CALVIN: *Institutes*, book iv. chap. xiv. 23.

While the former *shadowed* forth a promised Christ, the latter bears testimony to Him as already come and *manifested*. . . . There is no doubt that if you compare time with time, the grace of the Spirit is now *more abundantly displayed*. . . . Both testify that the paternal kindness of God and the grace of the Spirit are offered in Christ, but ours more *clearly and splendidly*. In both there is an exhibition of Christ, but in ours it is more *full and complete.* — *Ibid.*, 20, 22, 26.

per. The generic name of "sacraments," as now used by the whole Christian Church, separated and sanctified from its original uses, includes all that is taught in Scripture and in Christian experience in regard to these holy ordinances. All Protestants hold that there are only two sacraments, not seven, as the Church of Rome teaches. But the contention between us at this point is chiefly one of definition. We believe that marriage and ordination to the ministry are Divine and sacred ordinances. But we do not call these things "sacraments;" for according to our definition, which is based upon the facts recorded in the New Testament, " a sacrament is a holy ordinance instituted by Christ, wherein by sensible signs Christ and the benefits of the new covenant are represented, sealed, and applied to believers."

Baptism and the Lord's Supper are the only ordinances instituted by Christ for these specific purposes. They are committed to the visible Church as Divinely appointed instruments for the gathering and perfecting of the saints in this life to the end of the world; and Christ by His own presence and spirit, according to His promise, makes them effectual for these ends. We therefore separate baptism and the Lord's Supper from all other Divine ordinances, and distinguish them by the name of "sacraments." We are not strenuous for the name, but for the revealed truths, the recorded facts, and the blessed experiences which it represents. While the sacraments are not *merely* badges of distinction between Christians and the world, and of union among themselves, their office as outward signs is not to be ignored nor undervalued. They are by Christ's appointment the *insignia* of His Church and kingdom in the world.[1]

[1] The kingdom Christ was founding was to be everywhere

The preaching of the Word and the observance of the sacraments "are the symbols by which the Church is discerned; for these cannot anywhere exist without producing fruit and prospering by the blessing of God."[1]

Nor can the preaching of the word be separated from the observance of the sacraments. They are counterparts in one consistent system. Christ has joined them together, and for any man to put them asunder or to exalt one above the other as a Divinely appointed means of grace, is to contemn Christ's authority, to ignore the example of His Apostles, and to mutilate the marks by which the Church may be identified. No less presumptuous is the refusal to recognize these marks where they do exist. Where the Gospel is faithfully preached and the sacraments administered with a manifest regard to Christ's own words in their institution, and where these means of grace evidently bring forth the fruits they were designed to produce, there, says Calvin, "the face of the Church appears, without deception or ambiguity; and no man may with impunity spurn her authority, or reject her admonitions, or resist her counsels, or make

---

imperium in imperio; its members were to be at the same time members of secular states and national bodies. It was therefore a matter of extreme importance to preserve the distinctness of the Christian society, and to prevent its members from being drawn apart from each other by the distraction of worldly claims and engagements. For this purpose certain *sacramenta,* or solemn observances, renewing and reminding them of their union, were most desirable, and Christ ordained two, — the one expressing the distinctness of the Church from the world, and the other the unity of the Church within itself. — *Ecce Homo,* p. 186. This is a very incomplete account of the design and function of the sacraments, but it is true, and highly important so far as it goes.

[1] Calvin's Institutes, book iv. chap. i. 10.

sport of her censures, far less revolt from her and violate her unity. For such is the value which the Lord sets upon the communion of His Church that all who contumaciously alienate themselves from any Christian society in which the true ministry of His Word and sacraments is maintained, He regards as deserters of religion."[1] This is strong language, but none too strong for the case. To admit that the Gospel is preached, and that the sacraments are administered with a sincere purpose to conform to the terms of their institution, and that the gracious fruits these ordinances were appointed to produce do actually appear in connection with them, and yet to maintain that, because some theory of church order or some ceremonial of worship not explicitly enjoined in Scripture is rejected, therefore the Christian communities which bear these marks of the visible Church are no part of the Church at all, and the sacraments they observe are no sacraments at all, is something more than inconsistency; it is the very essence of schism.[2] From such schism "good Lord, deliver us!"

[1] Calvin's Institutes, book iv. chap. i. 10.

[2] When we say that the pure ministry of the Word and the pure celebration of the sacraments is a fit pledge and earnest, so that we may safely recognize the Church in every society in which both exist, our meaning is that we are never to discard it so long as these remain, though it may otherwise teem with numerous faults. Nay, even in the administration of the Word and sacraments defects may creep in, which ought not to alienate us from its communion. — CALVIN: *Institutes*, book iv. chap. i. 12.

As if for the purpose of rebuking and putting to shame the disdainful exclusiveness which is so apt to infect certain ecclesiastical bodies, the Lord seems to take pleasure in raising up choice saints and admirable divines, powerful preachers and apostolic missionaries, not only in the great historical churches, but occasionally also in the obscurest of the Christian denominations. — *Binnie on the Church*, p. 16.

The sacraments being among the Divinely appointed marks of the visible Church, it is very important for us to understand, —
1. The grounds of their obligation.
2. By whom they are to be administered.
3. The mode of their administration.
4. The conditions of admission to these sealing ordinances.

1. The observance of the sacraments is obligatory upon all who profess the true religion, and is part of that profession. This obligation rests primarily upon the explicit precepts of Christ. For the precept to "baptize all nations, teaching them to observe all things whatsoever I have commanded you," is an integral part of the commission to preach the Gospel; and among those things which Christ commanded, none is more explicit than "this do in remembrance of Me." The administration of the sacraments is, therefore, an essential part of preaching the Gospel, and the faith which believes the Gospel is inseparably connected with their observance.

But the obligation does not rest only upon prescriptive rule. All Christian obedience, through the gracious reward inseparably connected with it, rises above the hard lines of duty into the broader and brighter sphere of privilege. And this is especially true of positive as distinguished from moral precepts. A Divine commandment which translates the law written on the heart, and appeals for its sanctions to the approval of reason, the monitions of conscience, and the natural consequences by which sin becomes its own punishment, is not more sacred to a true believer than one which has no basis in the constitution of our nature, but is designed by sovereign grace to express the love and pledge the favor of God. Such precepts, just because their only sanctions are the Divine authority and the Divine blessing which accompanies obedience, appeal with peculiar force to the "law of the spirit of life in Christ Jesus." Whatever force there may be in the Scholastic distinction between *the necessity of precept* and *the necessity of means*, we cannot admit that it has any application to the observance of the sacraments; and above all, we cannot agree with the Zwinglian writers on the subject who insist that our obligation to observe them rests simply on the necessity of precept. If we must choose between the two, our views of the nature and design of the sacraments would compel us to base their observance rather on the necessity of means. But we do not admit in this case the distinction between these two grounds of obligation; we insist equally upon both. The Saviour's precept implies and includes the promise of special blessing upon a loving obedience, and Christian experience confirms the promise. It is true, indeed, that God is not limited in the dispensation of His grace by any outward form, even when it bears the seal of His own authority. But *we are limited* in the rightful expectation of His blessing by His positive appointments. We have no right to plead the gracious exceptions He has made, under entirely different conditions, as a ground of hope for ourselves. There is no comparison between our case and that of the penitent thief on the cross. We are not cast away upon a desert island, where there are no ordained ministers and no Christian ordinances. See, here is water: what doth hinder us to be baptized? The table of the Lord is spread before us by the same Providence that has brought us within the hearing of the Gospel, and the voice of Christ comes ringing down to our ears through all the Christian ages, saying, without qualification or exception, " *This do.*" To insist that this precept is not binding upon *us*, and not necessary to *our* salvation, because God has not enforced it upon others who never heard it or had no opportunity to obey it, is to set up our private judgment against Christ's holy ordinances, and to impeach His wisdom in their institution. With the same propriety the blind man might have refused to be anointed with clay or to go wash in the pool of Siloam. All such reasoning belongs to the same school of philosophy with the contention of Naaman about the waters of Jordan.[1]

All the Reformed Confessions teach that the sacraments are *effectual means* of grace and salvation. They are "institutions which God has ordained to be the ordinary channels of grace; that is, of the supernatural influences of the Holy Ghost to the souls of men."[2] As means and channels of grace, the sacraments stand on precisely the same footing with the preaching of the Gospel. "This do in remembrance of Me" was spoken by the same lips that said, "Go, preach My Gospel." The two precepts rest on the same authority, and are designed to accomplish the same end.

"Let this," says Calvin, "be a fixed point, that the office of the sacraments differs not from the office of the Word of God; and this is to hold forth and offer Christ to us, and in Him the treasures of heavenly grace."[3] The Word and the sacraments are in the same line; they are means of grace in the same sense and in the same way.[4] In this all the Reformed theologians

[1] See Appendix, Lecture VII. (A).
[2] Hodge's Theology, iii. 416.
[3] Institutes, iii. 503.
[4] The efficacy of the sacraments depends upon their Divine

are agreed; and some who are called High Churchmen claim no more.[1] Why, then, should we hesitate to affirm that the Lord's Supper has the same necessity of means with the Word of God?[2] It is nothing to the purpose to insist that the Scriptures speak more frequently of the importance of the Word than of the sacraments. One such precept as "Go, teach all nations, *baptizing* them," "This do in remembrance of Me," is just as binding as a thousand would be. The hearing and believing of the Word is thus joined with baptism, and the remembrance of Christ is joined with the observance of the Lord's Supper; and that not by an arbitrary command, but by a gracious appointment which makes the sacraments equally with the Word instruments, channels, and effectual means of grace. The sacraments and the Word have this in common, that they are exhibitions and conveyances of saving truth. Jesus Christ "is set forth evidently crucified among you," in the one as in the other. "A sacrament," says Augustine, "is a visible Word, because it presents

appointment as means and channels of grace. They were not devised by man as suitable in themselves to produce a moral impression, but they were appointed by God, and we are commanded to use them as means of grace. — Dr. A. A. HODGE: *Commentary on the Confession*, p. 454.

[1] The Lord's Supper is an actual channel or vehicle of grace to the soul. It stands in *this respect on the same footing* with prayer, reading the Scriptures, public worship, and sermons. Only we believe that it takes precedence of them all as means of a higher grace and the instrument of a closer communion with God. — GOULBURN: *Personal Religion*, p. 18.

[2] Many who do not scruple to speak of the Word of God as a means through which a direct and supernatural power is exerted on the hearts of men, refuse to say the same of the sacraments, because they think it is not warranted in the Scripture, and tends to superstition. — *Candlish on the Sacraments*, p. 39.

the promise of God as in a picture." Calvin calls it
"a living sermon." If God has chosen two methods of
revealing His truth, one by articulate words and the
other by sensible signs, what right have we to say that
we will hear the one and not observe the other? And
how vain is the attempt to justify our self-will and
vindicate our private judgment against God's express
appointment by insisting without any warrant of Scripture that the one method of revelation is more efficacious and important than the other? It is no answer to
this question to say that the sacraments have no inherent efficacy. This is equally true of the Word.
There is no Divine power in the syllables or sound of
the Gospel, any more than there is in the bread and
wine of the communion. The truth, indeed, of which
the words of the Gospel are the outward signs, has a
natural adaptation to the mind, as the light has to the
eye; and this also is equally true of the visible Word
in the sacraments. But the mind of man, in his fallen
and unregenerate state, is blind to things of the Spirit of
God, however they are exhibited. The Gospel, whether
in the Word or the sacraments, is the wisdom and
power of God to salvation, only by the blessing of
Christ and the working of His Spirit in them who by
faith receive it. God *can* give all that is represented in
the sacraments without the use of them, and He *can*
give all that is revealed and promised in the Gospel
without the hearing of it. He does this, as we all believe, in the case of all who die in infancy; and how
much farther the aboundings of His grace may reach,
we are not competent to affirm.[1] The question is not

---

[1] We know from the Bible itself that God is no respecter of persons, but in every nation he that feareth God is accepted of Him (Acts x. 34, 35). No one doubts that it is in the power of God to

what He *can* do, but what we have reason to believe He *will* do in behalf of those who have the opportunity both to hear His Word and to observe His sacramental ordinances. It seems to us the height of presumption to teach men that they may wilfully neglect and set aside any of the means of grace He has chosen and consecrated, and yet hope for the benefits of His salvation. If the sacraments are not only signs, but seals of Christ and His benefits, when we refuse to receive and apply them, we presumptuously rest our hopes of salvation upon an unsealed title which has not been ratified and delivered to us according to the law of the new covenant.

2. The universal obligation of the sacraments being conceded, it becomes a very important question, *Who are authorized to administer them?* To this question the Westminster Confession gives an emphatic answer: " Neither sacrament may be dispensed by any but by a minister of the Word lawfully ordained."[1] For this position there is no very explicit warrant in Scripture. The two most important passages quoted in its support are Christ's command to " Go, teach all nations, *baptizing* them " (Mat. xxviii. 19), which was given, not to the whole body of the disciples, but to the eleven, and Paul's saying, " Let a man so account of us as of the ministers of Christ and *stewards of the mysteries* of God," — " the mysteries of God " being understood by many expositors as synonymous with the sacraments. It must be confessed that these proof-texts are not conclusive. The most that can be claimed for them is that they fall in with the idea that the administration of the sacraments

call whom He pleases from among the heathen, and to reveal to them enough truth to secure their salvation. — HODGE: *Theology,* iii. 476.

[1] Confession, chap. xxvii. 4.

is the prerogative of the ministry. That idea is according to the eternal fitness of things. While it is not plainly expressed in Scripture, it is assumed and implied. Whether the sacraments are among "the mysteries of God" or not, they are certainly the most sacred rites of Christianity, and belong to the innermost sanctuary of Christian worship. There is therefore a manifest propriety in committing their administration to the Christian ministry. All Christians feel this in regard even to marriage. They wish to have the ceremony performed by one who officially represents the sanctions of religion and is authorized to pronounce its benediction. And if this universal Christian sentiment is well founded, much more so is the opinion that the sacraments, which signify and seal the union of the soul with Christ, ought to be dispensed only by "a minister of the Word lawfully ordained." The force of this reasoning is universally felt and practically recognized. Christian denominations (for example, the Methodists) who have "lay preachers" as part of their working force, do not commit the sacraments to them. Those Presbyterians who hold the highest views of the office of ruling elder, making it co-ordinate with that of the minister, and insisting that, as presbyters, ruling elders ought to participate in the ordination of ministers, have never, so far as we know, carried out their theory to its logical conclusion, by claiming that ruling elders ought to administer baptism and the Lord's Supper. Even denominations (for example, the Baptists) who hold theoretically that any member of the royal priesthood of believers has the inherent right to administer the sacraments, are careful to restrict the exercise of the right by the special appointment of the church, and to limit such appointment to an *emergency.* Dr. A. H. Strong says: "Although the pastor administers the ordinances, this is not his main work, nor is the church absolutely dependent upon him in the matter. In an emergency, any other member appointed by the church may administer them with equal propriety, the church always determining who are fit subjects of the ordinances, and constituting him their organ in administering them."[1] In practice, if we are correctly informed, the emergency rarely occurs. There is, however, a notable exception to this prevailing rule. The Church of Rome authorizes lay baptism in the case of dying infants when a priest cannot be obtained; and some Episcopal writers defend the practice. The late Dr. Henry Hopkins, bishop of the Episcopal Church in Vermont, was a strenuous advocate of such lay baptism, the special object of his contention being a protest against the practice of rebaptizing proselytes from other denominations. How far his views are adopted, we are not informed. The ground of this exception in regard to infants, when made by Romanists or Episcopalians, is the supposed necessity of baptism to salvation. It is a concession to parental anxiety in behalf of dying children. But the concession is more creditable to the kindly feelings than to the doctrinal consistency of those who make it. It cuts the root of their whole theory concerning the validity of the sacraments. If, as they maintain, the efficacy of these holy ordinances depends, as an essential condition, upon the grace of orders, and this grace is transmitted from its depository in the Apostles only through episcopal ordination, how is it possible in any case to set aside this Divine constitution, and yet retain the validity of the sacraments? And if this may be done in one case, why not in another? If baptism may be lawfully and

[1] Strong's Systematic Theology, p. 511.

effectually administered by the physician or the nurse to a dying *infant*, why not, under similar circumstances, to a dying *man*? And if to the *dying*, why not to the *living*? — who are, in fact, all dying, seeing that " in the midst of life we are in death." Moreover, if one of the sacraments may be lawfully administered by those who are not episcopally ordained, why not both? It will perhaps be answered that the one is more necessary to salvation than the other. But even if this distinction be admitted, it has no pertinency to the question we are considering, which is not the *necessity* of the sacraments to salvation, but simply their *validity*. The theory which bases that validity upon the grace of orders received from an apostolic depository through a particular mode of ordination, breaks down and is abandoned by its strongest advocates as cruelly impracticable when it is put to the test of an *emergency*. Blessed be their tender-hearted inconsistency! If they would only carry out that inconsistency a little farther, and enlarge their views of what constitutes an emergency, the inconsistency would change into harmony, the "contumelious maledictions" of the Church of Rome and their echoes among nominal Protestants would die out, and beyond these discordant voices there would be peace.

3. We proceed to consider briefly the form under which the sacraments are to be administered. This brings us to the margin of the great and bitter controversy concerning *immersion* as the only mode of baptism. But we decline to go very far into these deep waters. We hold, of course, to "one Lord, one faith, one baptism." But this one baptism is not confined to any particular mode of administration; its validity does not depend upon the quantity of water employed, nor upon the way in which the water and the person are

brought into contact.[1] The Westminster Confession takes very broad ground upon this subject when it declares (chap. xxviii. 3) that "dipping the person into the water is not necessary, but baptism is rightly administered by pouring or sprinkling water upon the person." We cannot now rehearse the exegetical and historic proofs of this position. It will be sufficient to say that we claim to be just as capable of understanding the meaning of the original words of Scripture, and the records of the Christian Church from the days of the Apostles, and quite as sincere in our desire to know and obey the truth, as those who insist that *dipping* is the only mode, and belongs to the very essence of the sacrament. If, because we cannot see this subject in the light of their eyes, they insist that we, with the great majority of the Christian Church in all ages, are unbaptized; and if, notwithstanding they admit that we have

---

[1] The word βαπτίζω, as a religious term, means neither dip nor sprinkle, immerse nor pour, nor any other external action in applying a fluid to the body, or the body to a fluid, nor any action which is limited to one mode of performance. But as a religious term it means at all times, to purify or cleanse, — words of a meaning so general as not to be confined to any mode, or agent, or means, or object, whether material or spiritual, but to leave the widest scope for the question as to the mode; so that in this usage it is in every respect a perfect synonym of the word καθαρίζω. — DR. EDWARD BEECHER: *Mode and Subjects of Baptism.*

The testimony of the Didache in regard to the mode of baptism prevalent when it was written is as follows: Chap. VII. "1. Now concerning baptism, baptize thus: having first taught all these things, baptize ye in the name of the Father, and of the Son, and of the Holy Ghost in living water. 2. And if thou hast not living water, baptize into other water; and if thou canst not in cold, then in warm water. 3. But if thou hast neither, *pour water* thrice upon the head, in the name of the Father, and of the Son, and of the Holy Ghost."

received the Holy Ghost as well as they, and are partakers with them of all that baptism is appointed to signify and to seal, they continue to exclude us from their communion, we can only marvel at their inconsistency. Meantime, we will continue cordially to invite them to sit with us at the table of our common Lord, hoping for the dawning of a brighter and a broader day, when so small a matter as the mode of administering a sacrament will no longer be permitted to mar the visible unity of the Church of Christ. In the universal longing for Christian unity, this exclusiveness is beginning to weaken, and we believe it must ultimately give way, as the iceberg melts in the warm currents of the Gulf Stream. And the same remark applies to the question of ordination to the ministry.

Our Lord has given no specific instructions as to the forms and ceremonies to be used in the administration of His Holy Supper. "This do" has reference simply to the eating and drinking of bread and wine in remembrance of Him. The time of the day or of the year when this is to be done, the dress and posture and words of the administrator, and the bodily attitude of the communicants, are left to the decision of Christian discretion.

It was undoubtedly the practice of the Church, in the days of the Apostles and for a long time after, to celebrate the Lord's Supper on every Lord's day, and frequently on other occasions. "To break bread" was one chief object in the assembling of Christians. In the Church at Jerusalem, in the new joy and sweet fellowship which followed the Pentecost, it was a daily observance. Such frequent communion is generally regarded by Presbyterians as a fruit and evidence of "Ritualism." Yet Calvin maintains that once a week is not too often to observe the sacrament, and he condemns a yearly interval in the severest terms.[1]

Kneeling in the reception of the sacred elements, as practised in the Episcopal and Methodist churches, is certainly as appropriate and as nearly conformed to the reclining posture of Christ and the Apostles at the first Lord's Supper, as the sitting attitude observed by Presbyterians. The prejudice that it involves a superstitious reverence, and is a mark of popery, is neither intelligent, nor just to those who practise it.

While we believe that everything in the administration of the Lord's Supper not prescribed by the precept and example of Christ and His Apostles is left to the decision of Christian liberty, and desire to cultivate the broadest and tenderest charity toward all Christians with whom we differ in the exercise of that liberty, we feel bound to observe and defend whatever Christ and His Apostles have enjoined upon us; and this applies especially to the elements the Saviour chose and consecrated as the symbols of His body and blood. Aside altogether from their natural suitableness for the purpose, "the giving and receiving of *bread* and *wine* according to Christ's appointment"[2] is essential to the celebration of the sacrament. His death cannot be showed forth *according to His appointment*, nor can we be made partakers of His body and blood by the sacramental use of anything but bread and wine. It is the *bread* which we break that is the communion of the

[1] The sacrament might be celebrated in the most becoming manner if it were dispensed to the Church very frequently, at least once a week. . . . Most assuredly the custom which prescribes communion once a year is an invention of the Devil, by what instrumentality soever it may have been introduced. — *Institutes*, book iv. chap. xvii. sections 43-46.

[2] Shorter Catechism, p. 96.

body of Christ, and the *cup of blessing* which we bless which is the communion of the blood of Christ. But suppose Christians are placed in circumstances in which bread cannot be obtained: may they not substitute for it some other article of food, such as flesh or fruit? Most assuredly not. " Christ took *bread* and brake it, and gave to His disciples, and said, *This* do in remembrance of Me." If bread cannot be procured, we are precluded by Divine Providence from the use of the sacrament; and surely the Saviour will not hold us responsible for the failure, nor withhold His grace from us on that account. The use of bread in the communion is precisely analogous to the use of water in baptism. We cannot baptize a man with milk or with sand; for "except a man be born of *water* and the Spirit, he cannot enter into the kingdom of God." Better to remain unbaptized than under the plea of necessity to attempt to amend Christ's positive institutions. The obligation to observe the sacrament ceases when Divine Providence renders it impossible; and God's grace is not so tied to the outward ordinance that He cannot separate them. What is true of bread in the Holy Communion is equally true of wine. That "the cup" and "the fruit of the vine" mean *wine*, and nothing else, no candid reader of the New Testament would ever question, if it were not necessary to do so in order to maintain a foregone conclusion. And what is wine? Let us answer in the sober words of Dr. Hodge:—

"By wine, as prescribed to be used in this ordinance, is to be understood 'the juice of the grape,' and the juice of the grape in that state which was and is in common use, and in the state in which it was known as wine. It was not the juice of the grape as it exists in the fruit, but that juice submitted to such a process of fermentation as secured its preservation, and gave it the qualities ascribed to it in the Scriptures. That οἶνος in the Bible, when unqualified by such words as 'new' and 'sweet,'[1] means the fermented juice of the grape, is hardly an open question. It has never been questioned in the Church, if we except by a few Christians of the present day. . . . Those in the Early Church whose zeal for temperance led them to exclude wine from the Lord's table were consistent enough to substitute water. They not only abstained from the use of wine and denounced as *improbos atque impios* those who drank it, but they also repudiated animal food and marriage, regarding the Devil as their author. They soon disappeared from history. The plain meaning of the Bible on this subject has controlled the mind of the Church, and it is to be hoped will control it till the end of time."[2]

Under whatever forms it is administered, the true spirit of the Lord's Supper ought to be preserved. It is not a fast, nor a funeral, but a feast in God's banqueting-house under His banner of love, — a feast of all that is life-giving in the person of Christ, and all that is cheering and delightful in the Gospel of His grace. There is no *damnation* in it, and no more danger in its use than there is in any other means of grace. It is not the crucifixion again, either of the Saviour or of His disciples. Its design is to turn our sorrow into joy, and fill us with all the fulness of God. Its associations are not merely with "that dark and doleful night" when the Son of Man was betrayed, but rather with the glory which followed and swallowed up His sufferings. He does not say, "Do this in remembrance of My death," but

---

[1] It is evident from Acts ii. 13 that even the new wine would intoxicate when used to excess. "These men are full of new wine." "These are not drunken, as ye suppose." The "new wine" was the wine of the last vintage, which at the time of the Pentecost was six months old.

[2] Theology, iii. 616. See Appendix, Lecture VII. (C).

"in remembrance of *Me*." We come to this feast, not to eat of a dead sacrifice, but to receive and feed upon Him "who liveth and was dead, and is alive for evermore." For the sacrament signifies and effects our communion with Christ in His person, in His offices, and in all their precious fruits. It is on our part a eucharistic sacrifice, an oblation of all possible praise and thanksgiving. And so, as Calvin says, the Lord's Supper is medicine to the sick, comfort to the sinner, bounty to the poor; while to the righteous and the rich, if any such could be found, it would be of no value.[1]

4. *The Grounds of Admission to Sealing Ordinances.* — Baptism is commonly spoken of as "the initiatory rite" of the Christian Church. This language is correct when we use the word "initiate" in its true meaning, to signify, not the creation, but the acknowledgment and first exercise of an existing right.[2] This is admirably expressed in Fisher's Catechism: —

"Does baptism make or constitute persons church members? No. They are supposed to be church members before they are baptized; and if they are children of professing parents, they are *born* members of the visible Church. Why must they be church members before they are baptized? Because the seals of the covenant can never be applied to any but such as are supposed to be in the covenant, nor can the privileges of the Church be confirmed to any that are without the Church. Why then do our Confession and Larger Catechism say that the parties baptized are solemnly *admitted* into the visible Church? Because there is a vast difference between making a person a church member who was none before, and the solemnity of the admission of one who is already a member. All that our Confession and Catechism affirm is that by baptism we are

[1] Institutes, book iv. chap xvii. 42.
[2] See Appendix, Lecture VII. (D).

solemnly admitted into the visible Church ; that is, by baptism we are publicly declared to be church members before, and thus have our membership solemnly sealed to us."

But while baptism is the formal acknowledgment of visible church membership, this is but a part, and the lowest part, of its meaning and its use. It is "a sacrament of the New Testament ordained by Jesus Christ, to be continued in His Church until the end of the world, not only for the solemn admission of the party baptized into the visible Church, but also to be unto him a sign and seal of the covenant of grace, of his engrafting into Christ, of regeneration, and of remission of sins."[1] "It is a sign and seal of our regeneration and engrafting into Christ, *and that even to infants.*"[2] To

[1] The efficacy of baptism is not tied to that moment of time wherein it is administered; yet notwithstanding, by the right use of this ordinance, the grace promised is not only offered, but really exhibited and conferred by the Holy Ghost to such, whether of age or infants, as that grace belongeth unto, according to the counsel of God's own will in His appointed time. — *Westminster Confession,* chap. xxviii. 6.

[2] Westminster Confession, chap. xxviii. 1, and Larger Catechism, 177. We call attention, especially of our Presbyterian brethren, to these statements of our Standards. Candor compels us to admit that they are stronger and more explicit in the declaration that baptism signifies and seals the regeneration of infants than the statements of the Episcopal liturgy. We are bound to accord to our Episcopal brethren the right to define their own terms. The great majority of their most esteemed expositors understand the word "regeneration" to mean, not a moral, but an ecclesiastical change, which secures indeed certain spiritual blessings, but does not involve either the renovation of the child's nature or the certainty of its salvation. In other words, they mean by "regeneration" what we mean by "church membership," coupled with the reception of what we call "common," as distinguished from "saving" grace.

Waterland, who was one of their ablest writers on the subject in the last century, maintains this (see Works, iv. 424). Dr. Harold Browne,

apply that sacred sign and seal to any whom we know or believe to be *unregenerate*, is a solemn mockery. But, it will be asked, how can we know that an infant is regenerate and grafted into Christ? I answer by asking, How can we know that an adult is regenerate? We *cannot know* it in either case, for only God can read the heart. We baptize both the adult and the infant, not upon demonstrative, but upon probable evidence; and we do not hesitate to affirm that the Divine completeness of the sacrament, the union between the outward sign and the inward and spiritual grace, fails oftener in the case of adults, who are baptized upon their own confession, than in the case of infants, who are baptized upon the confession of parents and trained according to covenant promises. The infant is not regenerated *by the baptism*: we have no sympathy nor toleration for any such mechanical religion; but the *presumption* that it is regen-

---

whose exposition of the Thirty-nine Articles is a text-book in Episcopal seminaries in this country, sustains the same position (see Browne on "Thirty-nine Articles," p. 633). Bishop Brownell, in his elaborate "Commentary on the Prayer-Book," sanctions the same opinion, and quotes many authorities to show that it is the accepted doctrine of the Episcopal Church (see "Commentary on Prayer-Book," p. 418).

Whether this is a right use of the word "regeneration," is a question not pertinent to this discussion. According to them the right to define their own terms, and admitting that this definition is a sufficient answer to the charge that their service teaches "baptismal regeneration" in the sense that is so offensive to Presbyterian ears, our objections to that service are based upon other grounds: (1) that it seems to ignore the whole idea of the household covenant; (2) that it puts the children of the Church and the children of the world upon a common level; (3) that it substitutes the awkward and unscriptural device of "sponsors in baptism" for the sacred relations of believing parents and of those who stand *in loco parentis*.

erate, which is in all cases the antecedent ground of baptism, is co-extensive with the Divine warrant for its reception of the sacramental sign. Wherever God authorizes us to apply the Divine seal, He makes Himself responsible for writing the spiritual document with His own finger on the heart.

The one essential condition for the baptism of a child is a sufficient security that it will be trained by precept and example as a child of God and an heir of the kingdom of heaven; and upon the assumption that this condition is honestly stipulated and will be faithfully fulfilled, we have a right to assume also that the child either is or will certainly be regenerated.

Our hesitation to believe this indicates, not a high, but a low, view of regeneration as a work of God's sovereign grace. We limit the Holy One of Israel in this mighty work by connecting it inseparably with what we call "conversion," and by judging of its existence by our tests of religious experience. The Divine grace, which abounds in Christ beyond the abounding of sin, and beyond our ability to define or even to conceive of its working, is stronger in every point of human existence than the fallen and corrupt nature we inherit from Adam. We all admit in theory that this Divine grace *can* change the nature of a child, before its birth, or at its birth, or at the time of its baptism, as easily as at any subsequent period of life. We all see the evidence that, in consistency with the law of heredity, God fulfils not only His threatening to visit the sins of the fathers upon the children unto the third and fourth generation of them that hate Him, but also His promise to show mercy to thousands of generations of them that love Him and keep His commandments. The proverb of Matthew Henry, that "grace does not run in the blood, but deviltry does," is not altogether true. Hereditary gracious influences control and modify the nature of children born of Christian parents. The doctrine of total depravity is not the absurd notion that any one is *as bad as he can be*, nor that all are *equally bad* at their birth. Some are born less depraved than others. The grace of God makes them to differ. Samuel and John the Baptist and Timothy are not exceptional cases, but specimens of those who are filled with the Holy Ghost even from their mother's womb. "Of such is the kingdom of God" does not mean merely that the kingdom is composed of adults who have been converted and become as little children, but that it is largely composed, in heaven and on earth, of little ones whom the Saviour has taken into His arms and blessed. The typical little one whom He set in the midst was a "young Christian," and not merely an unsophisticated child who might one day become a Christian. Connecting the sovereignty of God's grace with His covenant promises to believers and their children, we maintain that every child lawfully baptized — not because of its baptism, but because of the relations and promises of which baptism is the sign and seal — is to be regarded and treated as a regenerate child of God, until the contrary is made to appear.[1]

[1] Principal Cunningham, in his essay on "Zwingli and the Doctrine of the Sacraments," contends that the definition of "baptism" in the Shorter Catechism "applies fully and in all its extent only to those who are possessed of the necessary qualifications or preparation for baptism, and who are *able to ascertain this*." He further declares that "the sacraments were instituted and intended for believers, and produce their appropriate beneficial effects only through the faith which must have *previously existed*, and which is expressed and exercised in the act of partaking in them." In order to harmonize these statements with the doctrine and practice of the Reformers and with the Standards of the Presbyterian Church, he

We repudiate the opposite doctrine that all children, whether baptized or not, are to be regarded and treated as unregenerate until they give what we may regard as satisfactory evidence of being born again. These two theories underlie and pervade two very different schemes of Christian education. According to the one, parents have a child of Satan, a fallen and unregenerate being, prone to all evil and incapable of all good, to restrain, to instruct, and to pray over, in the hope that it will one day be converted and made fit to join the Church.[1]

asserts that "the case of infant baptism is special and peculiar;" that it "really occupies a sort of subordinate and exceptional position." Wherein it is subordinate and exceptional he does not undertake to show, nor does he quote a word from the Presbyterian Standards or from any of the Reformed creeds to prove that the views he advocates are consistent with the doctrines of the Reformers. He makes it plain, however, that in his opinion baptism, as applied to infants, is not to be regarded as a *seal*, because in their case there is nothing whatever to seal. How such opinions could be held and openly advocated by a leader and a teacher in the Free Church of Scotland, and how far such advocacy accounts for the prevalence of low views of the baptism of infants in the Presbyterian churches of this country, are questions which cannot now be discussed. It is sufficient for our present purpose to set over against such opinions the explicit and strong statement of our Standards that "Baptism is the sign and seal of our regeneration and engrafting into Christ, and *that even to infants.*"

As an exposition of this confessional statement, we quote the following sentence from Dr. Hodge: "The status of baptized children is not a vague or uncertain one, according to the doctrine of the Reformed churches. They are members of the Church; they are professing Christians; they belong *presumptively* to the number of the elect. These propositions are true of them in *the same sense in which they are true of adult professing Christians*" (Princeton Review, 1858, p. 389).

[1] Principal Cunningham, carrying out his views as to the subordinate and exceptional character of the baptism of infants, insists that "every child, whether baptized or not, should be treated and

According to the other scheme, the child is a fellow-member with its parents in the Church of Christ, a participant with them in the covenant of grace, a joint heir with them to the same covenant promises, a child of God whom He has committed to them to be nursed for Him. The reflex influence of the aim pursued will determine the whole educational process, and temper the whole atmosphere of the Christian home. Dr. Bushnell, in his admirable book on "Christian Nurture," does not put the case a whit too strongly when he says: "It is the very character and mark of all *unchristian* education to train up a child for future conversion." And he is no less correct when he adds, "The true idea of *Christian* education is that a child is to grow up a Christian, and never to know himself as being otherwise." These opposite aims will not only control the

dealt with in all respects as if they were unregenerate and still needed to be born again of the Word of God *through the belief of the truth*" (Reformers and Theology of the Reformation, p. 291). And yet, notwithstanding the intimation in the words we have italicized, that there is no other way to be born again except through the belief of the truth, he insists in the same passage that "believers are warranted to improve the baptism of their children in the way of *confirming their faith in the salvation of those of them who die in infancy.*" How can these two positions be reconciled? Does death change the moral character and relations of its subjects, and make credible in regard to them that which was incredible before? Can even an infant enter heaven without being born again? Does baptism really add anything to the grounds of our faith in regard to the salvation of infants? If a child dies before its believing parents have an opportunity to have it baptized, must they have any less faith in its salvation than if it had been baptized?

To all which questions we answer, No. And for the same reason we utterly reject the dogma that the children of the covenant are to be judged and treated as unregenerate, unless, happily for them, death comes into the higher court of the believer's heart to plead against his head for a reversal of the cruel judgment.

hopes of parents, and the instructions through which they seek to be realized, but they will make themselves felt with peculiar power in our treatment of children's faults. It must make a vast difference in our discipline whether we regard their shortcomings and misdoings as the lingering remains of sin in a young Christian, or as the living seeds of all evil in one who is still in the gall of bitterness and the bonds of iniquity. The assumption that they are already within the covenant, regenerate and holy, that grace is struggling in them for mastery over sin, will give a Divine tenderness to our rebukes. It will make us pray with them in the assurance that they are partakers with us of the same grace, even as we share with them in the same passions and infirmities. It will bring us together to Christ in the faith of the Syrophœnician woman, saying, "O Lord, have mercy upon *us*." Our sympathy will be to the child the sign and seal of Divine mercy, and our kiss of reconciliation the sacrament of God's loving forgiveness. But if we assume that the faults we would correct are the evidences of their unregenerate state; if we constantly tell them that they are wicked, and drill into their tender souls the unevangelical falsehood that "God does not love naughty children;" if we warn them continually that they are in great danger of growing up reprobates and are in perishing need of a new heart, — such religious training will discourage and harden their sensitive nature more effectually than the indiscriminate use of the rod. Even under the kindest personal treatment, multitudes of the children of the covenant are placed by the inexorable logic of the popular creed in the most anomalous and hopeless condition. They are taught to believe that the mark of the Lord Jesus is upon them, but that they are still excluded from His fold. They are bound by all the *obligations* of religion; but they are warned not to claim its *privileges* until they have undergone a change of whose nature they can form no clear conception, for which they can discover no necessity in their present simple and childlike religious experience, and the symptoms of which they are taught not to expect until that ill-defined period shall come when they will be "old enough to join the church."

The telling of experiences, the fixing of the time, the discovery of the causes, and the description of the process of conversion, have become, to a large extent, synonymous in the mind of the Church with the tests of piety and the evidences of Christian character; while the value or even the possibility of a true Christian experience running back into springs that are hidden and Divine, gradually developed, like a grain of mustard-seed, under the steady influence of Christian culture, and eluding by its very depth and pervading power all attempts to fix its times and seasons or describe the successive stages of its growth, is ignored, undervalued, and even condemned as unevangelical. Our children are afraid to claim their birthright privileges, because they have no experiences to tell, and can give no account of their conversion. Instead of being taught that they already belong to the Church, and that if they love the Saviour it is their privilege to come to His table as soon as they understand the meaning of the ordinance, they hear the changes rung about being converted and joining the Church; and getting their ideas of conversion from what they hear of the experience of adults brought into the Church from the world, they sadly number themselves with Christ's enemies, even while their hearts ache to be recognized among His friends.

It is time to take down the bars with which the tables have been fenced to the exclusion of children, and to substitute for them the plain and wise instructions of our Presbyterian Standards:—

"Children born within the pale of the visible Church, and dedicated to God in baptism, are under the inspection and government of the Church, and are to be taught to read and repeat the Catechism, the Apostles' Creed, and the Lord's Prayer. And when they come to years of discretion, if they be free from scandal, appear sober and steady, and to have sufficient knowledge to discern the Lord's body, they ought to be informed that it is their privilege and duty to come to the Lord's Table."[1]

There is certainly a wide departure from the spirit and the letter of these instructions. For proof of this we need look no farther than the forms for a public profession of faith, which in their freedom from a prescribed liturgy our ministers invent for themselves. So far as our observation goes, these forms, with few exceptions, ignore the church membership of the children of believers, and assume that they all grow up to years of discretion unbelieving and unregenerate. One of these forms, which has been in use in a prominent Presbyterian Church for fifty years, may serve as a sample. It makes no distinction whatever between the children of the Church and the children of the world. It assumes that admission to membership, and coming for the first time to the communion, are contemporaneous and identical. It demands the same "confession and covenant from all who are thus 'added on profession,'" and among other things it requires them all to adopt the following declaration: "In this public manner you do humbly confess and bewail the original and

[1] Directory for Worship, chap. ix. sect. 1.

total depravity of your nature, the past enmity of your heart against God, the unbelief which has led you to reject a Saviour, and the manifold transgressions of your life: all which sins you do condemn, and in your purpose renounce." Now, without stopping to inquire whether the acceptance of the doctrine of original and total depravity is essential to salvation, and therefore a term of communion in the Church of Christ, it is sufficient for our purpose to observe that confessions like this, as applied to children born within the pale of the visible Church, and trained in the nurture of the Lord, are without warrant of Scripture and contrary to experience. I have received scores of such children to the Lord's table, — many of them at an early age. There was not one of them, so far as I can now remember, who was conscious of having ever rejected the Saviour or of cherishing enmity against God. While they all confessed and bewailed their sins, most, if not all of them, declared that they always believed in and loved the Saviour, and had never ceased from their earliest recollection to pray for His forgiving and sanctifying grace. My experience and observation in this matter cannot be peculiar. Surely it is not right to put such a confession between the Lord's table and the tender souls of children whom Christ has taken into His arms and blessed, and concerning whom He has said, "Of such is the kingdom of heaven." How can a child who has always, so far as memory goes, believed in and loved the Lord Jesus Christ, publicly confess, bewail, and renounce "enmity against God and the unbelief that rejects a Saviour," without contradicting his inmost consciousness and denying the grace of God which is in him? If there is only *one* such child in the Church, is it right either to keep that child away from the Lord's table, or to bring it there with a confession on the lips to which there is no response in the heart? But such forms of admission are not only an offence against the little ones who believe in Christ, they are a practical repudiation of what we profess to believe concerning the household covenant, the efficacy of the ordinance, and the sovereignty of God. They are manifestly based upon the assumption that original depravity is never counteracted by Divine grace, in the case of those who live, till they come to years of discretion; that none of the children of the Church are born again in infancy, except they *die* in infancy, and that their baptism does not in any case really signify and seal their actual engrafting into Christ. These assumptions seem to me to be monstrous. They are far more inconsistent with the doctrines of grace and with the sovereignty of God than any theory of baptismal regeneration.

APPENDIX.

LECTURE I.

A.

The Salvation of Infants.

Dr. Hodge's argument on this subject is as follows: "All who die in infancy are saved. This is inferred from what the Bible teaches of the analogy between Adam and Christ. 'As by the offence of one, judgment came upon all men to condemnation, even so, by the righteousness of one, the free gift came upon all men to justification of life. For as by one man's disobedience many (οἱ πολλοί = πάντες) were made sinners, so by the obedience of One shall many (οἱ πολλοί = πάντες) be made righteous' (Rom. v. 18, 19). We have no right to put any limit on these general terms, except what the Bible itself places upon them. The Scriptures nowhere exclude any class of infants, baptized or unbaptized, born in Christian or in heathen lands, of believing or unbelieving parents, from the benefits of the redemption of Christ. All the descendants of Adam except Christ are under condemnation; all the descendants of Adam, except those of whom it is expressly revealed that they cannot inherit the kingdom of God, are saved. This appears to be the clear meaning of the Apostle, and therefore he does not hesitate to say 'that where sin abounded, grace has *much more* abounded;' that the benefits of redemption far exceed the evils of the fall; that the number of the saved far exceeds the number of the lost. Not only does the comparison which the Apostle makes between Adam and Christ lead to the conclusion that, as all are condemned for the sin of one, so all are saved by the righteousness of the other, those only excepted whom the Scriptures except, but the principle assumed throughout the whole discussion teaches the same doctrine. That principle is that *it is more congenial to the nature of God to bless than to curse, to save than to destroy.* If the race fell in Adam, much more shall it be restored in Christ. If death reigned by one, much more shall life reign by one. This 'much more' is repeated over and over. The Bible everywhere teaches that God delights not in the death of the wicked; that judgment is His strange work. It is, therefore, contrary not only to the argument of the Apostle, but to the whole spirit of the passage (Rom. v. 12–21), to exclude infants from the 'all' who are made alive in Christ. The conduct and language of our Lord in reference to children are not to be regarded as matters of sentiment or simply expressions of kind feeling. He evidently looked upon them as the lambs of the flock, for which, as the Good Shepherd, He laid down His life, and of whom He said, they shall never perish, and none could pluck them out of His hands. Of such, He tells us, is the kingdom of heaven, as though heaven was, in a great measure, composed of the souls of redeemed infants. It is therefore the general belief of Protestants, contrary to the doctrine of Romanists and Romanizers, that all who die in infancy are saved."[1]

The argument for the salvation of all dying infants is still more broadly stated in the following extracts from a book entitled "God and Little Children," by Dr. Henry Van Dyke, pastor of the Brick Church, New York:[2]—

"It has been audaciously asserted and commonly believed that the doctrine of the perdition of infants originated with those theologians who are called Calvinists, and that the Presbyterian Church is peculiarly responsible for it. Never

[1] Hodge's Theology, ii. 26.
[2] Published by A. D. F. Randolph & Co.

was there a more ignorant assertion, never an assumption more at variance with the facts.

"It has been piously claimed, on the other hand, that the Calvinistic theology has never recognized this doctrine, and that the Presbyterian Church has kept itself entirely free from the shadow of it. Never was there a claim made with more amiable intentions or with less substantial proofs.

"The simple truth is, that the responsibility for this doctrine rests, not upon any one branch of the Church, but upon theologians at large, from Saint Augustine down to the end of the seventeenth century. Here and there you will find men who were bold enough to deny and disavow it. But everywhere you will find men who not only accepted, but taught it. That is the amazing fact. You will not discover those dreadful words, 'Hell is paved with infants' skulls,' in the works of any ancient writer. It is merely a waste of time to try to run that gray-headed falsehood to earth. But you will have no trouble in finding theories and statements which imply or declare that some infants pass through death unto perdition, in the writings of Roman Catholics, Lutherans, Presbyterians, and Episcopalians, down almost to the present century. . . .

"1. The doctrine of the perdition of infants is false, because there is nothing in the Word of God to support it. Search the Scriptures from end to end, and you will not find a single word, a single syllable, which implies that children are to be sent into everlasting death.

"2. But this argument is only negative, and we must pass on at once to the second point, which is positive. The doctrine of the perdition of infants is false, because it is condemned by natural justice. It is not to be assumed for a moment that our human sense of justice is perfect and infallible, or that we are acquainted with all the considerations which enter into the judgment of God. But there is, in spite of all ignorance and defect, a perception of equity in the human soul which corresponds to the attribute of righteousness in God. And this is what we affirm: the more highly this moral sense is educated, the more clearly and unequivocally does it reluctate against the notion that God will condemn the soul of one little child to everlasting death, either on account of the guilt of Adam's sin, or on account of the neglect of its parents to have it baptized. How could we believe such a morally insane doctrine as that the final outworking of God's justice will be to spare the original offender and damn his helpless children? For that, in plain language, is what it all amounts to. Adam is saved. The Church has given him a place among the saints. Raphael has painted him among the blessed who sit around the throne, in the great fresco of the Disputa della Trinità. Dante has described him as the first in that happy circle which surrounds the mystic Rose of Paradise. From these pictures of celestial bliss we are told to drop our eyes downward and contemplate the miseries of myriads of Adam's children who have been cast into eternal torment solely on account of his sin. The vision is a dream of madness. It is a nightmare monstrosity of error. Before I could believe in it I should have to annihilate my conscience and commit moral suicide.

"3. But there is a still stronger argument against the perdition of infants. It is directly contrary to the principles of judgment as they are revealed to us by Jesus Christ. Let us understand very clearly that Christ teaches that there is punishment in the future world, and that this punishment is so great that it passes the power of human thought to conceive it. But let us never forget that He teaches also that this punishment is just and righteous, and that not a single stroke of it will ever fall upon any who have not deserved it by their own sins and refused deliverance by their own impenitence. And it is for this reason that the loving and gracious Christ tells us of their perdition, in order that we may know that we also must give account to God of the deeds done in the body. Now, if you introduce another principle of judgment, — if you say that any soul may be lost for the sin of Adam, for not accepting an invitation which it could not understand, for not receiving a baptism which was never offered, for not repenting and believing before repentance and faith were possible, — you absolutely cancel and obliterate the teachings of Christ, and leave the future world a moral chaos, dominated solely by a blind and brutal terror. If judgment means anything, it means that this is forever impossible. If the words of Christ mean anything, they mean that not one helpless, harmless child will ever be banished into the outer darkness by the just God.

"4. And this brings us to the fourth and last reason for rejecting the doctrine of infant perdition. It is false because it is contrary to the revelation of the love of God which is given unto us in Christ Jesus our Lord. There has been a time when men have refused to accept this revelation in its integrity because it would not fit into their theories. Coming to the text, 'God so loved the world,' they have cut it down to suit their logic, and said, 'This means the world of the elect.' But by the gracious Spirit of God the darkness of that time has been dispelled. We believe that Christ meant just what He said. We believe that God is love, and that His mighty heart broods over all the world with an infinite tenderness, willing to save and bless it. Everywhere that love is flowing, following, seeking, calling for its children. Into every soul that does not refuse it, it will come. In every life that does not reject it, it will accomplish its Divine purpose. And sooner shall our hearts learn to forget and hate the children that have nestled beside them, sooner shall our hands be ready to cast them into the flames, than God's heart shall forget them, — than God's hand shall cast away one of the little souls that pass, helpless and harmless, out of the shadow of their brief mortal life into the light of His loving presence."

B.

"The Holy Catholic Church, the Communion of Saints."

THE Apostles' Creed is part of the Standards of the Presbyterian Church, and is included among the elementary formulas which children born within the pale of the visible Church are to be taught to repeat as part of their preparation for admission to the Lord's table.[1] The revived use of this most ancient creed in our Sunday schools and assemblies for worship is to be hailed as a hopeful sign, pointing backward to the faith of our fathers, and forward to the ultimate unifying of Christendom. It has been affirmed that this Creed, so far from setting forth the Church as a visible society in one specific form, does not present it under the idea of an external society at all. The clause, "the communion of saints," is often printed without a pause following it, as though it were not a separate article, but only a synonymous and explanatory phrase for "the Holy Catholic Church." We believe, with Dr. Schaff, that this is a mistake.[2] The clause in question was one of the later additions to the Creed, — not earlier than the fifth century. It surely could not have been intended as a mere repetition; still less could it have been designed and accepted at that time as a denial of the existence of the visible Catholic Church. But regarded as a separate and additional article of faith, it recognizes the communion of saints as something more than any outward organization.

Calvin says: "When in the Creed we profess to believe in the Church, reference is made *not only to the visible Church*, of which we are now treating, but also to all the elect of God, including in the number even those who have departed this life."[3]

[1] See Directory for Worship, chap. ix.
[2] See Creeds of Christendom, vol. i. p. 22; vol. ii. p. 52.
[3] Institutes, book iv. chapters i. ii.

Canon Westcott says : " We believe there is a Holy Catholic Church, a communion of saints, or, in other words, a body of Christ, *seen and unseen*, by which the truth is on the one side presented *outwardly before the world*, and on the other brought home with concentrated power to the souls of believers."[1]

As adherence to this creed is one of the marks by which we recognize the Roman Catholic communion, in spite of its corruptions and the usurpations of the papacy, as a part of the visible Church of Christ, so this article, whether it is so intended or not, is a confession that every true believer is a saint of God and a member of the invisible Church.

C.

Thou art Peter, and upon this rock I will build My church. — MATT. xvi. 18.

OF course this language is highly figurative, but that is no reason why it should be wrested from its context, and treated as a dark saying, covering a meaning entirely different from that which lies on its surface. Many devices have been found to set aside that meaning. In the first place, it is arbitrarily assumed that the "church" here spoken of is not the same to which the offended brother is directed to take his case,[2] for that is evidently an outward and visible organization ; nor is it the kingdom of heaven spoken of in the very next verse, the keys of which are given to Peter ; but the "church" spoken of in this particular sentence must be regarded as altogether spiritual and invisible. Then, *secondly*, it is affirmed that this spiritual and mystical temple cannot be built on Peter or any other man, because Christ Himself is expressly declared to be its one foundation : " other foundation can no man lay than that is laid, which is Jesus Christ." And *thirdly*, these premises being as-

[1] Historic Faith, p. 115.
[2] If he neglect to hear them, tell it unto the Church. — *Matt.* xviii. 17.

sumed and read into the text, something more occult must be substituted for its obvious meaning. An antithesis is imposed upon it; "and" (καί) is made to signify "but" (δέ). Christ said to Peter, "Thou art a rock, *and* [that is, as these interpreters would have it, *but*] on *this* rock [meaning something else than Peter] I will build My church." Some say the "rock" is Christ Himself, and go so far as to affirm that when He uttered the words He made His meaning plain *by pointing to Himself*. This is the device of Augustine, to which even his great name cannot reconcile us. Others think the "rock" is the truth of Peter's confession, separated entirely from his personality and future agency. And this is defended by the supposed significance of the change in the termination of the original word from *Petros* to *petra*. "Thou art *Petros*, and on this *petra* I will build My church." The reason for this change is a mere matter of conjecture. Mr. Goulburn's explanation is the most plausible. "Houses are not built upon single stones; they may, however, be built upon a rock, and the word for 'rock' in Greek is the same as that for a stone, only with a feminine termination, *petra* for *petros*" (Holy Catholic Church, p. 30). Whether this be true or not, the mere change in the termination of the word is no reason for changing the obvious meaning of the passage.

"It seems certain that the words themselves (ἐπὶ ταύτῃ τῇ πέτρᾳ), though occasioned by the confession, refer to Peter himself. The change of person, 'on *this* rock,' instead of 'upon *thee*,' is the natural result of the sudden transition from a direct to a metaphorical address, and is in exact accordance with our Lord's manner on other occasions. He said, not 'destroy Me,' or 'the temple of My body,' but 'destroy *this* temple' (John ii. 19)."

It is not necessary, nor indeed possible, to separate Peter from his belief and confession of the truth. It was not upon Peter as denying his Master, but upon him as confessing and

[1] Stanley's Sermons on the Apostolic Age, p. 113.

truly believing that Jesus is the Christ, the Son of the living God, that the Church in its New Testament form was to be built. Neither, again, can Peter be separated from the rest of the Apostles, whose representative and mouthpiece he was, answering a question addressed to them all, "Whom say ye that I am?"[1] And hence, while Christ says, "I will give unto thee the keys of the kingdom of heaven : and whatsoever thou shalt bind on earth shall be bound in heaven," a little while after He repeats and applies the same words to *all* the Apostles : "Whatsoever ye shall bind on earth shall be bound in heaven" (Matt. xviii. 18). Our Confession of Faith applies the same words to all church officers (chap. xxx. 1, 2).

The interpretation we have given is adopted by all modern commentators of note. Take a specimen from Alford : "The name Petros, the termination being altered only to suit the masculine appellation, denotes the *personal position* of this Apostle in the building of the Church of Christ. He was the first of those foundation-stones (Rev. xxi. 14) on which the living temple of God was built; this building itself beginning on the day of Pentecost by the laying of three thousand living stones in the very foundation. That this is the simple, only interpretation of our Lord's words, the whole usage of the New Testament shows ; in which not doctrines, nor confessions, but *men*, are uniformly the pillars and stones of the spiritual building (1 Pet. ii. 4–6 ; Gal. ii. 9 ; Eph. ii. 20). Nothing can be farther from any legitimate interpretation of this promise than the idea of a per-

[1] Peter is called the foundation of the Church only in the same sense as all the Apostles are called the foundation by the Apostle Paul (Eph. ii. 20) ; namely, as the first preachers of the true faith concerning Jesus as the Christ and Son of God; and if the man who *first* professed that faith be honored by being called individually the 'Rock,' that only shows that the *faith*, and not the man, is, after all, the true foundation. That which makes Simon a *Petros*, a rock-like man, fit to build on, is the real *petra* on which the ecclesia is to be built. — BRUCE : *Training of the Twelve*, p. 170.

petual primacy in the successors of Peter; the very notion of a *succession* is precluded by the form of the comparison, which concerns the person, and him only, so far as it involves a direct promise."

LECTURE V.

A.

WE make the following extracts from an article in the "Lutheran Review" for January, 1889, by Rev. Dr. I. B. Reimensnyder: "'The Didache,' says Schaff, 'fills a gap between the apostolic age and the Church of the second century, and sheds new light upon questions of doctrine, worship, and discipline.' All the proofs would fix its chronology from 70 to 100 A. D. Hitchcock and Brown assign it to the period between 100 and 120 A. D., Farrar to 100 A. D., Lightfoot to 80–100 A. D., and Schaff fixes it at 90–100 A. D. It is earlier than Clement of Alexandria (200); earlier than the Shepherd of Hermas (100 to 150); and earlier than the epistle of Barnabas, — for all these quote from it; and it is older than Ignatius, for the ecclesiastical order he describes has not yet arisen. Its place in order of time is, then, immediately after Clement of Rome and Polycarp. It thus becomes one of the most authoritative of the patristic writings, giving us a reflection of the state of affairs immediately subsequent to the era of the Apostles. . . .

"Bishops and deacons are referred to in the Didache as the only regular, permanent officers of the church. With reference to these the testimony is clear and precise. Chap. xv. says of *bishops* and *deacons:* 'Appoint, therefore, for yourselves *bishops* and *deacons* worthy of the Lord, men meek, and not lovers of money, and truthful and proved. Despise them not, therefore, for they are your honored ones.' We observe here, —

" 1. That only two ecclesiastical orders are in existence.

The presbyter is not mentioned, because he is, according to New Testament usage, synonymous with the bishop, and therefore included under that title. Nothing is known of three orders, the episcopate, the presbyterate, and the diaconate,—a distinction which arose in a later age.

"2. The use of the word χειροτονέω, 'appoint,' 'therefore, for yourselves,' shows that the custom still prevailed of a choice by the congregation.

"3. There is nothing said of ordination, least of all of episcopal ordination, as essential to legitimate introduction to the ministry.

"Certainly we discover nothing hierarchical here, no indications of that rigid episcopal order which subsequently became prevalent. Professor Riddle says of the Didache in this respect: 'The church polity indicated in the "Teaching" is less developed than that of the genuine Ignatian epistles . . .; this theory must admit that there existed for a long time great variety of church polity and worship.' Bishop Lightfoot says: 'When our author wrote, "bishop" still remained a synonym of "presbyter," and the episcopal office, properly so called, had not been constituted in the district in which he lived.'[1]

"The ecclesiastical order, then, disclosed in the 'Teaching' is that indicated in the New Testament. The extraordinary offices and spiritual powers of that time linger in some shadowy sense in the itinerant and temporary preachers, variously called apostles, prophets, and teachers. The regular ecclesiastical officers are but bishops, or presbyters, and deacons, and these are appointed by the people, instead of being ordained by a bishop. There is no episcopate as a higher clerical order. The 'Teaching' thus differs distinctly from the Ignatian writings, Irenæus, etc., which show a sacerdotal church order existing in the second century. And it accordingly becomes a powerful additional and corroborative proof as to the church government bequeathed by the Apostles.

[1] Expositor, Jan. 5, 1885.

"The facts as to the so-called apostolic episcopate are then these: The New Testament, and especially the Pastoral Epistles, hint nothing of the kind, regarding the bishop and presbyter absolutely one and the same. All the earliest patristic writings, Clement, Polycarp, the Didache, and the Shepherd of Hermas — those of the immediate sub-apostolic age, to about 120 A. D. — show positively by their assertions and references that no distinct episcopal order as yet existed. It is only subsequent to this period that, with Irenæus and Ignatius, we begin to find the changed order. The conclusion is irrefragable that the historic episcopate originated later than the Apostles, and accordingly lacks scriptural and inspired authority. It cannot be insisted on, then, as obligatory and essential, nor can the want of it illegitimatize any ministry, or unchurch any body of Christians. As Dean Alford (Episcopalian), the great Greek scholar, writes, 'men by legitimate appointment are set to minister in the churches of Christ, not by *successive delegation* from the Apostles, — *of which fiction I find in the New Testament no trace*, — but by their mission from Christ, the Bestower of the Spirit for their office, when *orderly and legitimately conferred on them by the various churches.*'

"With these incontrovertibly established facts admitted with practical unanimity by scholars of every church, including the most eminent Episcopalians, we may say, with the historian Kurtz, that it is 'little less than absurd' to ask Christendom to accept the episcopate as a succession of the apostolate necessary to the true Church."[1]

Mr. Gore, in his recent book on the "Church and the Ministry," wrestles hard to bring the facts recorded in the Didache, and in the epistles of Clement and Polycarp, into line with his theory of the apostolic succession and the exclusive right of ordination in diocesan bishops. He insists that the Didache "belongs at the latest to the first century." He admits that the only *local* officers in the

[1] Greek Testament, i. 904.

churches, as described in that document and in the epistles of Clement and Polycarp, are bishops and deacons, and that these *bishops* were nothing more than *presbyters*. But he contends that over these were prophets and teachers and apostles, in the sense of evangelists, — "men belonging to a ministry as yet unlocalized," "an itinerant episcopacy," "an unlocalized prophetic ministry." And he tells us that "we have evidence that cannot be resisted that the transition" from this "ambulatory ministry" of prophets, teachers, and evangelists to the localized episcopate was effected by *no less an authority than that of the Apostles* (page 285). Now note that he has already admitted that there were already in the churches a local body of bishops (ἐπίσκοποι) in the person of the presbyters; but these did not constitute a localized diocesan episcopacy distinct from and superior to the presbyterate. Let it be remembered also that at the time the Didache was written, and before there was any such localized episcopacy as he contends for, *all the Apostles except John were dead*, and, therefore, according to his own admissions, the "transition" could have been accomplished by the authority, not of the *Apostles*, but only of one *Apostle*. But what is the "evidence such as *cannot be resisted*" that the change from presbyter episcopacy to diocesan episcopacy was effected by apostolic authority? It is nothing more than a "*legend* handed down and preserved about John the Apostle," as recorded by Clement of Alexandria, " that after his return from Patmos he used to go away when he was summoned to the neighboring districts, in some places to establish bishops, in others to organize whole churches, in others to ordain to the clergy some one of those indicated by the Spirit " (page 286). And this *legend*, recorded a hundred years after the death of the Apostle, is "the evidence that cannot be resisted"! On this slender thread is suspended the enormous claim of "the historic episcopate," and the denial that any of the Protestant denominations but the Episcopal have any ordained ministry or any valid sacraments! "Here, then," exclaims Mr. Gore, as though his case were proved beyond contradiction, "we have Saint John *organizing episcopacy* in the district about Ephesus." Now, admitting all that is affirmed in this legend as "very history," how does it prove that the transition from the "itinerant episcopacy" to a "localized episcopacy" was effected by no less an authority than that of the *Apostles?* John was only one of them. The district about Ephesus was a very small part of the territory of the church. Certainly there was no room there for many diocesan bishops. And after all, may it not be that the bishops he "established in some places" were just the same old *presbyter* bishops whom Paul recognized in Ephesus, and who are spoken of in the Didache and in the epistles of Clement and Polycarp as being, with the deacons, the only permanent and localized officers of the Church? The attempt to prove that diocesan episcopacy was established by Christ or His Apostles is a miserable failure.

LECTURE VI.

A.

WE are thoroughly Protestant in our rejection of transubstantiation as defined by the Council of Trent, whether that doctrine was held by the Fathers or not. At the same time, we are not in sympathy with some of the Protestant arguments against it. Nothing is gained by our appeal to the Word of God from human authority embodied in ecclesiastical decrees, if in the contest between rival interpretations of Scripture we invoke that same authority expressed by individuals or by the masses of mankind. If we must submit to either, we prefer an organized court to a town-meeting or to the opinion of any number of individuals. Our Confession of Faith says "the doctrine which maintains a change in the substance of the bread and wine into the substance of Christ's body and blood is repugnant, not to Scripture alone, but *even to reason and common-sense.*"

What is the force of "even" in this statement? Does it indicate an authority above that of Scripture? If so, the statement repudiates the fundamental principle of Protestantism. What do we mean by "reason and common-sense"? If we mean simply our own perceptions and the inferences we draw from them, the statement is only a roundabout declaration that we as individuals reject the doctrine in question. If we mean the reason and common-sense of mankind in general, the argument is manifestly based on false premises, in view of the fact that the majority of nominal Christians, including multitudes of the ablest and purest of mankind, sincerely believe in transubstantiation. As to the vague proverb that a thing may be above reason and common-sense without being contrary to them, our opponents are as much entitled as we, under the storm and stress of the argument, to run into this refuge; for if a thing is above the apprehension of our senses and the grasp of our reason, how can we know whether it is contrary to them or not? It may, indeed, be assumed as a truism that the Word of God does not and cannot require us to believe anything which the constitution of our nature as God has given it to us forces us to reject as false or impossible. But "the constitution of our nature" is but another phrase for "reason and common-sense," and is equally indefinite. It may also be assumed that whatever God has revealed in His Word will be found ultimately to be in perfect harmony with all He has established in His works. But it does not follow from this that our present apprehensions, whether of sense or of reason, are the true measure of that final agreement. It is of the very essence of faith in the supernatural to admit that there are "more things in heaven and in earth than are dreamed of in our philosophy." The facts discoverable by our senses and the laws which are the generalized and scientific statement of these facts must be regarded as supreme in their own sphere; but when, in the attempt to apply natural law to the spiritual world or to the explanation of revealed mysteries, we go a step beyond the Word of God, we get beyond our depth, and are surrounded with the fogs of "philosophy and vain deceit." What do we know about substance in its last analysis? "Substance is nothing but the supposed but unknown support of those qualities which we find existing, which we imagine cannot subsist without something to support them."[1]

Admitting that there are only two substances in the universe, matter and mind, and that these two are essentially and forever distinct, what do we know about the relations they may sustain to each other in a sphere beyond our observation, and how far in these unknown relations they may be assimilated to each other? What do we know about the capabilities of a celestial and spiritual body? The phrase is self-contradictory, "and repugnant to reason and commonsense." Yet "there is a natural body and there is a *spiritual body*" (1 Cor. xv. 44). What do we know about the capabilities of a body begotten by the Holy Ghost and filled with all the fulness of God? Even before He rose from the dead and was glorified, the body of Christ was exempted from the ordinary restrictions of flesh and blood. When, after His resurrection, He stood suddenly in the midst of the disciples, "the doors being shut" (John xxi. 26), and permitted Thomas to touch the wounds in His hands and side, could they or can we tell how He came in? To insist, with some commentators, that the doors must have opened of themselves, or that a keeper was appointed to open them to friends, is a presumptuous addition to the record which explains away its chief point. The closed door is the definite and emphasized condition under which Christ came into the upper chamber. "τῶν θυρῶν κεκλεισμένων points to a

[1] Locke, quoted in Worcester's Dictionary.

miraculous appearance which did not require open doors, which took place while they were closed, — how, it does not and cannot appear. In any case, however, the ἄφαντος ἐγένετο in Luke xxiv. 31 is the correlative of this immediate appearance in the closed place; and the constitution of His body, changed, brought nearer to the glorified state, although not immaterial, is the condition for such a liberation of the Risen One from the limitations of space which apply to ordinary corporeity."[1] It was not His personal appearance, but the supernatural and incomprehensible mode of His coming in that terrified the disciples, just as they had been alarmed before when they saw Him walking on the waters. Understanding no better than we do how a human body could pass through a closed door, they hastily concluded that He was only a spirit; but Christ, knowing their thoughts, showed them His hands and His feet. We believe this story because "it is written." And for the same reason, if the Scriptures declared that the bread and wine of the communion are changed into the flesh and blood of Christ, we should believe that also, however repugnant it might be to "reason and common-sense." We therefore greatly prefer the statement of the Thirty-nine Articles on this subject to that of our Confession.

B.

THE Lutheran doctrine of the Lord's Supper is stated with admirable clearness in the following extract: —

"The Lutherans hold all that Calvin does, and something more; but that concerns almost entirely what unbelievers receive in the sacrament. In order to avoid the danger that seemed to them to lie in Zwingle's view, of making the blessing of the sacraments depend on our changing moods, they thought it necessary to maintain that the blessing was there, whether men believed it or not, and is *really given even to unbelievers*. Hence, since they have no faith, the

[1] Meyer on John xx. 26.

consequence followed that Christ and His benefits must be given or received in or with the outward elements; and thus the Lutheran doctrine in appearance approximates to the Roman Catholic one, though it is really very different in nature and spirit, and much more truly akin to that of Calvin. Lutherans agree with Calvinists as to what *believers* receive in and through the sacraments; their chief if not only difference is as to what *unbelievers* receive in them, and that surely cannot be an essential part of the Christian doctrine on the subject."[1]

While we greatly admire the breadth of his views and the catholicity of his spirit, we cannot agree with Dr. Candlish in passing over the difference between the Lutheran and Reformed doctrine so lightly. The doctrine that unbelievers receive the same thing with believers in the Lord's Supper cannot stand alone. It rests upon the assumption that the outward elements are so connected with the body and blood of Christ which they represent, that the reception of the one necessarily involves the reception of the other, whether the recipient have faith or not. When the Lutheran comes to explain the mode of this connection, it is not easy to understand him. When the Formula of Concord declares that the real presence of Christ's body and blood in, with, and under the bread and wine is not an impanation or local inclusion, not a mixture of the two substances, nor a permanent conjunction between them, but only a sacramental union which is confined to the celebration of the Supper, we can see no difference between these statements and the Reformed doctrine of Christ's real presence. But the Lutheran symbols and theologians go farther than this, and teach: (1) The local and material ubiquity of Christ's body, involving the communication of His Divine attributes to His human nature; and (2) the efficacy of the sacraments aside from the work of the Holy Spirit and the exercise of faith by the communicant. On this point the Lutheran is careful to

[1] Dr. Candlish on the Sacraments, p. 40.

avoid the Romish doctrine that a Divine efficacy is imparted to the elements in the Supper by *priestly consecration*, and that the consecrated elements produce the *same effect* in all who oppose no obstacle to their Divine virtue. According to his view, there is the same Divine power imparted by God directly to all the means of grace, to the Word as well as to the sacraments. The efficacy of the sacrament is due to this inherent virtue, independent both of the influences of the Holy Spirit and the faith of the communicant. Faith, indeed, is the necessary condition for the *improvement* and *beneficial effect* of what is received ; but it has nothing to do with the reception of all that is signified by the sacrament. Because it rests upon and involves these two dogmas, the ubiquity of Christ's body and the inherent efficacy of the sacrament, the Reformed Confessions and theologians unanimously reject the doctrine that unbelievers receive the same thing as believers in the Lord's Supper.

C.

It is not easy to ascertain what were Zwingle's views, and to determine precisely what doctrine of the Lord's Supper may fairly bear his name. He was a popular leader, not a profound theologian. He contributed very little to formulate the theology of the Reformation. His fame rests largely on his personal heroism and the tragic interest which gathers about his death in battle. His peculiar views of the Lord's Supper were not embodied in any of the Reformed Confessions,[1] and are not recognized to-day in the Standards of any Christian denomination known as evangelical, with the exception of the Reformed Episcopal Church.[2] How far his

[1] The doctrine that the Lord's Supper is a sign or symbol, and nothing more, became the characteristic dogma of the Socinian party. — BANNERMAN : *Church of Christ*, ii. 137.

[2] " We feed on Christ only through His Word, and only by faith and prayer ; and we feed on Him whether at our private devotions, or in our meditations, or on any occasion of public worship, or in *the*

earlier teaching about the sacraments was simply the recoil and protest of his ardent mind against the errors of Romanism, and therefore not intended to be a full exposition of doctrine on the subject; and how far his earlier teaching was modified by the influence of the other Reformers or by his own more mature reflections, we cannot undertake to determine. The learned witnesses on these points contradict each other, and are not always consistent with themselves. Bishop Browne affirms that Zwingle was not satisfied to reject a material presence of Christ in the Supper, but he denied a presence of any sort. With him the bread and wine were empty signs. Feeding on Christ was a figure for believing on Him. The communion was but a ceremony to remind us of Him.

"He probably may have modified these statements afterwards, but they thoroughly belonged to his system."[1] Dr. Bannerman says: "There is good reason to doubt whether Zwingle ever meant to deny that the Lord's Supper is a seal as well as a sign of spiritual grace."[2] Dr. Cunningham defends the Reformer against "the misstatements of Mosheim and Milner," which he condemns as "second-hand opinions" and "remarkable specimens of the *humanum est errare.*" And yet when he comes to give positive testimony in Zwingle's favor, he seems virtually to admit what Mosheim and Milner had affirmed; for the most he can say is that, "in his last work, 'Expositio Fidei,' Zwingle gave *some indications*, though perhaps *not very explicit*, of regarding the sacraments as not only signs, but also seals; as signifying and confirming something then done by God through the Spirit, as well as something done by the believer through faith."[3] Dr. Hodge says: *memorial symbolism* of the Supper" (Ref. Epis. Articles of Religion; Schaff's Creeds, iii. 823). "By the word 'sacrament' this church is to be understood as meaning *only a symbol or sign* Divinely appointed" (Ibid.).

[1] Browne on the Thirty-nine Articles, p. 701.
[2] Church of Christ, ii. 136.
[3] Reformers and the Theology of the Reformation, p. 228.

"According to the doctrine of Zwingle, the sacraments are not properly means of grace. . . . They were not ordained to signify, seal, and apply to believers the benefits of Christ's redemption. . . . They were to Him no more means of grace than the rainbow or the heap of stones on the banks of the Jordan. By their significancy and by their association they might suggest truth and awaken feeling, but they were not channels of Divine communication." [1] And yet Dr. Hodge afterwards says: "It should be remembered that Calvin avowed his agreement with Zwingle and Œcolampadius on *all questions relating to the sacraments.*" [2]

Of course these two statements can be reconciled only on the supposition that Zwingle before his death abandoned his earlier opinions, against which Calvin so earnestly contended; for no one can think that Calvin modified in any important particular the views so grandly set forth in his Institutes.

LECTURE VII.

A.

The Necessity of the Sacraments.

THOSE writers who hold to the Divine appointment of the sacraments, and believe that they are in any sense effectual means of grace and salvation, and yet insist that whatever is signified, sealed, and conveyed to the believer by their use may be obtained without their observance, are utterly inconsistent with themselves. Their word is yea and nay; they scatter with one hand what they have carefully gathered with the other. As an eminent but not singular example of this inconsistency we may cite Dr. Cunningham. He maintains that "the sacraments Christ has instituted are of imperative

[1] Theology, iii. 498. [2] Ibid., p. 647.

obligation, and that it is a duty incumbent upon men to observe them when the means and opportunity of doing so are afforded them ; so that it is sinful to disregard them." [1] Now, to a mind unwarped by theological controversy, it would seem that any one who lives in open disregard of an "imperative obligation," in habitual neglect of an "incumbent duty," in a voluntary and "sinful" refusal to use what Christ has appointed as an effectual means of salvation, must be destitute of the simplest elements of Christian character, and that the hope of salvation which may be cherished under such conditions must be, to say the least of it, without any well-grounded assurance. And yet Dr. Cunningham goes on to insist that the observance of the sacrament, while it is necessary *ex necessitate precepti,* is "not necessary *ex necessitate medii,* or in such a sense that the mere fact of men not having actually observed them either produces or proves the non-possession of spiritual blessings, — either excludes men from heaven, or affords evidence that they will not in point of fact be admitted there." [1] As this is a fair statement of the views of those Calvinistic divines who incline to Zwinglian views of the sacraments, and think with Dr. Cunningham that "the effort to bring out something like a real influence exerted by Christ's human nature upon the souls of believers in connection with the Lord's Supper is perhaps *the greatest blot* in the history of Calvin's labors as a public instructor," [3] it may be well for us to analyze and catechise its meaning. The question before us has no reference to those who are either ignorant of the Lord's Supper or have no opportunity to partake of it. It refers only to those whose observance of the sacrament is admitted to be an "imperative obligation" and "an incumbent duty," and whose neglect of it is declared to be "sinful." What does the author mean by "the mere fact of men not having *actually* observed" the sacraments? Is there any conceivable

---

[1] Reformers, and Theology of the Reformation, p. 235.
[2] Ibid., p. 236. [3] Ibid., p. 240.

observance which is not actual? And the same question may be asked in regard to the author's expression about being admitted to heaven *in point of fact*. We can conceive of no admission to heaven which is not a fact; and to our mind the suggestion of any such qualification, whether in regard to the observance of the sacraments or to the enjoyment of the salvation they signify and seal, only darkens counsel by words without knowledge. We pass from this to a more serious question: Can any one live in the sinful neglect of an incumbent duty and an imperative obligation, without thereby giving explicit evidence as to the possession or non-possession of spiritual blessings? Even if we admit the Scholastic distinction between the necessity of precept and the necessity of means, does not the one bind us equally with the other, and present as complete a test of Christian character? Can any one have the evidence or enjoy the fruit of regeneration by the Spirit and faith in the Lord Jesus Christ without at the same time having respect to all God's commandments; and upon what principle do we exclude from the application of this universal rule that command which comes to us from the lips of Christ on the eve of the crucifixion? But there is yet another question, which goes still nearer to the core of this discussion. What ground is there for denying that the Lord's Supper is necessary *ex necessitate medii* as well as *ex necessitate precepti?* Did not Christ institute it and make the obligation to observe it universal and perpetual upon all who hear the Gospel? And is it a mere arbitrary appointment, without any gracious design or any vital connection with our salvation? The whole contention on the part of those who would confine the necessity of the sacrament simply to the precept of Christ seems to us more Protestant than Christian, more rationalistic than scriptural. It is the falsehood of one extreme leaning backward from another. It grows out of a morbid fear lest the doctrine of the Lord's Supper should lead to what are opprobriously called "sacramentarian views." It is inconsistent with the plain teaching of the Confession and Catechisms of the Presbyterian Church.

As to the position that the Christian receives nothing in the Lord's Supper which he does not receive in the use of other means of grace, it may well be asked, Why, then, was this sacrament instituted? If as a means of grace it has no efficacy peculiar to itself, it is a superfluous form. If Christ does not fulfil in it some special promise, He holds out to us a mere empty sign. In answer to this it is usual to fall back upon the necessity of the precept, and to say that it is not for us to question the wisdom of Christ's appointments; He has commanded us to do this, and whether we receive any special benefit from it or not, it is our duty to obey. All this is true. But on what a low, hard level does it put the holy sacrament, and what a sapless and perfunctory service must its observance be to all who hold such views. If the obligation to keep this feast rests simply on the necessity of precept, it stands alone among all the Divine ordinances; it is an exception among the means of grace. All Christians admit that we obtain by prayer blessings that are secured in no other way, that we receive through the reading and hearing of the Word what comes to us through no other channel; and yet theologians insist, and make it a test of orthodoxy, that we are to expect nothing from the sacrament but what can be obtained without the use of it, — nothing, at least, beyond the satisfaction of knowing that we are doing what Christ has told us to do. The same men do not reason thus in regard to any other Divine institution. Paul does not reason thus in regard to the Lord's Supper. He does not rest the obligation for its observance upon the simple necessity of precept, when, applying to it language which is nowhere used in Scripture in regard to prayer, or hearing the Gospel, or to any other means of grace, he declares that the use of this consecrated bread and wine is the κοινωνία, or *participation*, of the body and blood of Christ. We agree, therefore, with John Owen that "herein is a peculiar participation of Christ, such as there is in no other ordinance whatever;"[1] and with Bruce, that the sacrament is appointed "that we may get a better grip of Christ than we get in the simple Word, that we may have Him more fully in our souls, that He may make the better residence in us."[2]

B.

Is the Lord's Supper a Converting Ordinance?

PROTESTANTS generally answer this question very emphatically in the negative. And the answer is unquestionably correct, provided the question be understood to refer to the *distinctive* design of the Lord's Supper, and if the word "conversion" is used in its restricted popular sense, to signify the beginning of the Divine life in the soul. The sacrament is intended primarily and chiefly for the comfort, the nourishment, and the confirmation of believers, for their growth in grace, and the enlargement of their personal interest in Christ. But in a too rigid and exclusive insistence upon this distinctive design we think many Protestant writers have overlooked the influences which belong to it in common with all the means of grace, and so have unconsciously limited the grace of God itself. (1) Strictly speaking, there is no such thing as a converting ordinance. The preaching of the Gospel never converted a soul. It is simply the instrument by which the Holy Spirit brings men to Christ and to salvation. In this respect all the means of grace stand on a common level.

(2) The Lord's Supper is in itself, and aside from any teaching which may accompany the administration of it, a graphic and powerful preaching of the Gospel. Have not many spectators of that solemn ceremony been convinced of sin and turned to Christ by this visible embodiment of the truth, and was it not to them a converting ordinance? We

[1] Owen's Works, viii. 560.
[2] Quoted in Candlish on the Sacraments.

admit and insist that no one ought to come to the Lord's table without faith and a full purpose of heart to lead a life of faith and holy obedience. But suppose some mistaken soul, through no contempt or carelessness, should come to the Lord's table, may not Christ, in the exercise of the same infinite mercy which instituted the Supper, make it the means of self-revelation and of conscious conversion to that soul? Or suppose some child of the covenant, without ever having been conscious of enmity or opposition to God, and therefore having no experience of conversion, and yet being free from scandal and having knowledge to discern the Lord's body, desires to acknowledge and confirm the obligation of its baptism by coming to the Lord's table, — must such a little one be kept back by the syllogism: Except ye be converted ye cannot see the kingdom of God : the Lord's Supper is not a converting ordinance; therefore these little ones which believe in Him must wait till they are converted.

(3) The truth is, that the word "conversion" in its popular use in our churches has assumed a narrow, technical sense, for which there is no warrant in the Scriptures nor in our doctrinal Standards. In the Scripture it is not applied exclusively to the beginning of a Christian life, but to any turning of the soul from sin to God. A Christian may and must be converted, a hundred times, after the manner of Peter, to whom Christ said, " I have prayed for thee, that thy faith fail not; and when *thou art converted*, strengthen thy brethren." In this Scriptural sense the Lord's Supper is pre-eminently a converting ordinance. Its very design is to nourish and renew our Christian life, to turn us more and more from self and sin to Christ and to holiness.

In our judgment it is a far greater injury to Christ and to the souls of men to prevent a true believer, however feeble and imperfect, from coming to the Lord's table, than by a mistaken judgment to admit one who has not true faith. It is better to have a millstone hanged about our neck and to be drowned in the depths of the sea than to put a stumbling-block in the way of Christ's little ones. The "fencing of the tables," as practised in many churches, is a human addition to the Divine ordinances. It is doubtful whether it ever excluded a hypocrite; it has certainly kept back many a weak and timid Christian. It is to be feared that many have come short of eternal life who, had they been received into the bosom of the Church and enjoyed its fostering and guardian care, might have been saved. It is a fearful thing to refuse to any sinner who sincerely desires to use them, any of the means of grace and salvation which Christ has appointed.

C.

The two Wine Theory.

THE theory that there are two kinds of wine spoken of in the New Testament, one fermented, and therefore intoxicating, and the other unfermented and unintoxicating, and that Christ made at the marriage in Cana and used in the institution of the Lord's Supper only the unfermented kind, is a mere figment of a zealous imagination. It has no basis in history, nor in classic literature, nor in Biblical exegesis. It rests entirely upon antecedent grounds. It assumes that "the known character of Jesus is a sufficient guarantee that He did not furnish a promiscuous gathering of men and women at Cana with an unlimited quantity of a liquid on which such of them as were disposed could get drunk." This is precisely the old Manichæan argument for dualism in creation. The character of a good God is a sufficient guarantee that He would not fill the world with things which men can so readily abuse to their own destruction; therefore the material universe is the work, not of God, but of the Devil. The argument is just as valid in its broader application as when it is applied to wine. It can be applied to the interpretation of the New Testament only by doing open violence to the plain meaning of its words. Even an ordinary reader of the

English Bible, if free from prejudice, must see that what John the Baptist abstained from, and the Son of Man came drinking, so that they slanderously called Him a wine-bibber, — *i. e.*, a drunkard (Matt. xi. 19) what the desecrators of the Lord's Supper at Corinth abused till they were "drunken;" what Paul recommended Timothy to take a little of, and forbade bishops to use in excess (1 Tim. iii. 3), — was not unfermented grape-juice, as harmless as water, but something that might be lawfully and beneficially used, but at the same time was liable to be abused. It was this drink, thus capable of being both used and abused, that Christ chose to be the symbol of His blood. We know what "the cup" in the celebration of the Passover contained as certainly as we can know anything pertaining to the history of the past. We know that "the fruit of the vine" was a proverbial name for wine in common use. It is mere trifling and evasion to insist that because it is not called wine, we have no proof that it was wine which the Saviour blessed and gave to His disciples.

But we are not left to the plain meaning of the Scripture on this question. The whole subject has been thoroughly and exhaustively discussed by men whose temperance in all things admits of no suspicion, and whose scholarship is as great as their reverence for the Word of God. Dr. John Maclean, in the "Princeton Review" of April and October, 1841, and Dr. Lyman Atwater, in the same Review for October, 1871, and January, 1872; Dr. Dunlop Moore, in his articles published in the "Presbyterian Review" for January, 1881 and 1882; the Rev. Dr. Edward H. Jewett, in two articles published in the "Church Review" for April and July of 1885, — have demonstrated that the two wine theory is utterly without warrant in Scripture or in classic literature.

The idea of abolishing the use of wine in the Lord's Supper, in order to remove temptation out of the way of the weak (even if we admit the exaggerated statements of the danger it involves, which we utterly deny), is contrary to

God's uniform method in the discipline of His people. He does not remove temptation out of our way; but surrounding us on every hand with that which may be abused, He strengthens us to use it lawfully, that in our own character and experience we may inherit the blessedness of the man who endureth temptation. The ascetic maxim, "Touch not, taste not, handle not," which is so often quoted as a motto of Bible temperance, is condemned and rejected by the Apostle as a doctrine and commandment of men (Col. ii. 21). "God pours out His bounty for all, and vouchsafes His grace to each for guidance; and to endeavor to evade the work which He has appointed for each man by refusing the bounty in order to save the trouble of seeking the grace, is an attempt which must ever end in the degradation of individual motives and in social demoralization, whatever present apparent effects may follow its first promulgation. One visible sign of this degradation, in its intellectual form, is the miserable attempt made by some of the advocates of this movement to show that the wine here [in the miracle at Cana] and in other places of Scripture is unfermented wine, not possessing the power of intoxication."[1] The substitution of something else for wine in the Lord's Supper, under the plea of removing temptation from the weak, destroys the typical significance of the cup of blessing as the emblem of joy, as an illustration of the manner in which Christ's blood was pressed out by His sacrificial agony, and as a fulfilment of the evangelical prophecy, "In this mountain shall the Lord of hosts make unto all people a feast of fat things, a feast of wines on the lees, of fat things full of marrow, of wines on the lees well refined" (Isa. xxv. 6). Whether this prophecy refers specifically to the Lord's Supper or not, it certainly applies to and includes this holy sacrament; and no ingenuity of interpretation can so torture "wine on the lees well refined," which God makes the symbol of all Gospel blessings, as to make it mean unfermented grape-juice.

[1] Alford's comment on Second Chapter of John.

D.

Forms of Admission to Sealing Ordinances.

UPON the whole subject of the conditions and rights of church-membership Dr. Charles Hodge has conferred a great and lasting benefit on all denominations of Christians, and especially on Presbyterians. He has demonstrated that nothing should be made a term of communion which is not declared in Scripture to be a term of salvation; that all who make a credible profession of faith in Christ — *i. e.*, a profession which *may* be believed — are entitled to be regarded as members of the visible Church; that the Church does not consist exclusively of communicants, but includes all who, having been baptized, have not forfeited their membership by scandalous living nor by any act of Church discipline; that baptized infants are professing Christians and members of the visible Church in the same sense that their parents are; and that we are bound to admit to the Lord's table all members of the visible Church who express an intelligent desire to partake of it. The application of these simple principles would sweep away at once many of the bars by which that table is "fenced," and most of the covenants by which individual ministers and churches have supplemented God's covenant of grace and salvation. The enforcement of the adoption of the Confession of Faith as a condition of membership in the Presbyterian Church and of admission to the Holy Communion has no warrant in our Standards nor in the Word of God; and the same may be said of most of the extemporized and mutilated confessions which individual ministers and churches have substituted for it. Many ministers have felt this so profoundly that they have abolished the custom of a public confession on the part of baptized persons coming to the Lord's table. This, we think, is going to the other extreme. Such a confession is manifestly appropriate in the case of adults coming into the Church by baptism. It seems to be equally so in the case of those who have been baptized in infancy and come in years of discretion to ratify their baptism and claim their birthright privileges. In the latter case a public confession is simply an act of *confirmation*, according to the early practice of all the Reformed churches. The Presbyterian Church greatly needs, and we trust will one day have, uniform and authoritative formularies for the administration of baptism and for the admission of professed believers to the Lord's Supper; so that all things may be done decently and in order, and the Church, in these solemn transactions, may teach a form of sound words rather than the rambling effusions of individual ministers.

That the general instructions given in our Directory for Worship do not supply this need is evident from the fact that there is a constant issuing of new books of forms, some of which have received the *quasi* indorsement of the Church through its Board of Publication. Opposition to such forms is practically dead.

E.

Whose Children are to be baptized?

A SUFFICIENT guarantee for the Christian education of a child is the Divinely appointed and indispensable condition of its baptism. The Presbyterian Church, in common with most of the churches of the Reformation, has always insisted that parents, or those who actually stand *in loco parentis* — that is, those who really intend to bring up the child — are the only persons who ought to be accepted as its sureties in this solemn transaction.

It seems shocking to us that one who has only a passing interest in the little one, who has no responsibility for its education, and does not expect to have a controlling influence in the moulding of its character, — one who in many cases does not expect to see the child again after the ceremony, — should assume these solemn obligations and make these solemn promises in its behalf. No such practice prevailed in the early Christian Church. Bingham in his "Christian Antiquities" shows that up to the time of Augustine parents were, in all ordinary cases, sponsors for their own children.

"The extraordinary cases in which they were presented by others were commonly such cases where parents could not or would not do that kind office for them; as where slaves were presented for baptism by their masters, or children whose parents were dead were brought by the charity of any one who would show that mercy on them, or children exposed to death by their parents, which were sometimes taken up by the holy virgins of the Church, and by them presented for baptism. These are the only cases mentioned by Saint Augustine in which children seem to have had other sponsors and not their parents, — which makes it probable that in all ordinary cases parents were sureties for their own children."[1]

It being admitted that the indispensable condition of baptism is a sufficient guarantee for the Christian education of the child, it remains to consider what are the qualifications on the part of parents, natural or adopted, which entitle them to give such a guarantee. Whose children have a right to baptism? There is an ambiguity in this question which it is very important to clear up. It is exactly parallel with the question, Who have a right to be recognized as members of the visible Church? This question may refer either to the abstract right in the sight of God, or to the concrete and prescriptive right in the sight of men. In God's sight none have a right to visible church-membership and to a participation in the sacraments but those who are regenerate and made members of the invisible Church. Ministers are to preach this doctrine. But from the nature of the case they cannot enforce it upon individuals,

[1] Bingham's Christian Antiquities, i. 552.

because they have not the gift of discerning spirits. They are bound to recognize as members of the visible Church and to admit to all its ordinances and privileges all those who make a credible profession of their faith in Christ, not upon the certainty, but upon the presumption that they are regenerate and members of the invisible Church. The responsibility for the truth or falsity of such a profession rests not upon the Church or the minister who accepts it, but upon the individual who makes it. The same is true of the children of professed believers and of the profession which they make representatively through their parents. They are members of the visible Church, and presumptively regenerate upon the same grounds that their parents are. They are included in the covenant whose sacraments the minister is to dispense. If the acceptance of the covenant is a mere outward form, without the inward reality, then the sacramental seal, whether applied to the parent or to the child, is merely an outward sign, without the inward and invisible grace, and the essential element being wanting, it is, in fact, no sacrament at all. But the minister cannot discriminate between the false and the true. He can only act upon the presumption in the case. The Westminster Confession and Catechisms answer the question whose children are to be baptized as definitely as the nature of the case will allow. The Confession (chap. xxviii. 4) declares that "not only those who do *actually profess faith in and obedience to Christ*, but also infants of one or both believing parents, are to be baptized." By believing parents is evidently meant those who *actually profess* to believe, as distinguished from those who profess in and through their representatives or sponsors. The Shorter Catechism says (Question 95), "The infants of such as are *members of the visible Church* are to be baptized." And the Larger Catechism (Question 166) still further explains this position: "Infants descending from parents, either both or but one of them *professing faith in Christ* and obedience to Him, are in that respect within the covenant and are to be baptized." Now this is in exact accordance with the requirements of the Abrahamic covenant in regard to the circumcision of children; and it throws upon the minister the responsibility of deciding in every case whether those who ask for the baptism of their children are members of the visible Church and make a credible profession of faith. It is easy to renounce this responsibility by baptizing all who are presented, asking no questions for conscience' sake. It is easy also to evade it by baptizing only the children of those who are *communicant members* of some particular church. But where is the warrant in Scripture for making church-membership and the profession of faith identical with coming to the Lord's table?

After much study of this question I have come deliberately to the conclusion to baptize the children of all who have themselves been baptized, who have never repudiated their covenant obligations, and *who at the time of the administration of the ordinance are prepared to make a credible profession of their faith in and obedience to Christ.* If any parents will deceitfully or carelessly make such a confession and assume such vows, the accountability is on them, not on us. The instances in which non-communicants will ask for the baptism of their children on these conditions are not many. But there are such cases in which the known character of the applicants inspires far more confidence in their sincerity than we are able to feel towards many who have "joined the church." We dare not exclude their children from the one sacrament because they have timid or erroneous views in regard to the other. Coming to the Lord's table and having our children baptized are both privileges of the covenant. It is not for us to say, nor can we find anything in the Word of God which lays down an invariable rule as to which of these privileges must be first embraced. The refusal in all cases to baptize the children of those who are not communicants can be justified only upon the assumption that membership in the visible Church is identical with coming to the Lord's table. This, we know, is the popular notion on the subject; but it is contrary to the doctrine of all the Reformed Creeds and of the Scriptures, which agree in teaching that the children of professing Christians are born members of the visible Church according to Paul's declaration in 1 Cor. vii. 14 : "Else were your children unclean, but now are they *holy*," — *i. e.*, separated from the world and consecrated to God by virtue of the household covenant.

Dr. Ashbel Green, in his lectures on the Shorter Catechism, admirably discusses this subject. We quote his words as an exposition and defence of our views : —

"I have no belief in such a thing as a *half-way covenant*, nor am I prepared to say that the essential qualifications for a participation in both sacraments are not the same; and I distinctly say that baptism, in my judgment, ought not to be administered to those of whom there is no reasonable ground to believe, after examination and inquiry, that the requisitions of duty in chap. vii. of our Directory for Worship will be solemnly regarded and their performance conscientiously endeavored. All this notwithstanding, I cannot make abstinence from the Lord's table the ground, in all cases, for precluding from the privilege of devoting their infant offspring to God in baptism, some who are desirous of doing it, although they cannot, for the present, view themselves as prepared to go to the table of the Lord."[1]

Our venerated teacher, Dr. Hodge, fully indorses these views : —

"The sacraments, as all admit, are to be confined to members of the Church; but the Church does not consist *exclusively of communicants*. It includes all those who, having been baptized, have not forfeited their membership by scandalous living or by an act of church discipline. All members of the Church are professors of religion. . . . Those,

[1] Green's Lectures, ii. 378.

therefore, who having been themselves baptized and still professing their faith in the true religion, having competent knowledge and being free from scandal, ought not only to be permitted, but urged and enjoined, to present their children for baptism."[1]

[1] Hodge's Theology, ii. 578.

INDEX.

ABRAHAM, covenant with, the perpetual charter of the Church, 89-98: everlasting, 90; all-inclusive, 91-92; a covenant of grace and salvation, 92-94; includes the church-membership of infants, 94-95.
Act of Uniformity, enforced with relentless cruelty, 154.
Alexander, on the Acts, quoted, 142-143 note.
Alford, Dr., on the two-wine theory, 251.
Anabaptists, the, 76.
Angels, the, of the seven churches of Asia, 143-144.
Apostles, the, baptized households, 101-104; not ordained in the technical sense of the word, 117; never claimed the power of ordination, 133; no Scriptural evidence that they claim the exclusive power of ordination, 145-146; frequency with which they observed the Lord's Supper, 207.
Apostles' Creed, the, contains an admirable and universally accepted summary of essential truth, 16-17.
Apostolic Succession, doctrine of, 131 et seq.
Ascension gifts, 49.
Assembly of the Redeemed, as seen by John in the Apocalypse, 10.
Augsburg Confession, the, on the Sacraments, 172.
Augustine, on infant baptism, 80.

BANNERMAN, his "Church of Christ," quoted, 3 note; on the real presence, 182 note.
Baptism, no one mode of, enjoined by Scripture, 68, 69; identical with circumcision, 96-98; why restricted to the children of believers, 108-110; the Christian equivalent of circumcision, 193; the initiatory rite of the Christian Church, 211; a sign and seal of the covenant of grace, 212.
Baptism and the Lord's Supper, the only two Sacraments instituted by Christ, 194.
Barrow, Isaac, quoted, 19 note.
Beecher, Dr. Edward, on "Mode and Subjects of Baptism," quoted, 206 note.
Bellarmine "On the Church," quoted, 55 note.
Bingham, on ancient rites of baptism, 254.
Binnie, on the Church, quoted, 196 note.
Bishop and presbyter, synonymous terms, 135.
Bishops, no exclusive right to ordain men to the Christian ministry, 144 et seq.
Blunt, "Annotated Prayer-Book," quoted, 132.
Bread and wine, essential to the observance of the Lord's Supper, 209.
Briggs, Dr., "Whither," quoted, 135 note.
Browne, Harold, Lectures on the Thirty-nine Articles, 165-166, 177 note.
Bruce, Dr., his "Kingdom of God," quoted, 31; on the *Petros*, 231 note.
Bruis, Peter de, leader and founder of the Waldenses, 76-77.
Bushnell, Dr., on Christian Nurture, quoted, 217.

CALVIN, John, 36 and *note;* his "Institutes," quoted, 16, 24-25 *note;* his doctrine of the Lord's Supper, 176-178, 181 and *note*, 184 *note*, 185 *note;* on the Sacraments of the Old and the New Testament, 193 *note;* on Gospel preaching and the administering the Sacraments, 195-196 and *note;* on the frequency of observing the Lord's Supper, 208 *note;* on the communion of saints, 228.

Candlish, Dr., his "Kingdom of God," quoted, 41; on the Sacraments, 200 *note;* his statement of the Lutheran doctrine of the Lord's Supper, 239-240.

Catechism, Fisher's, quoted, 211.

Charles II., his solemn promises broken, 154.

Children, of believers, how to be regarded and treated, 217-222; whose are to be baptized, 253-258.

Chiliastic theory of the Church and kingdom, 44-47.

Christ, cosmic relations of, as indicated by the Scriptures, 11-12; his sacrifice the centre, though not the circumference, of Christianity, 29; His kingship underlies both His prophetic and priestly office, 29-30; His humiliation on earth did not annul His authority, 30; visible Church of, in what it consists, 31; what He established and proclaimed, 31; incarnation of, in its relation to infancy, 104-107; His body and blood, how received in the Lord's Supper, 188-191.

Christendom, unity of, how much to be desired, 65-66; by what means to be promoted, 66-73.

Christians, real and nominal, 2.

Chrysostom, on baptism, 80.

Church, derivation of the word, 1, 2; divine idea of, 1, 2; the true, a mixed society, 2; of whom it consists, 2, 3, 5; as spoken of in Scripture, 3; definition difficult, 3; for best analysis of complex idea of, see twenty-fifth chapter of Westminster Confession, 3; knits individuals into one body, 3; a living organism, 4; branches of, 4; Christ likens it to the kingdom of heaven, 4; consists of "particular churches," 4; recognized in Scripture, 4; "vegetable theory," 4-5; the whole body of the redeemed, 6; as a divine institution in the world, 7; in the Scripture use of the name, reaches far beyond any earthly and visible organization, 7; not an aggregation but a body, or society, of believers, 8; Saint Paul's teaching concerning, 14-15; first reference to, in the New Testament, 18; inclusive character of, as stated by the Westminster Confession, 24-26; a particular, four things essential to its organization and life, 55; is it one in fact, as in theory, 57; perpetuity and identity of, as a divine institution in the world, 85-89; perpetual charter of the covenant with Abraham, 89-98.

Church and State, true relation between, 34 *et seq.*; why attempts to unify, have failed, 38; demonstration by America that each can stand alone, 160.

Church government, no particular form of, essential to the existence and unity of the visible church, 51-52.

Church, Holy Catholic, invisible, 3, 4, 9.

Church, the invisible, Dr. Goulburn's remarks upon, 7-8; the elect people of God, 8; entrance into, is with Christ, 27.

Church of Christ, fully organized and equipped, 18-19; has the world for its empire, and all nations for its subjects, 26; and Kingdom of Christ, mutual relations discussed, 33 *et seq.*; analogy between it and the human body, 50-51.

Church of England, isolation of, by its own act, 154.

Church of God, Saint Paul's teaching concerning, 14-15; synonymous with kingdom of God, 18.

Church of Rome, the, dream of, 57;

INDEX.

not the *Catholic* church, 58; largely responsible for existing divisions of Christendom, 58; its doctrine of the Lord's Supper, 164-168; authorizes lay baptism, 204.

Church, visible, 3, 4; Congregational or Independent theory of, 5 *note*; and invisible, distinction between, 5, 13; called the Body of Christ, 6; not the limit of God's elect, 8; as much a true church as the invisible, 17; first announcement of, 17-18; of whom it consists, 17, 24; foundation of, prepared by Jesus, 18; Peter most successful promoter of, 20; referred to by Paul as "the Jerusalem which is above," 21-22; separated from all forms of human government, 25; identical with the kingdom of our Lord Jesus Christ, 26; its unity considered, 48 *et seq.*; what constitutes its unity, 50.

Circumcision, identical with baptism, 96-98; the seal of righteousness by faith, 193.

Citizenship, what it implies, 48.

Communion of Saints, the, 228-229.

Constantine, Emperor, 35.

Conversion, not necessarily the test of piety or the evidence of Christian character, 219; wrong ideas concerning, 248.

Co-operation, a means of promoting church unity, 70-71.

Covenant, Solemn League and, 37.

Creed, a, no part of the divine constitution of the visible church, 51.

Cunningham, "Reformers and Theology of the Reformation," quoted, 162 *note*; 177 *note*.

Cunningham, Principal, on infant baptism, 216-217 *note*.

Cunningham, Dr., on the Sacraments, 243-244.

Cyprian, on the baptism of infants, 79-80.

DELITZSCH, on the Pentateuch, quoted, 91 *note*.

Denominationalism, an evil to be deplored, 62; Saint Paul condemns, 62; local example of, 63; its effect upon the Sacraments, 64; its dire effect upon churches and ministers, 65.

Didache, the, opinions concerning, 232-236.

"ECCE HOMO," quoted, 194 *note*.

Ecclesia, of the New Testament, 1, 2, 13, 18; synonymous with *Kahal* of the Old, 85.

Edwards, Jonathan, "Qualifications for Full Communion Work," quoted, 9-10.

Election to the pastoral office by the people of a particular church no part of ordination to the Christian ministry, 123-125.

England and Scotland, churches of, 37.

Episcopal Church, its attitude toward non-episcopal ordination, 155-161; one of the bulwarks of genuine Protestantism, 161; its doctrine of ordination, 127 *et seq.*

FAITH, unity of, an attribute of the true Church, 15; does not depend upon exact agreement in doctrine, but upon an essential minimum of truth, 15-16.

Fasting, no part of the ceremony of ordination, 121-122.

Fathers, the Church, on infant baptism, 81; contradictory teachings of, as to the Lord's Supper, *etc.*, 165.

Federation, a means of promoting Church unity, 71-73.

First-born, the general assembly and Church of, existing only in the city of the living God, the heavenly Jerusalem, 7.

Fisher's "Christian Church," quoted, 36 *note*.

GARDINER, Bishop, on the Catholic teaching of transubstantiation, 166.

Gieseler, "Ecclesiastical History," quoted, 164 note.
Gore, "Church and Ministry," quoted, 44 note, 130.
Gossip, an ecclesiastical term, 64 note.
Goulburn, Dr., his idea of the invisible Church criticised, 7-8; his "Holy Catholic Church" quoted, 7-8, 126 note; on the Lord's Supper, 200 note.
Green, Dr. Ashbel, on subjects of baptism, 257.

HADDON, "Apostolic Succession," quoted, 116, 135-136, 144 note.
Hall, Bishop, on the divine right of Episcopacy, 152.
Hatch, Bampton Lectures quoted, 151.
Hodge, A. A., "Outlines of Theology," quoted, 9; "Popular Lectures," quoted, 10-11.
Hodge, Charles, quoted, 10; "On Denominationalism," 60-61; his "Church Polity," quoted, 52, 68 note, 115-116.
Hodge, Dr., "Commentary on Romans," quoted, 88-89; on the Lord's Supper, quoted, 163 note, 164 note; on the efficacy of the Sacraments, 199 note; on the use of wine in the observance of the Lord's Supper, 209-210; on the status of baptized children, 216 note; on the salvation of infants, 223-224; his views of whom the Church consists, 257-258.
Holiness, an attribute of all true believers, 14; qualification of this statement, 14-15.
Holy Catholic Church, the, consists of the whole body of professed believers on earth, 15.
Hooker, "Ecclesiastical Polity," quoted, 16 note, 124 note, 137-138; on the episcopal power of the Apostles, quoted, 146 note.
Human race, the great majority of, will be saved through Christ, 10.

IMMERSION, regarded as the only mode of baptism, discussed, 205-207.
Incarnation of the Son of God, its bearing upon the Sacrament of the Lord's Supper, 178-181.
Infant baptism, a practice as early as third century, 78; alleged silence of Scripture in regard to, 82-85; argument for, put into a nutshell, 97-98; the profit accruing from, 110-114; obligations of parents in consequence of, 111; the one essential condition of, 214; subjects of, to be regarded as regenerate until the contrary is made to appear, 215 and note.
Infants, church membership of, 74 et seq.; baptism of, 74 et seq.; the unbaptized, are they saved, 75; history of the doctrine of the church membership and baptism of, 75 et seq.; salvation of, most Christians believe in, 83-84, 223-227; silence of Scripture in regard to, 84.
Irenæus, on the nature and scope of Christ's redemption, 105.

JEROME, on the origin of Episcopacy, quoted, 144.
Jesus of Nazareth, his claim to be the Messiah, 27-28.
John the Baptist, first to announce the establishment of the visible Church, 17-18.
Judaism and Christianity, not different, much less hostile, religions, 85.

KAHAL, the, of the Old Testament, 1, 2; synonymous with the *Ecclesia* of the New, 85.
Kingdom of Christ, not the universal sovereignty of God, 30; synonymous with the Church visible and invisible, 32-33; yet there is a difference between them, 33-34; what the term "kingdom" indicates, 33-34; as applied to the Church, 43.

INDEX.   263

Κλητοί, 2, 13.
Κυριου οἶκος, 1.

LAMBETH Conference, quoted, 131 note.
Lang, Marshall, on the Last Supper, quoted, 189 note.
Laud, Archbishop, his attempt to enforce exclusive episcopal ordination, 153.
Lay baptism, authorized by Church of Rome, 204; defended by some Episcopal writers, 204.
Laying on of hands, the, an essential element of ordination, 121.
Lightfoot, Bishop, quoted, 135 note, 137 note; on the Christian ministry, quoted, 147 note; on "bishop" and "presbyter," quoted, 151 note; on circumcision and baptism of infants, quoted, 101 note.
Litton, Dr., "Church of Christ," quoted, 5 note.
Lord's Supper, the, silence of Scripture on the admissibility of women to, 83; four theories of, 163 et seq.; points in which these theories agree and differ, 163–164; Romish doctrine of, 164–168; Lutheran doctrine of, 170–173; Zwinglian doctrine of, 173–176; Calvinistic, or Reformed, doctrine of, 176–177; what the believing and the unbelieving communicant receives in, 185-188; is the Christian passover, 193; no specific instruction from Christ as to the mode of its administration, 207; frequency of its observance in apostolic times, 207; kneeling in the reception of, 208; the scope of Christian liberty in regard to, 208; the true spirit of, to be strenuously preserved, 210-211; Lutheran doctrine of, 239-241; Zwingle's doctrine of, 241-243; is it a converting ordinance, 247-249.
Luther, Martin, his doctrine of the Lord's Supper, 170-173.

MARRIAGE, a divine institution, 82; no form of ceremony of, prescribed by Scripture, 83; the divinely appointed means for propagating the Church, 113.
Mason, quoted, 49, 50; on the Church of God, quoted, 86 note.
Mercy, gates of, not to be shut by human authority, 11.
Millenarian theory of the Church and kingdom, 44–47.
Miller, on infant baptism, quoted, 81–82 note.
Ministry, Christian, all the great Protestant denominations agree is of divine appointment, and essential to the existence of the visible Church, 115; ordination the symbol and seal of, 115; divine call to, how given, 116; not to be entered upon save by lawful ordination, 120 and note.
Mitchell, on the Westminster Confession, quoted, 177 note.
Montanists, the, 77.
Morality, an essential part of religion, 42.
Mount Sinai, covenant made at, superseded by that with Abraham, 90.

OLD Testament economy, the, full of natural symbolism, 192.
Ordinances, sealing, forms of admission to, 252-253.
Ordination to the ministry, no one mode of, enjoined by Scripture, 68, 69; what it is, 115-120; Scriptural forms of administering, 115; who are entitled to administer it, 115, 125 et seq.; appropriate only to those whose call to the ministry is unattended by any miraculous sign, 117; the Romish doctrine of, 118; not a Sacrament, but an effectual means of preparation for the work of the ministry, 118; case of Timothy, 119; Dr. Smythe on, 118 note; the only lawful path to the ministry, 120 and note; the true outward form of, 121-125.
Origen, on the baptism of infants, 79, 81.

Owen, John, on infant baptism, quoted, 107 *note;* "Plea for Scripture Ordination," 137 *note;* on the Lord's Supper, quoted, 191.

PALMER, "On the Church," quoted, 56 *note.*
Parables, our Lord's, outline the history of His kingdom, 32.
Parental office, religious importance of, 113-114.
Passover, the, the seal of righteousness by faith, 193.
Paul, Saint, his teaching concerning the Church, 14-15; nature of his ordination to the apostleship, 122-123.
Pelagius, on infant baptism, 80.
Petros, the rock-foundation of the Church, discussed, 229-232.
Presbyter, the word interchangeable with "bishop" in apostolic times, 150-151.
Presbyter and Bishop, synonymous terms, 135.
Presbyterian Church, the, its doctrine of ordination, 127 *et seq.*; its idea of valid and irregular ordination, 157-158; undergoing changes, 161; in the United States, 38.
Presbyterian Directory for Worship, quoted, 220.
Presbyterian doctrine of the form of Church government, 53 *note.*
Presbytery, discussion as to the meaning of, 149-151.
Public profession of faith, some forms of, stated and criticised, 220-222.
Puritan dream, the, of a visible Church on earth, 58.
Puritan intolerance, 59-60.

QUAKERS, the, incompleteness of their profession, 56.

REAL presence, doctrine of the, discussed, 181-185.
Recognition, a means of promoting church unity, 67-70.

Redeemed, the, the Apocalyptic vision of, 10.
Redeeming grace, not to be limited by man, 106-107.
Reformers, the, agreement among, as to the doctrines of grace, 168; bitter strife among, as to the Sacraments, 169-170.
Reimensnyder, Dr. J. B. on the Didache, 232-234.

SACRAMENTS, new, the Church no right to institute, 74; doctrine of, different to-day from what it was in the creeds of the Reformation, 162-163; drift in the direction of a vague formalism, 162; great need of a sacramental revival among all denominations, 163; all Protestants hold that there are two, not seven, 194; baptism and the Lord's Supper the only two, instituted by Christ, 194; the *insignia* of Christ's Church and Kingdom in the world, 194; the preaching of the word inseparable from the observance of, 195; obligatory on all who profess the true religion, 197; effectual means of grace and salvation, 199; exhibitions and conveyances of saving truth, 200; who were authorized to administer them, 202-205; their administration the prerogative of ordained ministers, 203-204; inconsistency of the Romish and Episcopal churches on this point, 204-205; mode of their administration, 205-211; conditions of admission to, 211; necessity, efficacy, and significance of, discussed, 243-247.
Sacramentum, the Latin translation of the Greek μυστήριον, 193.
Salvation, ordinary possibility of, not commensurate with God's power, 9; of every human soul whom it is possible for God to save, 9; of all dying infants, not an abstract theory. 11; not ceremonial or mechanical, but by grace, 113.
Saved, the, the number of, greater

INDEX.

than that of professing Christians, 8; not few, 10.
Saviour, the, his great commission, 98–101.
Schaff, "Creeds of Christendom," quoted, 76 *note*; " Creed Revision," quoted, 37 *note*; "History of the Christian Church," quoted, 25 *note*; on the Lord's Supper, 172 *note*, 177 *note*.
Schism, among presbyters, the "only remedy" for, 139–140; Paul's treatment of, 140–143.
Scriptures, the, diffuseness and variety of, 1; they recognize the Church as both invisible and visible, 17.
Sermon on the Mount, 29.
Smythe, Dr., "Presbytery and Prelacy," quoted, 118 *note*.
Stanley, Dean, "Christian Institutions," quoted, 175–176.
State, a Christian, 34–35; three attempts to realize, 35 *et seq.*; is it realizable, 39.

TERTULLIAN, 77; denounces marriage, 77; author of the earliest extant treatise on baptism, 78; advises against baptism of infants, 78–79.
Testament, Old and New, organic and vital connection between, 85–87.
Thirty-nine Articles, their definition of the visible Church, 56 *note*; on transubstantiation, 166; on the effect of receiving the Sacraments, 186 *note*.
Timothy, nature of his call to the ministry, 119; ordination of, 148–149; whether as bishop or presbyter, 148 and *note*.
Total depravity, doctrine of, stated with qualification, 215.
Transubstantiation, doctrine of, defined and confuted, 166–168; some Protestant arguments against it considered, 236–239.

Trent, Council of, its decree of transubstantiation, 166, 167 *note*, 168 *note*.

VAN DYKE, Dr. Henry, on the salvation of infants, 224–227.

WALDENSES, the, 76–77.
Walker, his "Scottish Theology and Theologians," quoted, 5 *note*, 39.
Water, essential in the administration of baptism, 209.
Westminster Assembly, its theory of a Christian State, 36–37.
Westminster Confession, quoted, 3, 24, 26; imposed upon England by Act of Parliament, 37; on the visible Church, 56 *note*; on the Sacraments of the Old and the New Testament, 193 *note*; on the efficacy of baptism, 212 *note*; on whose children are to be baptized, 255.
Wilberforce, on the Eucharist, 168 *note*.
Wine, essential to the observance of the Lord's Supper, 209–210; the two kinds spoken of in the New Testament, 249–251.
Wiseman, Cardinal, on the Eucharist, 167 *note*.
Witherow, Dr., "Form of the Christian Temple," quoted, 20 *note*, 130 *note*.
Wordsworth, Bishop, on Apostolic Succession, quoted 159 *note*.
Worship, no prescribed and uniform mode of, essential to the organization and unity of the visible Church, 53–54; must have rights and ceremonies, 192; implies not the absence of form, but its subordination to the Spirit, 192.

ZWINGLE, his doctrine of the Lord's Supper, 173–176; his views as to the Lord's Supper, 241–243.
Zwinglianism, essentially rationalistic, 174.

www.ingramcontent.com/pod-product-compliance
Lightning Source LLC
Chambersburg PA
CBHW031946230426

43672CB00010B/2065